MARTIN LUTHER

MARTIN LUTHER
From a painting by Lucas Cranach the Elder, 1528

MARTIN LUTHER

A Biographical Study

by

JOHN M. TODD

THE NEWMAN PRESS
WESTMINSTER · MARYLAND
1965

First American Printing, 1965

NIHIL OBSTAT: JAMES A. REYNOLDS, PH.D.
CENSOR DEPUTATUS
IMPRIMATUR: FRANCIS CARDINAL SPELLMAN
ARCHBISHOP OF NEW YORK
APRIL 30, 1964

PRINTED IN THE UNITED STATES OF AMERICA

Contents

Introduction: Facts and Theories about Luther.
The Aims of this Book   *Page* xiii

Part I

CHILDHOOD, SCHOOL AND UNIVERSITY

Chap.
1 His Home and his Parents   3
2 Religious Background: Devotional Life, Spirits,
   Sacraments and Superstition   7
3 Boarding School   14
4 University, Depression and the Vow   19
   Note on the Vow   26

Part II

YOUNG FATHER LUTHER

5 The Priory   31
6 The First Mass   37
7 Student and Lecturer at Wittenberg   42
8 Theology at Erfurt
   1. The 'Justice of God' and the Human Predicament   45
   2. Scholasticism   51
9 Visit to Rome   59
10 Dr Luther   65

Part III

DOCTOR AND PREACHER

11 Anguish and the End of an Age   71
12 Luther's Crisis   74
13 The Solution: The Theology of Justification   78
14 Justification—A Catholic Doctrine   81
15 Lectures and Status, 1511–18   85

16	The Psalms, 1513–15	87
17	The Epistle to the Romans. Tauler	90
18	Spalatin	96
19	The Church in Need of Reform	98
20	Luther and Reform	102
21	Galatians and Hebrews	104
22	All Saints' Eve 1516–October 1517	109
23	The St Peter's Indulgence	114
24	The Ninety-five Theses	118
25	The Reaction	124

Part IV

THE PUBLIC FIGURE

26	Into the Arena	133
27	Luther in relation to Church, State and Society	137
28	The Literary Spate begins: January–August 1518	141
29	The Man becomes Reformer and Prophet	144
30	Towards a Showdown	146
31	The Meeting with Cardinal Cajetan	151
32	After Augsburg	158
33	Luther's Position consolidated	161
34	The Bull *Exsurge Domine*	165
35	Luther's Reply; Bonfires; To Worms	168
36	Writings, December 1518–Summer 1520	171
37	Luther considers Christian Society	178
38	The Church, Sacrament and Faith	180
39	Writings, November 1520–April 1521	187
40	The Diet of Worms and the Beginning of the Reformation	189

Part V

THE NEW WORLD

41	Luther and the Universities	197
42	The First Year	201
43	1521–1546: Loosening and Binding	208

44 Luther and the Papacy, 1521–1546 220
45 The Reformed Mass 228
46 The Bible 230
47 Wittenberg: The University, the Parishes
  (and Civil Authority), Luther's House 233
48 The Religious Left and Luther's Idea of the Church 242
49 Erasmus and 'Free Will' 247
50 Luther's Later Theology:
  The Commentary on Galatians 259

51 Summing Up 271
  Appendix 1: Indulgences 277
  Appendix 2: By what Authority? 282
  Index 289

Illustrations

Martin Luther in 1528   *Frontispiece*
 1. Margaret Luther, Martin's mother   *Facing page* 76
 2. Hans Luther, Martin's father   77
 3. Spalatin   92
 4. Frederick the Wise   93
 5. Luther in 1520   172
 6. Pope Leo X in 1521   173
 7. The Emperor Charles V in 1519   188
 8. Luther disguised as 'Junker George', 1521   189
 9 and 10. Luther and his wife, Katherine von Bora,
        in 1525   204
11. Melanchthon baptizing   205
12. John Tetzel   220
13. Zwingli   220
14, 15 and 16. Title-page, opening of St. Paul's First
        Epistle to the Corinthians and illustration from
        Luther's Bible of 1534   221
17. Erasmus   252
18. A composite group   252
19. Luther holding the Bible   253
20. Luther preaching   268
21. Luther dead   269

In the text

Signatures to the Marburg Convention, 1529   *Page* 193
Interpretation by the Cranach School of the distribu-
    tion of the Lord's Supper to the Protestant Saxon
    Princes   270

Sources of the Illustrations

Albertina, Vienna, 2; Deutsche Fotothek, Dresden, 4; Devonshire Collection, Chatsworth, 6; Foto Marburg, 19; Kunsthalle, Karlsruhe, 3; Kunstverein, Winterthur, 13; Lutherhalle, Wittenberg, 5, 9, 14, 15, 16, 21; Mansell Collection, 17, 20; Museum der Schönen Kunste, Budapest, 7; Staatliche Bildestelle, Munich, 11, 12; Staatliche Kunstammlungen, Weimar, Frontis.; Staatliche Museen, Berlin, 8, 10, 18

Abbreviations

Bainton. *Here I Stand*, by Roland H. Bainton, 1955, Mentor Books, U.S.A.

Böhmer. *Martin Luther: Road to Reformation*, by Heinrich Böhmer, 1957, Meridian Books, U.S.A.

Bouyer. *The Spirit and Forms of Protestantism*, by Louis Bouyer, 1956, Harvill Press, London; Newman Press, U.S.A.

Clark. *Eucharistic Sacrifice and the Reformation*, by Francis Clark, S. J., 1960, Darton, Longman & Todd, London; Newman Press, U.S.A.

Jedin. *The Council of Trent*, by Hubert Jedin, Vol. I and Vol. II, 1957 and 1961, Nelson and Sons, London.

Mackinnon. *Martin Luther and the Reformation*, by James Mackinnon, 4 Vols, 1925–30, Longmans, London.

Palmer. *Sacraments and Forgiveness* (Sources of Christian Theology), edited by Paul F. Palmer, 1960, Darton, Longman & Todd, London; Newman Press, U.S.A.

Rupp, R. G. *The Righteousness of God*, by Gordon Rupp, 1953, Hodder and Stoughton, London.

Schwiebert. *Luther and his Times*, by E. G. Schwiebert, 1950, Concordia, U.S.A.

Introduction

FACTS AND THEORIES ABOUT LUTHER.
THE AIMS OF THIS BOOK

IT is a lifetime's work to read all Luther's books, pamphlets, lectures, the notes of lectures, the table talk, the letters and the rest which have come down to us, in the original German or Latin, and to master all the detail of his life and achievement. But knowledge of Luther is not confined to those who have the opportunity of devoting their whole life to gaining it. Many of those who have set themselves the task in the past four hundred years of reading Luther's works and knowing well his life have published the results of their studies. Scholarship has continued to add many to these in a number of languages up to the present day. Slowly the works of Luther are being put into English.[1] But with this we are still faced with a reading task for which only more or less complete commitment is adequate. The present work is for the many who have either no wish or no means to commit themselves in this way, or anything like it.

Amongst the authors of the studies on which the present work depends are men who have studied Luther's life and works intensively over long periods; such specialists are trusted at many points.[2] It is happily possible on numerous issues both of fact and interpretation to compare specialist with specialist and to become reasonably certain of the truth of a solid core of material, agreed to virtually by all; and this now applies to many previously controversial matters. As an instance we may cite the fact that no one now thinks that Luther failed to keep his vow of celibacy whilst in the priory from 1505 to 1521; most authorities would say he did not find it particularly difficult.

Matters which were at one time thought to be settled but are

[1] Concordia Press, U.S.A.
[2] Discussion of MSS and sources is out of place in this book. I have tried to indicate the authors to whom I am indebted, and in their books will be found discussions of MSS occasionally, and references to the Weimar edition of Luther's *Works* regularly.

now generally considered to remain open are obviously more difficult. But one may point to Luther's doctrine of the relationship of the Church to the individual Christian; on this matter it is certainly no longer possible to say without qualification that the Church is something logically subsequent to the individual in Luther's teaching, that it is merely a congregation of individual Christians. This has been a standard idea amongst both Anglicans and Roman Catholic historians.[3] Another open matter must be that of the precise influence on Luther of Nominalist philosophy; this cannot be properly stated without further studies of the works of the Nominalist philosophers of the time.[4]

These three matters, his celibacy in the priory, his ecclesiology, the influence on him of Nominalism, are typical of very numerous matters about which all reputable authorities agree—either that they are now settled, or are still subject to further research. Together these and numerous other matters combine to leave us with a new Luther—a man quite different from the variable mythical figure in the popular mind, whether that mind be Protestant, Anglican, Roman Catholic, agnostic or Marxist.

An understanding of Luther is still of fundamental importance for European history and in particular for the history of Christianity; and every age must necessarily have an interest in the great historical figures rather different from previous ages. More important, as the tale of secondary studies mounts the portrait gradually needs to be re-done. Erroneous general impressions, due to work now outdated, need to be righted. This must not be overdone; Gordon Rupp devotes seventy-five pages to 'The Historian's Luther' and points to the value of some of the works

[3] See *Catholicity* (1947), an Anglican pamphlet, and Gustaf Aulen's critique of it in *World Lutheranism Today* (Blackwells, Oxford, England, 1950, and Augustana Book Concern, Rock Island, Ill., U.S.A., 1950). See also, for a Roman Catholic example: Yves Congar, *Vraie et Fausse Reforme dans l'Eglise* (Editions du Cerf, 1949), where the idea is put forward in diagram form, as held by Protestants, that the Church is the simple product of a gathering of Christians.

[4] See *The Spirit and Forms of Protestantism* (Harvill, London; Newman Press, U.S.A., 1956), by Louis Bouyer, translation of *Du Protestantisme à l'Eglise* (Editions du Cerf), where Nominalism plays the major role, and criticism of this by Francis Clarke, S.J., in *Eucharistic Sacrifice and the Reformation* (Darton, Longman and Todd, London, and Newman Press, U.S.A., 1961) which also reports other criticisms; also Gordon Rupp's criticism in *Protestant Catholicity* (Epworth Press, 1960).

of the older English historians, J. A. Froude, Charles Beard, T. M. Lindsay, in spite of the defective material they had to work with.[5] Perhaps in previous ages when religious presuppositions were still nearly universal in the sense that all had a nodding acquaintance with them even if they did not believe, it was easier to assess Luther's central place. Today he is much less easily understood, and much more easily misinterpreted by purely secular historians,[6] and by Christian writers who follow a prejudice or a party line and are not so generally subject to the intelligent criticism of most men of culture.

It is only quite recently that passions have really begun to cool within the Protestant and Catholic traditions over Luther's life and works. It is true that almost every work published about him even up to the present time has been making out, or assuming a 'case' on one side or the other—and committing itself in the process to a number of historical inaccuracies. The beliefs of authors have in the past made it almost inevitable that Luther would be treated either as a hero or a villain. More recently this has been mitigated a little but, even so, all authors who are themselves in the Catholic tradition, if they have not 'exposed', have tended to 'explain' or perhaps apologize or patronize Luther.[7] On the other hand even the most recent Protestant studies still fail to evaluate properly the Catholic world from which Luther came or continue to make hoary mistakes about the nature of indulgences;[8] and Luther is for them primarily a 'providential' figure, the first 'Protestant'. All this is natural, and not always deplorable. It is impossible to be unbiased. However, the present book attempts to take advantage of the recent cooling of

[5] *The Righteousness of God* (Hodder and Stoughton, 1953). This is the best book in English on Luther's theology.

[6] Tribute must be paid to the accuracy of the play *Luther* by John Osborne, virtually all of which corresponds with historical fact. He makes brilliant use of one of Tetzel's specimen sermons for preaching the fateful indulgence. See pp. 114–124.

[7] See Josef Lortz's *Die Reformation in Deutschland* (1949) for the best modern book. The eirenic *One and Holy* of Karl Adam (London and New York, 1954) tries to find and preserve the Catholic essence in Luther: however well this may be done, it is bound to mis-read something of the reality of Protestantism.

[8] Ronald Bainton in *Here I stand* (Mentor Books, 1959) speaks wrongly of some bulls of indulgence actually forgiving sin, not merely abrogating punishment. Similar errors occur in many other books. The only book in English on Luther, other than works (nearly all polemical) by Roman Catholics, which can be relied on for accuracy on Catholic background and doctrine is Gordon Rupp's *The Righteousness of God*.

temperatures to give a brief record of the life, describing and doing justice to the central religious issues, without being merely dissectionist on the one hand or partisan on the other.

It is not usually wise for a historian to try to trace what he may believe to be the influence of the good angels or the bad angels, and to discern the 'providential'. Is anything not 'providential'? Can God ever be understood as defeated or indifferent? Some idea of the possible answers to these perennial questions must be glimpsed in the course of a biography of Luther. But the point here is simply that an attempt to label any man in a special sense 'providential' or in some other special sense 'disastrous', even 'diabolical',[9] is usually very hard to square with the facts; and yet until recently it has been very difficult for a Christian not to think of Luther precisely in terms of one of these two categories. This book tries to stick to the facts whilst not holding itself stonily apart from the religious issues. If the author were compelled at the point of a gun to express his opinion of the results of Luther's life, whether they were good or bad according to his Christian scale of values, the answer would still be variegated, that some were good and some were bad. He might even murmur that Luther was *justus et peccator*.[10]

But someone might then put the ultimate questions: 'Was Luther right to leave the Roman Catholic Church? Was he right to set up Christian communities out of communion with Rome? Is the Protestant tradition something established with God's blessing, is it in fact a part of his Church?' Or the questions would be put the other way: 'Was the Church of Rome right to condemn Luther's doctrines? Was the excommunication of him just? Can the Church of Rome claim to be the one true Church, and what is the limit of its possible future change of mind, and recognition of Protestant tradition?' These are partly theological questions, the concern of theologians in the ecumenical dialogue today. They are also partly questions which God alone can answer. Men can make objectively valid moral judgments but cannot judge

---

[9] Would the psychopath Hitler be an exception?
[10] Luther's key phrase to describe the Christian, justified by God, but still human and a sinner, able and bound to do objectively good works but not thereby able to 'merit' anything in God's eyes.

other individual men, ultimately. In both cases it is not for a biography to answer these questions.

One may, however, make a brief comment before leaving the ecumenical dialogue aside. The theological questions have only begun, in the last thirty years, to be posed in such a way as to engage the minds of a fair number of Protestant and Catholic theologians other than in a negative or polemical way. Even now the vast majority of Christians in both traditions are wrapped round with prejudices such that it could still not occur to most Free Churchmen that there could really be anything 'Christian', in such a plenary way, about Rome's actions and 'claims', that it must concern them, and a similar phrase could describe the attitude of very large numbers of Roman Catholics in relation to Protestants. But the real questions at issue are now being formulated more widely, and in Germany a dialogue has been going on for decades. Whilst declining to attempt answers to the theological questions (or the matters of divine judgment), formulated above, one may perhaps state the theological dilemmas which the facts of Luther's life present to both traditions in the following way.

1. For *Catholics*: 'If Luther's criticism of the Roman Catholic Church and his separation from it and his foundation of a reformed tradition provided the main impetus which led the Roman Catholic Church to undertake measures of reform which everyone had admitted to be necessary for the previous century and which she had failed to achieve, and if the Lutheran tradition has been fruitful in Christian lives, then the Protestant tradition can hardly be lacking some divine and Christian sanction.'

2. For *Protestants*: 'If Luther wanted a reformed Church, but not a multiplicity of sects, then a 'reformed' Church of Rome could with justice claim at least the serious attention of Protestants, if she invited them to consider reunion.'

With these remarks we leave aside the great questions which will increasingly engage Christians in the coming half century, hoping, rather than to light ecumenical fireworks, to shine as steady and bright a light as we can on the facts of Luther's life. Someone might say that there could hardly be a less satisfactory way of approaching Luther, the great prophet who should either be expounded or contradicted. And such a judgment has been passed on one great impartial biographer of the past.[11] If the present work can be held guilty of something approaching impartiality the author will be very pleased—though less pleased if it also incurs the judgment of dullness, for the life of Luther seems above all one to excite the imagination.

But the excitement will be intellectual and theological, rather than emotional or religious in the partisan sense. For Luther's controversial position, generating so much emotion and so many partisan positions, stems ultimately from his concern with the great theological questions. This concern, though its ramifications are complex, is at root simple; the witness of C. V. Wedgwood[12] and Gordon Rupp[13] is significantly in agreement about this simplicity. No political, economic, social or psychological interpretations can replace or cancel its essentially spiritual and theological nature. If the historian wants to understand Luther and his influence he must appreciate the meaning and excitement of the religious controversies.[14] The basic simplicity of Luther's insight is only fully intelligible in its religious context. The analogy is not altogether apt but the full significance of a symphony by Mozart, the wonder of its simplicity, obvious and delightful as it is to the musically uninitiated, is only appreciated fully by competent

---

[11] Rupp, R. G., p. 53, referring to *Luther and the Reformation* by James Mackinnon, vols. I–IV, London (1927–30): 'He commits the one unforgivable sin of Luther study, which is to make Luther dull, and provokes the reflection that his brand of theological and historical liberalism singularly unfits him to interpret Luther's theology'.

[12] *Velvet Studies*, the chapter on 'Martin Luther'. 'Like all great revelations, his was a very simple one and not new, though to *him* it was new. . . .'

[13] '. . . Luther's problem lay, not in how to combine the divine justice with the mercy (misericordia) or the goodness (bonitas) of God, but in the conception of justice itself. Luther's mental clarification came when he saw this to be not simply a divine attribute, but a divine gift to men. . . . The history of four centuries of Protestant churchmanship . . . attest the richness and many-sidedness of the spiritual tradition which stems from this moment. This is not at all to assert that Luther's mental illumination at this point was some intricate theological matter. It was perhaps rather simple, and perhaps one of the reasons why Luther towers above so many other Christian teachers is that he was, after all, a rather simple person. He never claimed for this particular moment of insight that it was of universal novelty. "Nevertheless", says Joseph Lortz (*Reformation in Deutschland*), and a Catholic testimony at this point is helpful, "it was new for him".' *R.G.*, p. 128.

[14] See the astringent remarks of Gordon Rupp on some modern historians, Christopher Hill, E. J. Hobsbawm and A. L. Rowse, in his Cadoux Lecture: 'Behind this contemptuous dismissal of Protestant and Puritan theology there is, one suspects, real ignorance, and a funking of the chore involved in mastering the intricate code form of an alien ideology' (*Protestant Catholicity*, the Epworth Press, 1960).

musicians. So, the simplicity of Luther's insight is immediately obvious, but its historical importance is only fully understood when its technical theological significance is penetrated at least to some extent. Luther's contribution to Christian theology is of fundamental importance for an understanding of European history, and still exercises an enormous influence throughout the world. Its power springs partly from its simplicity, a simplicity mirroring the basic simplicity of parts of the New Testament, partly from its revolutionary novelty and its suitability to the new age, with its emphasis on the predicament of the individual.

It is hoped that this book will be useful to those, whether Christian or not, who have time only to read one book about Luther before reading something of Luther's own. It is hoped that it will communicate something of the essential issues involved. Its reviewers will not hesitate, it is hoped, to correct it when the author has himself made these hopes impossible of proper realization by some inaccuracy.

Part One

CHILDHOOD,
SCHOOL AND UNIVERSITY

I. *His Home and his Parents*

MARTIN LUTHER was born late at night on November 10, 1483, the second son of Hans Luder (as the name was then spelt) and Margaret (*née* Ziegler). This was at Eisleben on the edge of the Thuringian forest, in the south-west of Saxony. Hans had, almost certainly, lived on the family farm in Möhra, not far away, until shortly before this. But the farm had gone, according to the local custom, to his younger brother; Hans, now in his late twenties, had migrated with his young wife to the nearby town, and decided to try his fortune in the mines. Others had made good locally in both the silver and copper mines. He went, then, to Eisleben where his second son was born. On the morning after his birth the baby was taken to the neighbouring church of St Peter and baptized by Bartholomew Rennebecher, the parish priest, in the name of Martin, it being the Feast Day of St Martin.

The following year Martin's father moved to the town of Mansfeld and, it is thought, worked for a time as an employed miner in one of the copper mines. This is not certain. But we do know that within seven years, not later than 1491, Hans had taken a lease of one of the foundries, along with a partner, the capital for this having been advanced by a local copper merchant. Hans was also by then a shareholder in one of the small firms founded to mine copper. Mining was a growing industry in a district where a more or less democratic tradition enabled local communities to run their affairs without paralysing demands or interference from their overlord, the Elector of Saxony.

Sometime during the first eight years of his life, Martin began to attend the local town school—it was probably on St Gregory's day, March 12, 1488, when he was four and a half. Martin's father must have been earning more than a bare minimum, and already have been determined to provide the children with a schooling which would enable them to live at least as well as he was living. Martin was taught, in a rough and ready fashion, with many other children of a fairly wide age-range, to read, write and sing, and to understand Latin. The teacher had to educate older boys in the same room and the younger boys were taught everything possible simply by memorizing. They were beaten fairly often, it seems, when they did not know their lesson. We know very little for certain about these early years at school. But they perhaps were in mind when Luther said in later life, 'Who ever loved a school-master?'[1]

The family grew year by year. Sometimes the new baby would die, and the number who died could not in fact be remembered. By 1505 (the year in which Luther would enter the monastery at twenty-two) the family was composed of four boys and four girls. The family life was lived out against a background of its own slowly rising social and economic status. Father was a leading citizen of Mansfeld. Sometime before 1491 he had been elected by his fellow citizens to be one of the *Vierherren*, the Four Citizens, who represented his fellow townsmen on the town council. In 1497 he was associated with the other men of Mansfeld in seeking for an indulgence to be attached to the local church by the bishop. Business was continually increasing and Hans presumably had to work hard to reach the position he occupied in 1511 when, with his partner or partners, he owned at least six mines and two foundries. Six years previously he had come forward with a hand-some gift of twenty Guldens (the price of ten or more oxen, or perhaps £110), when Martin was clothed as a friar. Life at home was based on the kind of economy to which Hans had been used on the family farm; Frau Luther always went out to the forest to collect the firewood herself. Herr Luther's enjoyment of beer, which Martin declares brightened the family atmosphere and was sometimes taken to excess, was not a sign of poverty and incom-petence but rather a normal indulgence resulting from the family's success in its venture into the mining industry and the life of the little town.

It is difficult to be certain about the quality of the family life, its atmosphere. What we know derives from statements of Luther himself written thirty or forty years later. Luther said his father was 'by nature a jovial companion, always ready for fun and

[1]Rupp, *R.G.*, p. 86.

pastimes'.[2] But he also speaks of the severity of his parents, specifying two particular occasions, once when his mother beat him for stealing a nut, and this drew blood, and again when his father beat him so that Luther bore a grudge against him until his father managed 'to accustom me to him again'. In later life, Luther seems to have had a sense of a certain injustice done to him both at home and at school, but he directs this against the social and religious system which taught his parents to behave as they did, rather than against them themselves. He always had a respect for his father, allied with a certain fear, and there was undoubtedly some emotional tension here. In spite of what he considered their harsh treatment of him Luther said that his parents 'meant heartily well by him'.

Biographers have sometimes built much on Luther's relation with his father. A recent book[3] is concerned solely with Luther as a psychological case and builds its theme of Luther's relation to his father on the very few strictly relevant texts, and a large number of other texts, with their obvious psychological aspects. Its thesis really draws on a vast common experience of children's relationships with their parents, particularly as ordered and interpreted by Freud and the whole psychoanalytical school. Analysis of this sort should enable us to get a better overall image of a man, but unless we are dealing with a definitely pathological case, a real psychotic, it will not enable us to identify fully either the meaning and significance of his actions, nor all his motives and springs of action. If it did this in Luther's case, it would make of his life simply a function of his psychological condition. This can only be maintained today with any seriousness by a historian writing from a completely positivist position, in which the religious dimension properly speaking is supposed not to exist.

But an important element is added to our understanding of the man if we accept the thesis of a particularly sharp emotional tension between father and son, and if we understand the psycho-

---

[2] Heinrich Böhmer, *Martin Luther: Road to Reformation* (London and New York, 1957), translation of *Der Junge Luther*, p. 11: a good source for many of the basic facts about Luther up to the Diet of Worms.
[3] Erik H. Erikson, *Young Man Luther* (London, 1959), which in spite of close acquaintance with some of Luther's works contains elementary errors of historical fact.

analytical approach to Luther. We can see with greater understanding the full emotional force behind Luther's desire for justification in God's sight, his despair and terror at the thought of his guilt and unworthiness, his eventual rejection of obedience to Roman authority, his whole counter-weighted theology of faith alone, of the free gift of justification. If we see all this as, in the personal aspect, a projection of his relationship with his father we have an added insight into Luther's life and into the attraction he exercised on others. The theology itself and the decisions and actions related to it still have an objective significance, historical and religious, of primary importance. The psychological thesis enables us to understand better the tremendous emotional force which was put behind this theology, these decisions, whose first significance lies in the conscious, rational, and religious sphere.

The psychological factor, like the economic and political factors, predisposes. Of Luther it made a man who was specially sensitive about authority. Yet we find in Luther also insight into himself and his own sensitivity. He could laugh at himself and admit his own deficiencies. '*Barbarus*' he called himself at the age of forty-two, as a writer by comparison with Erasmus—though he was also making a subtle point against Erasmus at the same time. At another time, about five years later, he considered he was hardly fit for negotiations with the Zwinglians which he preferred to leave to his young colleague Melanchthon; though his enthusiasm for the negotiations was not great. Luther had a nervous and sympathetic personality abounding in mental energy. It tended to build up a defence in the form of abuse of others, expressed in the common vocabulary of coarse and excremental expletives, to which he was particularly addicted. This was, no doubt, partly due to a kind of exhibitionism; Luther always shuttled between shyness and a compensating self-assertion. The coarse expletives were also by implication a statement that he came from and remained one with rough and ready Saxon folk; his grandfather and uncle still farmers, his father a self-made small mine-owner. They had no time to cultivate a silvered speech.

We may conclude that Luther's father was a forceful character, dominating at home as he must have dominated at work. Luther was frightened of him at times; later he was often grateful, realizing that his father's success had enabled him to go to school. For the first twenty years of his life his father was a rather overbearing influence, but by no means so much as to stamp out all individuality in Martin, or to promote a simply pathological reaction.

2. Religious Background: Devotional Life, Spirits, Sacraments and Superstition

LUTHER was baptized within twenty-four hours of his birth, according to custom, in the parish church. It seems certain that the Luther family followed the normal religious observances, and had something of the same inner religious life as those around them. We may take it that as Martin was baptized, so he went to Mass on Sundays and feast days, believed with everyone else in the real presence of Jesus Christ in the bread and wine at Mass, went to confession, received communion, was confirmed, prayed to the Virgin Mary and the saints (St Anne, the mother of Mary, was the patron saint of miners), recited the rosary, reverenced the relics of saints, gained indulgences, and said prayers at home. In later life Luther remembered particularly the teaching about rewards and punishments after death, which were said to follow from a good or bad life on earth. He was frightened by this. The belief seems to have been general that substantial numbers of people suffered either the eternal pains of hell, or at least very long and painful retribution in purgatory. We cannot be certain about the extent to which preaching at Mansfeld concentrated on this so as to overshadow all other aspects of the Gospel. But it certainly gained a central place in Luther's memory.

All was not gloom. The daily religious life was in general rather joyful than gloomy. Christmas, Easter, Ascension, Whitsun and the saints' days provided plenty of scope for celebration. Popular devotion to Jesus (with the emphasis on his passion it is true), to the Virgin Mary, to the saints, and the regular round of the liturgy provided the daily warp and woof, leading both to a general workaday piety and occasionally to deeply prayerful lives manifesting great charity and goodness. Luther's later life was by no means all gloom, and it seems reasonable to suppose that as a child he was not lacking sometimes in the gaiety normal to a child. No doubt the depressions of later life may have had their counterpart in childhood, but equally so his jolly phases. He enjoyed an occasional prank. His poetical temperament and love of music responded to the Church services. We know he had a special love of the *Magnificat*.

This daily life of piety had much of superstition about it, and this on two counts; first in regard to a belief in spirits which was in some ways pagan; second in regard to an attitude to the sacramental and devotional life which tended to be mechanical, even 'commercial', to use Luther's own later description.

First, then, there was a general belief in malicious spiritual powers which were thought to reside in particular places, or people (witches), and to delight in particular kinds of evil actions. These powers were sometimes believed to be immediately responsible for natural phenomena, the immediate causation of which we now know to be natural. When there was thunder and lightning, Luther's father and mother would say, 'The devil is loose'. Luther himself continued all his life to give absolute credence not only to Satan as an objective reality, frequently plaguing him, but also to what might best be called the haunting of places by evil spirits. 'Many regions are inhabited by devils. Prussia is full of them, and Lapland of witches. In my native country on the top of a high mountain called the Pubelsberg is a lake into which if a stone be thrown a tempest will arise over the whole region because the waters are the abode of captive demons.'[1]

All this sounds very 'medieval' and tends to make us believe that Luther's whole world is too remote for us to be able to

---

[1] Quoted by Bainton, p. 19, who gives a reference in the *Table Talk*. Luther sometimes talked big and indulged his hearers, but there is no reason to doubt that in principle he believed what is here reported. But care has to be exercised in using the *Table Talk*. It is quite easy to make a selection of passages, combine these with excerpts from the work of admitted enemies and produce a lurid picture of a coarse blasphemer. Such a picture does not tally with the evidence as a whole and cannot be taken seriously.

understand it or even to take it very seriously. Indeed to trace such beliefs to pagan origins is probably reasonable. But to call them merely superstitious and to suggest that they are incompatible with any intelligent outlook, or with Christian belief as held today, would be to beg a question and make a grave mistake, one to which historians are perhaps too easily prone. Belief in spirits is not in itself superstitious, though to attribute natural phenomena to their activity may often be so. Belief in spirits is not incompatible with the New Testament which speaks of devils and angels. Today many Christians commonly believe in the objective reality of angels and devils. They pray to angels for their assistance, and they rely on help from God to protect them from what evil spirits may be abroad. If they stand in the Catholic tradition this reliance will extend to the use of the sacraments and to such sacramentals as holy water and to the invocation of those believed to be already in God's glory, the Blessed Virgin and the other saints, whether canonized or not, all others whom we believe to be in heaven, and of the angels.

Yet there is a great difference between the belief of a Christian today in the existence of spirits, and the belief of Luther's parents. The difference seems to lie primarily in two things: (1) The absence in those days of modern scientific knowledge; (2) an overmastering conviction of their domination by a spiritual world, which included pagan elements, a conviction shared by virtually the whole of society. Today the natural sciences enable virtually everything observable to be attributed to an immediate natural cause. This simply did not exist, and its place was filled to some extent by more or less 'pagan' spirits, by devils and angels and the interventions of providence. In the highest intellectual reaches an embryonic idea of an ordered and mobile physical world had been conceived; but the popular mind knew nothing of it. If in later years anything of this scientific world filtered through to Luther he would probably not have paid much attention to it since in any case his concern was precisely with the world of the spirit. The world of the spirit is the world of ultimate reality and God is in principle able to do what he may wish throughout creation.

In one sense, then, there is little difference between the attitude of a Christian today and that of Hans and Margaret Luther. Christians still pray for natural phenomena to occur, such as fine weather or rain. They still believe in the world of spirits, and still believe that God is so much all in all that they ought to pray to him, not only for their consolation as though they were children merely permitted to go through some act or charade, but because such prayer has an objective and dynamic value in the affairs of individuals and society. An intelligent and religious man may still look on every event in his life as part of a spiritual or 'supernatural' history—all experience, every event, every person, every thing, is sacramental for him. But the difference in practice is great. The number of unaccountable phenomena was then so great that it was easy for someone to be very much preoccupied in a sinister rather than in a sacramental sense with the spiritual world. There could be a sense of waiting for the unexpected, the unpleasant, the accident, the blow, in the physical world (Hans Luther saw the terrible marks supposedly made by devils in the mines on a miner, and was very severely upset by the sight). A person so preoccupied easily moved from thinking the milk had been pinched by a pixie to supposing that a deformed birth had been preternaturally caused or that a sickness would lead inevitably to death because of the work of a devil, or perhaps of a witch (Luther's mother spoke of a witch murdering one of her babies). We reach here the borderland beyond which lies the land of superstition, where supposedly malevolent or autocratic spirits have to be placated with arbitrary ritual actions or sacrifices. Theologically the difference is significant. Spirits, angels, saints, were then thought of as having a power almost independent of God. Today this has been giving way to a sense of such power being exercised only under God.

With us, then, is the ordered framework of events all foreseeable, explainable, nearly all actually expected—the unexplainable and unforeseeable lies purely in the 'spiritual' or the human volitional sphere, in manifestations of human personality, in the arts, in human work, in religion, in saintliness and sinfulness, and even here the sciences of genetics, psychology, and cognate sciences, promise further explanation and foresight.[2] With them on the other hand was a world in which malevolent spirits were so close that they could account for storms and were a matter of daily recognition. Life was all 'other' and strange, from the souring of the milk to the spiritual help of a good priest, from the trickery of a minor devil to the charity of Christ.

Yet, how hard it is to draw hard and fast lines. It is possible to predicate diabolical possession of some kinds of mental illness today. Exorcism is still practised. Buildings are believed to be haunted, especially by those who have experienced the phenomena. And exorcism has been known to end this. But these are exceptions to daily life which, nearly all the time, runs on the smooth ball-bearing wheels of modern science. So, what is exceptional to us was an everyday matter to them. But again it must have had a different quality, just because it was in fact an 'everyday' matter. The devils and witches were taken for granted as part of life, and were perhaps more easily digested and coped with than we might suppose. Yet they were, presumably, as frightening as the psychological states, neuroses, psychoses, which many modern Europeans and Americans experience or come near to experiencing at some time in their lives. The terror of which we know today in the lives of primitive tribes is perhaps evidence of what the medieval superstition may have led to at its worst. There still lingers on in the rural areas of many 'Christian' countries relics, sometimes quite widespread and powerful, of the 'spookey' superstition which was the context of Luther's life.

We pass now to the second count on which we can say that the daily life of the Luther family must have had something of superstition about it. The sacramental and devotional life tended to be mechanical, even 'commercial'; it was treated in fact, sometimes, as though it were magic, and this again ties back to a pagan past.

This matter is controversial in that it concerns precisely something which Luther himself set out to reform, first as to practice, and then finally as to doctrine—though the exact relationship between the Lutheran sacramental doctrine and Catholic

---

[2] The 'unexpected' is also present of course in the world of scientific research, but this is an 'unexpected' for which men search, already in another sense 'expected', not one which they wait for fearfully and passively.

sacramental doctrine is not easy to define, not least because both systems have been subject to changing interpretations. It is generally agreed that certain abuses were current, indeed so widespread as almost to have supplanted in common daily practice what was stated in theory, and it is not difficult to establish the facts. Briefly it may be said that men and women very often treated the sacraments as an automatic pass to 'salvation', to heaven. They tended to be ignorant of the doctrine that they should respond to and co-operate with the grace received in the sacrament. 'Grace' is received by 'faith'. If the Christian has no inner life the whole ritual then suffers debasement near to the level of mere magic, and becomes something to be done to placate an arbitrary God in whose plan love has no real place, something with no relation to the biblical doctrine of the importance of the life of each individual Christian as a member of Christ's body. Instead of a meeting-place with God, sacred and spiritual occasions, gifts from a loving God, the sacraments are treated pharisaically, as legal obligations, the prescribed rituals of an autocratic pagan god. It is impossible to generalize with absolute assurance. Whilst there were very numerous exceptions and a widespread piety, and sincere love of the person of Jesus Christ as far as he could be discerned, the superstitious attitude to the sacraments is widely attested.[3]

That Mass stipends led to abuse we may be sure from the frequency with which they were denounced at the time, also by the severity of the later denunciation by the Council of Trent.[4] When a man pays money to a priest at the same time as asking him to offer Mass for a special cause there is a natural tendency on both sides towards devaluation of the exclusively spiritual nature of the priest's act, and there must be a tendency to conclude that something which can be measured is received in return for the tangible gift of money.

Then it was often said and written that a specified number of Masses would achieve some object, usually the release of some soul from purgatory. This again was severely denounced at the

[3] See Francis Clark, S.J., *Eucharistic Sacrifice and he Reformation* (England and U.S.A., 1960).
[4] Clark, p. 57.

about the world? Probably little that would make an impact. His father, no doubt, was the master of Martin's world, a man with 'business' and a voice in the little town, who went out to his foundries and mines and came home again. Little seems to have occurred to disturb the family life, apart from its personal joys and troubles. War did not threaten to take the master of the house away to fight; no other lesser disturbances seem to have threatened Hans Luther's property or business. Demand for metal was steadily increasing. But we should not overemphasize the stability. Towns sometimes experienced a rule, so autocratic, of the little 'capitalists', the masters, that the apprentices or the journeymen revolted, and upset the whole economic structure. As Herr Luther's possessions increased, he must have had increasing worries about protecting and maintaining and further developing his property. In fact, however, he succeeded and prospered.

There was abroad a certain pride in the achievements of the age, a certain civic pride in the cathedrals and churches. The standard of domestic housing was improving, wood giving way to stone and brick even for the houses of people in a modest position. The social, economic and religious structure was taken for granted, but it was also growing, and the growth was mirrored in Herr Luther's own circumstances. Born and bred on a farm, he was now able to send a thirteen-year-old son forty miles across country to the city on the Elbe, the Elbe which flowed down to Hamburg and the sea which he had never seen. And within this slowly changing structure were strong forces tending towards much more far-reaching, more rapid change.

Luther always remained more or less uninterested in the artistic renaissance, and geographical discoveries, becoming positively opposed to the renaissance in its purely intellectual aspect on account of its spirit of detachment from the Reform. But it is impossible not to see him as one of the great 'individuals' of the sixteenth century, a protagonist of liberty, and so, as a child of his age. And we must say something of these forces of change of which his father must have known a little, and of which Luther himself must have heard during his school-days, however little each made of them. But above all we must remember that this small-town mine-owner of central Germany, and this small-town schoolboy, then student, then friar of central Germany, were for a time, the father always, playing a very small part in the middle of it all. They knew nothing of the Renaissance as we know it, or of the New World as we know it. They could have had no integrated knowledge, in their small-town circumstances, of the changes on all fronts which the historian now, and a few cosmopolitan people in those days themselves, could connect together in a single vision.

Perhaps the extent of interconnection between the various changes can be overdone. But it is certain that medieval society was bursting its seams in all directions. Exploration overseas made possible a vision of a new freedom and independence which also led to trade and so to the reaping of a benefit for and from the homeland. At the other end of the scale, the appeal of the Gospel, especially of the Sermon on the Mount, which had led to the foundation of the Franciscans and the Dominicans three centuries earlier, to some extent as a protest against the over-legalized and too-worldly ecclesiastical life, now drew men to a new vision of a simple mystical life. The Brethren of the Common Life, with whom Erasmus started his life and who taught Luther at Magdeburg, were a more recent example. Then there were the humanists with their looking back to pagan Greece and Rome, who hoped through a cultivation of the arts and the intellectual life to work out a practical 'Philosophy of Christ', a good life, which enabled them to sit loosely to some of the crudities of late medieval religion, if not to the whole structure itself.

For centuries revolt against overbearing social and religious forces had taken the form of occasional rebellions, sometimes religious, sometimes economic. For a century ecclesiastics had been trying to reform the Church. Intellectually it had been possible as long as two centuries previously for Marsiglio of Padua to work out a completely simplified theory of State and Church—one which stirred the admiration of late-nineteenth-century historians.[1] After two more centuries the practical possibility of

[1] See the pages on Marsiglio in R. Lane Poole, *Medieval Thought and Learning* (London, 1884 and 1920).

catastrophic changes was at last reached. The kettle could reach boiling point, and actually boil.[2]

Perhaps some distant echo of all this crept into Hans Luther's house; if it did, it was probably an echo of the geographical freedom, an echo of the ships in Hamburg harbour, an echo of Portuguese explorers, a commercial echo. This is only a guess. For all we know Hans Luther may have looked with admiration on a Dürer, or even some painting of the Italian renaissance—or even have pondered religious reform. But if anything of this was so, Martin recorded nothing of it, either of his father, or of himself either at home till the age of twelve and a half, or at Magdeburg.

Luther tends to be ironical about the works of man. The mind impressed him more than physical works. The religious aspect would have been the aspect of freedom most likely to strike him. As it is, the only thing he remembers and records of his schoolboy life at Magdeburg is indeed religious, typical of the late Middle Ages.[3] Prince William of Anhalt had become a Franciscan in the town, twenty-three years before Martin went there, and the boy met him once in the street as 'the noble penitent' (to use Böhmer's phrase) was going on his routine round, begging 'bread in God's name'; he was 'the picture of death, mere skin and bones', although by no means old in years yet. So Luther said nearly forty years later. A great impression, he remembered, was made on people by the penances which the Prince must have imposed upon himself. Luther probably went to the Cathedral school; he was taught by members of the Brethren of the Common Life. He lodged with one of the Archbishop's officials—this was made possible perhaps by his father's status at Mansfeld. Martin provided money for his keep by joining a little choir which went round singing in the street and, like Prince William the Franciscan, begging according to the custom.

[2] Cf. the striking image used by Teilhard de Chardin in *The Phenomenon of Man* to give some idea of the achievement of a new stage in any evolutionary process. The water in a kettle is at the temperature of boiling water for a second or two before it actually starts to boil; then without any further immediate cause the transformation takes place.

[3] The basic facts given here about the schooldays and Luther's time at the University are taken from Böhmer and from *Luther and his Times* by E. G. Schwiebert (Concordia, U.S.A. ,1950).

After a year at Magdeburg Luther was recalled home and was sent to another school in the other direction, at Eisenach, some fifty or sixty miles south-west of Mansfeld, right on the edge of the higher and wilder country of the Thuringian Forest. Exactly why a change of schooling was made after only a year is not certain. But it may possibly have been family reasons since his mother had an aunt living at Eisenach. Luther attended the parish school of St George there from about Easter 1497. Here he stayed during his adolescence until he was seventeen and a half in the Spring of 1501 when he went to university.

During these crucial years at school Luther was apparently happy—he always spoke later of his 'good city of Eisenach'; here he must have discovered for the first time the joy of good learning and of poetry. His school curriculum had at its centre the speaking, writing and versifying of Latin. Melanchthon says that 'he soon left all his classmates behind' but this is probably an exaggeration. He was on good terms with one of the teachers, Wiegand Guldennapf of Fritzlar, with whom he remained friendly for many years. The head of the school, John Trebonius, was a gifted man according to a statement of Luther's to Melanchthon.

At Eisenach Luther did not stay with his mother's relation, but at first at the school itself, and then in a pious household. Böhmer sees a special importance in these years in that the adolescent did not react against the religiosity of the family where he stayed, but went along with it. Possibly if his own father and mother had never been specially diligent in their piety, but somewhat mechanical (and we have no evidence that they were specially pious), then the pious yet warm atmosphere of the Eisenach household might have had a particular attraction for him. It is not certain whether Luther slept at the house of Henry Schalbe, merchant, and his wife, or at 'Kunz Kotta's' whose wife was a Schalbe. But Luther had much to do with the Schalbe family. He had to look after the son of Henry Schalbe in return for his board and had much to do with their religious goings-on which included close relations with the Franciscan House at the foot of the Wartburg, to which Herr Schalbe was devoted.

4. University, Depression and the Vow

FROM Eisenach school Luther went to Erfurt University. What is there to say about Herr Luther's choice of university for his son? The first point is to notice the remarkable fact that there was a choice and to appreciate the general prosperity of which this was a sign, a prosperity in which Herr Luther had taken his part. Whilst the English-speaking world had only two universities, and Italy and France not many, Germany had numerous universities[1] and Herr Luther had two to choose from within sixty miles or so—and in the course of the next year a third would be added in the district, the university of Luther's own future, Wittenberg, founded by the Elector of Saxony in 1502. Meanwhile there were Leipzig and Erfurt, the latter with apparently a higher reputation, the former nearer home. The family were used to Martin being absent and distance cannot have mattered greatly to them. Possibly the most important point is that Erfurt is only thirty-five miles from Eisenach and John Trebonius, Luther's headmaster, must surely have been known to some of the dons at Erfurt and been able to recommend Luther to a particular College, or Bursa as they were called. Indeed one of the best-known professors at Erfurt was a native of Eisenach, Jodocus Trutvetter. Leipzig, on the other hand, was ninety miles away from Eisenach.

Life at a university was strict, and more or less monastic. The hours and the reading of the undergraduates were carefully disciplined. The daily round was marked by morning and evening services in the college. Lectures, recitations, weekly disputations were the order of the day. Martin had first to pass the Bachelor of Arts degree, in language, logic and philosophy; the medieval trivium. He passed this as early as he was able, at Michaelmas 1502, being placed only thirtieth out of fifty-seven. He then started on the Master's course, studying the quadrivium—geometry, arithmetic, music and astronomy—and at the same time philosophy, natural, metaphysical and moral. Martin again passed the exam

[1] Böhmer, p. 21.

at the earliest moment, being second out of seventeen. That was probably January 7, 1505, Luther being twenty-one.

Aristotle and the later scholastics provided the texts. But the physical sciences had been brought up to date. Luther was taught that the earth was not a disk but a sphere and that the moon produces the tides. Classical poetry was allowed. Luther grew to be a lover of Vergil. Modern poetry too was allowed in one's spare time, if the master of the college was not opposed to it and considered the pupil was working sufficiently.

We have a few isolated facts about Luther's life at Erfurt University, but in general we may say that the absence of any striking information about his life then, or in the previous years at home or school, is strong evidence for the thesis that Luther was not an unusual youth. At any rate he did not distinguish himself in any special fashion that led anyone to record it, either for his blame or for his merit. We know he used to walk home, from time to time, to Mansfeld, covering the distance in three days or more. On one of these trips, half a mile from Erfurt on the return journey, he accidentally cut his leg on his sword (what was he doing?—cutting his toe nails with an unsuitable tool?), and only reached his college with difficulty. He lost much blood and was laid up for several weeks. Of this incident Luther relates simply the fact that he prayed to the Blessed Virgin and that whilst confined to his bed he taught himself to play the lute. We know that after this he often played the lute and sang songs with his friends, particularly John Jäger of Dornheim near Arnstadt, who many years later wrote the *Letters of Obscure Men*, a satirical exposé of the medieval spirit at such places as universities. Luther says he first saw a complete Bible when at the university, in the library. He was stimulated by what he had time to read and decided to read more in specifically religious matters and bought a Postil or book of sermons.[2]

Finally, like thousands of other undergraduates, Luther was im-

---

[2] The derivation of this word is from *post illa verba*—it was a name at first for a commentary on a particular Scripture passage. These commentaries commonly had a moralizing tone, and a person wishing to do some religious reading would look for such a book. The origin of the story about seeing a complete Bible for the first time is the *Table Talk*, and hence not absolutely reliable; some authorities date the occasion earlier.

pressed by degree day and its ceremony. 'Oh, what a majestic and glorious thing it was when the degrees were granted to the new masters and torches were carried before them in their honour.' Luther had become a real academic with a profound regard for intellectual truth. And he ever remained such, and this was quite in harmony with the forthright and rumbustious way he would later denounce those whom he considered to have abused their intellectual gifts. He received the Master's Brown Hat and delivered the Master's Address, early in February 1505. At home they were delighted and Martin's father gave up using the intimate 'thou' in favour of the formal 'you'—a little perhaps as some Catholics cease to call their son by his simple Christian name if he is ordained and speak of him as 'Father'. Luther was due now to spend two more years at the University so that he could follow a post-graduate course and be fully qualified for a professional vocation. It was settled that he should study Law.

The picture, then, is commonplace. We see an undergraduate who walks the fifty or so miles home every now and then, who has an accident which does not upset him, who plays music and sings songs with friends, who sees a Bible for the first time and decides to explore these paths further, who does well at his exams, is excited at receiving his degree and decided to study law which will assure him work in the future.

We have, however, omitted one matter, though up to this time it would hardly have distinguished Luther notably from other undergraduates some of whom must also have suffered from a chronic trouble of his—moods. But in Luther's case they became, later, one of the occasions of an examination of the bases of medieval theology and the jumping-off point for his whole personal achievement. Something must be said then of the particular form these moods took, of the things on which Luther brooded; and we now begin to have something like a firm account from himself to rely on.

We are concerned immediately with a depression into which he fell in May after he had taken his degree. It seems highly probable that he had gone home for Easter. On April 23 he was back at Erfurt starting to attend a few lectures assigned to him in the

Arts Faculty for the summer term. Those on the Law were not due to begin till May 20. As Böhmer observes: 'For the first time in his life, Martin had a whole month for introspection'. On Luther's own statement he 'wandered about sadly during that time'. Apparently a fellow student died about that time, and this perhaps directed Luther's thoughts especially to death, and the other three 'last things' of medieval piety, judgment, heaven and hell. At any rate Luther himself tells us that his mood was due to what he called *tentatio tristitiae*, literally the temptation to be sad. Thomas Aquinas says somewhere that *tristitia* is the most deleterious of all human passions; evidently its meaning had something of despair in it, the sadness which leads to self-pity, hopelessness and despair. Such depressions, deeply egocentric, are not uncommon to intellectual men at this age. Luther was now at a crucial point in his early manhood, having completed the major part of his task as a student. The horizon could no longer be bounded by an examination he must pass. Looking to the future he would think more deeply also about his own life—and in this month he had plenty of time to do it.

In this depression Luther became more deeply concerned with the problem of his own sinfulness. The subject eventually became an obsession, and in its fully spiritual aspect became what Luther called *Anfechtung* and we must describe this in greater detail later when it contributes directly to his theology.[3] It was for the moment, at least, a deep anxiety about the impossibility of ever measuring up to the goodness demanded by Christ, and a feeling of the horror of guilt, and of its penalties in life and after.What, actually, were his 'sins'? What was the grist to this agonizing mill? References to sex in Luther's writing, his eventual marriage, and his conversation makes it virtually certain at least that sex should not be excluded. It is reasonable to suppose that sexual temptation —temptation to masturbation perhaps rather than to sexual relations with others—was at least contributory to his feelings of guilt. But there are few grounds for thinking that sexual experience or temptation itself played a dominating rôle now or later. The guilt undoubtedly has its 'psychological' aspect, the tension

---

[3] See pp. 35–6, 71–8. An *Anfechtung* is literally, an 'attack'.

between himself and any authoritative father-figure. Luther was able to express it theologically and it became a fundamental despair in the face of a religion encouraging him to obtain spiritual merit, to 'propitiate' God—a thing that seemed almost impossible of achievement, by definition. His actual 'sins' were probably trifles—impatience and irritability no doubt among them.

In such anxiety there was one most obvious solution for Luther to turn to. The religious life was commonly seen as a sure way to heaven. And the solution lay all about one. Monks, friars, and other religious of many kinds were a normal feature of society, either in the streets or enclosed in their large community buildings. It was far from exceptional to think about joining one of these communities. However, even though some were lax, it did involve definite sacrifices, of freedom, of property and of marriage, sacrifices both a little frightening but also attractive to an ardent spirit. We have already referred to the impression made on Luther as a boy by the ascetic in the streets of Magdeburg; and we know he had some acquaintance with the Franciscans at Eisenach through the Schalbes.

There was a certain tension in medieval society between life 'in the world', a sort of second best which made up for its pleasures as best it could by much pious activity, frequently with a cash payment, and, on the other hand, the religious life, 'the life of perfection'. Preachers often spoke of the religious life as a certain means of attaining salvation and contrasted this with the more difficult way in society. This self-regarding piety was of course one of the things against which Luther was later to campaign, believing that basically all pious 'works', from the small devotional practices to the act of becoming a friar, were an attempt to 'merit' a reward from God, an attempt to subject God to man's will, in a spirit alien to the Gospel. He spoke bitterly of his own personal experience of this way. 'I was a good religious, and I kept the rule of my order so strictly that I may say that if ever a religious could have got to heaven by religious works it was I. All my brothers in the priory who knew me well will bear me out. If I had kept on any longer, I would have killed myself with vigils, prayers, reading and other work.'

We may reasonably suppose that it was during his later time at the University that Luther first began to experience these anxieties strongly. Sensitive, a lover of music and poetry, naturally of a spiritual cast, probably driven in on himself to some extent by the overbearing father, he now began to confront himself with the abyss between the creature and the Creator. It was a *tentatio tristitiae* then, and it would be surprising if Luther's mind had not turned to the religious life as the way for him, after his association through the Schalbes with the Franciscans at Eisenach, and considering the existence of six religious houses in Erfurt itself. Of his meditation on this possible solution we cannot be sure. But of the depression itself we know from Luther.

On May 20 Luther began his legal studies in the college of St Mary, near the cathedral. About four weeks later he went home—why we do not know; the term was not over, and he had only recently started his new studies. Was something special on his mind? Did he put the possibility of becoming a religious to his father? Did his father dissuade him? Possibly, but we can only guess from the events of the next month, of which we know the facts from Luther. Luther left Mansfeld about June 30 for the walk back to Erfurt. On July 2 he was at Stotternheim, not far from the university town, having nearly completed the walk in about his usual time. A thunderstorm blew up. Lightning flashed close by Martin. He was thrown to the ground. An exclamation came from his lips, an invocation to St Anne, asking her help and the words 'I will become a religious',[4] Böhmer suggests, and it seems most probable that the lightning was the catalyst of a decision which had been gradually forming itself in Luther's mind, in the previous months, perhaps even years. As we have seen, such a decision would follow naturally from an anxiety about salvation.

On arriving at Erfurt Luther consulted friends as to what he should do. Was he bound to a vow made in a moment of panic?

[4] Commonly biographers have translated this and other similar phrases of Luther's, using the word 'monk'. But 'monk' in English refers only to a member of one of the older Orders who use the Rule of St Benedict; it is not a generic term for all those who take the vows of religion. In this book I have tried to avoid this kind of inaccuracy. Luther became an Augustinian Friar. His 'vow' in the thunderstorm was a vow in general terms, to become a 'religious'. Today he would most likely have said: 'I will join an Order'.

He was, apparently, at first reluctant to be so bound. Many advised him not to enter a monastery. Others were of the opinion that morally he had bound himself. Luther decided to stand by the vow; and the kept vow is the beginning of Luther's life as a professional religious and theologian. The line is direct from his decision to stand by his vow to the conscientious honouring of other practical conclusions later in his life, including of course the decision to stand up for his theology and its practical conclusions, which eventually led him to marry. One can put too much direct weight on a man's decision at twenty-one, but Luther's life is a closely integrated whole. The kept vow is a pivot from which in general proceed all the later developments. A discussion of some of the issues involved is appended in the form of a note at the end of this chapter.

Table Talk, recorded in 1539, has the following words which are the principal source of our knowledge of Luther's view of the vow. He was talking on the anniversary of the day on which he entered the Augustinian Priory:

'Today is the very date on which I entered the priory at Erfurt', and he began to tell the story of conditions under which he had taken his vow: how nearly fourteen days before, on the road near Stotternheim not far from Erfurt he was so frightened by a thunderbolt that in terror he shouted: 'Help, dear Anne. I will become a religious.'

'. . . Afterwards I regretted my vow, and many of my friends tried to persuade me not to enter the priory. I, however, was determined to go through with it, and the day before St Alexius I invited certain of my best men friends to a farewell party, as on the next day they were to lead me into the priory.' To those, however, he left behind he said: 'Today you see me for the last time and then no more'. 'In tears they led me away; and my father was very angry about my vow, yet I persisted in my determination. It never occurred to me to leave the priory.'[5]

We have a picture then of Luther definitely reluctant to leave the world but spurred on by other motives, the motive of standing by his word, and back behind this the motives which had made

<hr/>

[5] Quoted by Schwiebert, p. 138.

it possible for the idea of the religious life to be in his mind at all, the motive of finding a secure salvation, and more generally, presumably, a wish to reach spiritual heights, to emulate the best of those monks and friars whom he had often met. In a sermon of 1534 Luther refers to the motive of seeking a secure salvation: 'I was never able to console myself regarding my baptism, but always thought: "Oh, when will you once become pious enough and do enough to obtain a gracious God?" Such thoughts drove me into the priory.'[6] As we shall see, Luther must have made his decision with some dispatch on his return to Erfurt and our picture in the end must be one of determination rather than of anguish, doubt or perplexity.

NOTE ON THE VOW

It will be instructive to consider what judgment moral theologians would make today on the nature of the obligations which Luther possibly incurred in his vow, for implicit in Luther's decision were issues leading to his later actions and doctrines and the whole Lutheran tradition. There remain important differences in the differing judgments which might be made today.

Some theologians today would probably say that Luther was morally bound to go on the course to which he had vowed himself although the vow was made in a moment when he was threatened with death. Böhmer himself appears to be one of these, for in discussing Luther's situation he says of the friends who were of the opinion that Luther had bound himself irrevocably, 'in all conscience he had to admit that these few serious-minded ones were right'. (Of course we set aside here the fact that some Protestant theologians might consider it ethically wrong to take the vows of poverty, celibacy and obedience in a monastic community—this is another question, which we are not discussing here.) This is the simple straightforward view that Luther had given his word and he must stand by it, even against his own subsequent disinclination.

Other theologians, and this would almost certainly include all Catholic theologians to a man, would say that the vow being made in a moment of panic and without the full consent of the rational being, and representing no firm and deliberate intention, could not bind a man. Catholic theologians would say that the Church has a certain authority in such matters, and follow the theory that the only thing which can finally and certainly bind a man is the formal call of the competent ecclesiastical authority, the bishop or religious superior, at the end of a period of training. But then it might reasonably be asked whether there was not some obligation to give the matter a trial, to undergo some of the preliminary training. But if such a matter were put to a

[6] Quoted by Schwiebert, p. 142.

spiritual director today the normal attitude would be to respect the external facts and to say that all inner urges may be of suspect psychological origin, even preternatural, or foolish self-opinionations. A man is either bound by the authority competent to bind him, such a director might say, or he is not. If he is not, he ·s free—free even to go against strong interior urges, and his own word if made in private without any witness. Such urges, such words cannot bind a man, and God will not punish a man for going the way he chooses, will not punish him for exercising his freedom. But the spiritually-minded Catholic will still have a doubt. Is the director just 'testing' him? It will be a crucial matter, particular to the persons concerned, to settle whether this is mere scruple to be ignored, or whether a definite preliminary step should be taken to try to enter the religious state.

The matters here are symbolical of, though not identical with, the later argument between Luther and Erasmus over the Freedom of the Will.[7] Erasmus would be for freedom to honour the vow or not: Luther for a subjection to a manifestation of the Word. They are also symbolical of the differences between Protestants and Catholics today on the question of authority. The Catholic contention is that man's whole life, his every act, all happen within the body of Christ, in a Christian orbit which is communitarian, and that the Church on earth has a real authority for the time of man's life here about the rights and wrongs of all morally significant actions. This 'say' is not arbitrary; it must be responsible, related to the Church's law, her moral tradition, all based ultimately on Scripture and the commission given there to the Church. Within these carefully and rationally defined limits a man may rely on the Church's advice or decisions on all matters of moral principle. He cannot submit every detail of his life for an oracular decision as from an astrologer, but he can ask for a statement of the relevant principles on every issue which he can then conscientiously apply to himself.

The Protestant might perhaps agree with most of this statement but say, with Luther's teaching to support him, that it has a wrong emphasis, omitting the extent to which each individual Christian is himself 'the Church' in a particular situation, and the degree to which, in this sense, the Word speaks directly to him, giving him a real authority, and precluding him from giving such continual and often decisive weight to objective historical tradition, with all its limitations of convention. The Church, he might say, in effect tends to make a man's decisions for him, in the Catholic tradition, and in this way to perpetuate the legalistic tradition and abuses which Luther overthrew. The Catholic might reply that the Church protects a man from his own foolishness. The Protestant might reply *Quis custodiet*—who will protect (control) the protectors (controllers)? And we come then to the ultimate crux—the Catholic believes in authority within the Church on earth as objectively final in matters of principle, in faith and morals, authority definable in human terms, in spite of the fact that this authority is essentially 'mediated' and must be defined analogically. The Lutheran would turn away from human authority to the Word, as the ultimate authority, in spite of the subjective danger.[8] In practice the two attitudes are liable to a large number of variations which can bring

[7] See pp. 247–59.   [8] See Appendix 2.

them very close to each other.[9] But there remains today in practice an out-standing difference between the two traditions.

Luther's decision to honour his vow was of course taken entirely within the old tradition, with the advice of friends themselves in the Catholic tradition. Many Catholic theologians would undoubtedly have argued at that time in a sense which would have meant that the vow must be honoured. There was for several centuries a school of Catholic theologians who maintained the authority of subjective inspirations. Probably, as Böhmer suggests, those who advised Luther to stand by his vow were the more responsible and serious-minded people—though they could have included the merely superstitious, or scrupu-lous, as well. On the other hand those who advised him to disregard the vow were quite possibly doing so for bad reasons, possibly implying the evanescent nature of all human activity and the small value that could be attached to such words, attacking not the circumstances but the status of any vow in itself.

[9] See 'Reformed Infallibility' by George Lindbeck in *Cross Currents*, U.S.A., Vol. XI, No. 4, a very striking current example of Protestant/Roman Catholic interpenetration. Dr Lindbeck, a Lutheran, is discussing in this article books by the Catholic theologians Küng and Rahner.

Part Two

YOUNG FATHER LUTHER

5. The Priory

FIFTEEN days after the thunderstorm, Luther entered the priory of the Augustinians at Erfurt. Even supposing that he had thought much about the religious life in the previous months, or years; even supposing he had decided that he would choose the Augustinians, in preference to the many other possible orders, in particular those which had houses at Erfurt, the Benedictines, the Carthusians, the Dominicans, the Franciscans, the Servites; it is still true that Luther acted rapidly in those fifteen or so days. They show us for the first time that the thinker, scholar, and the lover of music can take advice, weigh it, make his own judgment, and take the necessary actions to put his own conclusions into action with dispatch. He told his friends of his vow, listened to their advice, some one way some the other. He then followed the advice which coincided almost certainly with his own conviction. He informed the university authorities of his wish to break off his studies, to cease his lectures, and to be formally released from these engagements. The rapid release given was perhaps normal in the case of someone wishing to change his way of life. He wrote to his parents. Presumably he went to the Augustinian priory to tell them he wished to enter, and gained their assent to his entering at first as a postulant—not necessarily easy since they were careful about whom they admitted even to this pre-novitiate stage. He arranged to settle up and leave the house where he was staying; and he invited his friends to a party for the last evening 'in the world'. All these things take time, and particularly when we remember that there were no telephones. And Luther had been out of town for a week or two. It is not, I think, too much to see here a glimmer of Luther's unusual gifts peculiarly adapted to historical achievements. Possessing the interior sensitivity, imagination, and intelligence necessary to form careful and confident judgments, he can also summon movements of the will, and determination, and he has practical judgment and the ability to put all to precise and organized action. One must add the quality which eventually was among his greatest, a courage that enabled him to do what he saw to be right, regardless of all other considerations. This was Luther's first important action taken independently of his parents.

Böhmer tells us that the Augustinian priory 'was commonly considered the foremost centre in the town for the cultivation of the ascetic ideal' and enjoyed the highest prestige. Although the Order of Augustinian Hermits was a 'mendicant' order, depending by its regulations on charity, the priory at Erfurt was probably rich enough to make begging unnecessary. The friars at Erfurt were all educated men. They received Luther into the priory on July 17, 1505. A day or two later an angry letter came from Luther's father cutting him off from 'all paternal grace and favour'. He had plans for Martin's future, wishing him to make 'a respectable and wealthy marriage'; and this flouting of the family authority was not to be tolerated. It appears to be typical of his domineering but realistic spirit that a few days later a second letter came from his father to say that after all he had decided to resign himself to Martin's decision though 'with reluctance and sadness'. Two younger brothers of Martin's had died of the plague soon after Hans had written the first letter; and false news had come to him that Martin had been taken sick too. Fearing divine judgment, Hans retreated. His permission was not necessary to Martin's decision to enter, but Luther would no doubt have found it hard to bear opposition from his father.

About the beginning of September 1505 Luther was formally clothed as a novice. Perhaps he was reminded of his first days in the university at Erfurt. Now again he entered on a daily time-table which accounted for every hour of the day. But now it was more taxing personally and more exactly applied, though less exacting intellectually. Of the various small penances such as the limitation of eating to twice a day, and only once a day on the fast days (which amounted to perhaps a hundred a year), the worst he found was the cold in his cell. However, there was a warming room where one could go when one got too cold. Luther survived the novitiate and was formally admitted as an Augustinian Hermit probably in September 1506, after the usual year's testing. Thereafter the road to the priesthood was normally swift, much swifter than it would become a few decades later. The Council of Trent decreed a standard course of studies total-ling normally not less than six years. Luther studied doctrine on the Mass, and was ordained subdeacon probably by the Prior in December of the same year, deacon two months later on February 27, 1507, and the day of his ordination was April 4—nineteen months since his reception as a novice and in his own twenty-fourth year.

The step from layman to priest was not the same size as it is today. Biographers have emphasized the great divide between priest and laity in the medieval system but have failed to guard their readers against thinking in terms of modern priests, turned out all very much in the same mould, after many years of training which, coming at the end of adolescence, have a radical effect. The medieval priest was in some ways much nearer to the people than the twentieth-century priest. Indeed part of the claims of those who wished to reform the Church, and finally succeeded at the Council of Trent, was that the priest was much too near to the people, too liable to live just as they did, treating his priest-hood as a sort of incidental increment or accretion, a mere office, a sacramental (and in this sense very nearly a magical) 'power'. And it was also just this off-hand attitude to the supernatural which Luther so detested, the treating of God as though he were in the power of the Church, the giving of grace as though the Church truly had it within its power not only to forgive sins on earth but to rule also in purgatory, even in heaven. However, in practice there were wide variations and it seems likely that Luther's priory, although not exceptional in its devotion, stood well above the lowest standards; and the difference between a secular and a regular (belonging to a religious order) priest could be big. The training, though short, was serious. Its priests achieved a certain standard of reverence at Mass and considered some measure of dignity essential. Possibly this was general in Germany. At any rate we know Luther was deeply shocked when he saw the Italians saying Mass in Rome a few years later—counting seven Masses at one altar in an hour on one occasion.

Luther was possibly exceptional in the particular seriousness with which he approached the priesthood. He certainly earned the respect of his superiors during his novitiate. The year and a half before ordination seems to have turned his being wholeheartedly in the religious direction to which it had probably been tending for some years, perhaps since the school days at Eisenach. It seems pretty certain that Luther took his training with exemplary conscientiousness, and indeed that his behaviour in the priory subsequently was equally correct, even scrupulous. There is not a great deal of evidence, but it all tends to support this hypothesis, and there is no evidence or valid argument to support any other.

For the first months, even for much of the twenty-one months up to his ordination, Luther probably experienced a new, perhaps a profound content. His life now had a purpose, his religious feelings and thoughts a clear object, and he could pray for a long time. For the first year or so in a religious house it is common for the novice to feel at peace. The new surroundings, the regular discipline and framework, the absence of all questions about the future, the emphasis on simple obedience, and, perhaps very important, the absolutely regular meals, sleep and work, all conduce to physical and mental health. Spiritually, the novice is taken seriously by the novice master. He can discuss any difficulties he has and will be given careful advice and the reading of particular books may be advised. Luther was treated in this way himself, by his novice master, probably John von Grefenstein.

It is important to notice that Luther is a normal, even a specially good, religious, and it is no doubt partly as a result of this that he was able to be promoted so rapidly from one position of responsibility to another after his ordination. Luther himself tells us of his first months in the priory that all went well with him: 'I know from my own experience, and that of many others, how peaceful and quiet Satan is wont to be in one's first years as a religious or priest'. But within this calm lay the old moods, the depression and the worry about salvation, which now began to threaten to grow to the enormous proportions they eventually assumed, even though still only in the background.

We have referred to the essential content of these depressions, as we first know of them two months before the vow—despair at the impossibility of success in the task which the Christian apparently faced, the task of being good enough for God, the complete impossibility of a total purity of motive and of total perfection such as Jesus commands in the Sermon on the Mount. The depression involved an attitude of despair in face of the theology of 'merit', the theory which implied the spiritual validity of man's own unaided efforts. This *Anfechtung* is something more than a temptation for which the German word is *Versuchung*.[1] It is a human hopelessness which involves a deep spiritual conflict and struggle, a cosmic battle in the self, in the soul. 'If I were to live long enough I would write a book about *Anfechtung* without which nobody can understand the Scriptures or know the fear and love of God, nay, he cannot know what the Spirit is.'[2] One thinks of St Paul, 'It is a terrible thing to fall into the hands of the living God'.

But the teeth of Luther's *Anfechtung* are in the despair caused by the feeling that all one can do, all one sets one's hands to, is doomed, that God will have none of it. The *tentatio tristitiae* drew nourishment from the soil of the monastery, increasing its tentacles a hundredfold in the sharpened spiritual atmosphere of the religious life with its framework for a journey to perfection; the long hours of chanting and of private prayer, the little deprivations, the obedience, the whole structure, provided a fine

---

[1] See Rupp, *R.G.*, p. 106. All the references in this book to *Anfechtung* are invaluable, but this particularly so, with its further quotation from Vogelsang, and we therefore reproduce the whole paragraph: 'It is striking that Luther chooses the word *Anfechtung* with its suggestion of combat rather than *Versuchung* for "Temptation". For *Anfechtung*, says Vogelsang, "is a conception drawn from life, not doctrine. *Anfechtung* lies on the frontier where life separates itself from doctrine." We might call it an existential word since it concerns man as he grapples with himself and the universe. But we must not be misled into supposing that this is mere subjectivism. The whole meaning of *Anfechtung* for Luther lies in the thought that man has his existence *Coram Deo*, and that he is less the active intelligence imposing itself on the stuff of the universe around him, than the subject of an initiative and action from God who employs the whole of man's existence as a means of bringing men to awareness of their need and peril. It is God's eternity, holiness and power which thus endlessly threaten man at every moment in his whole existence, in his life and action, in the intention and decision of the moral life in the faith and hope of his religion. God's ever present judgment it is which holds a man in the loneliness of his conscience, and in absolute responsibility and which with his every breath consigns him to the Almighty and Holy One to prosper or destroy.'

[2] Rupp, *R.G.*, footnote, p. 106.

hothouse for any kind of disposition to reflect on one's own futility, in the face of a theology whose basic framework was that of the 'merits' of Christ and his saints, and the 'merit' which each Christian must try to earn.

Luther's spiritual director, probably John von Grefenstein, treated his troubles with seriousness, tried to help him and spoke frankly and kindly to him of many things, being a real counsellor and friend, advising him about books, the Bible, the Fathers, Cassian. Luther wanted to make a 'general confession' at an unusual time and John would not have it. We have his famous repartee, recorded and treasured by Luther who was well aware of the irritation he sometimes caused to others who must have looked on his complaints as 'belly-aching'; Luther had been complaining, more or less grumbling, perhaps more seriously anguishing, about the wrath of God, and John humourously and with some accuracy came out with: 'God is not angry with you, you are angry with God'—a remark which was very well directed to putting the trouble right if it had only been superficial, and which did in fact give Luther some immediate comfort. But Luther was already beginning to track the trouble down deep into the roots of theology and the whole contemporary practice of the Church. So, John's shaft did not help. As long as Luther accepted contemporary theology fully and sincerely as it was commonly preached and taught, with its primary emphasis on merit to be won, the wrath of God remained troublesome and a cause of those 'scruples' which were common amongst religious people in the Middle Ages, and remained quite common amongst Catholics even up to the present time.[3]

[3] Luther's *Anfechtungen* had roots, no doubt, in his own make-up, physical and psychological, and assumed in the end the role of a struggle with despair which recurred throughout his life. And this is no doubt a perennial human experience. Its form of 'scruples', particularly common amongst Catholics so subject as they were then and have been for the last four centuries to 'legalism', was less troublesome in Luther's later life, though doubt and despair became more severe.

6. *The First Mass*

THE spiritual struggle, *Anfechtung*, did not begin to assume really big proportions until after Luther's ordination, perhaps a year or more after, but the distant rumbles of the thunderstorm could be heard already. An important date is the occasion of his first Mass with its twofold incident, Luther's own experience during it, and his father's explosion at the meal afterwards.

Biographers who are keen to put great weight on the father-son relationship have devoted a very large number of pages to this occasion. Obviously his first Mass is a very important occasion to every man who is ordained as a Catholic priest. If his parents can be present it is a great joy, and the complex of emotions generated is naturally further increased, and there will be a certain anxiety, especially if the parents were originally in opposition to their son's decision. In Luther's case there were two unusual incidents. And the event stands out as one with a sub-stantial and unusual amount of historical detail (written down by Luther fourteen years later in 1521) in a period of about four years stretching from his reception into the priory at Erfurt till he began actively to teach theology there, a time during which no incident is described in comparable detail. Thus there is a temptation to the historian to overemphasize an occasion which was in any case naturally important to Luther himself.[1]

In prospect the occasion promised to be happy, although a little difficult. Herr Luther was invited to the priory for his son's first Mass. He asked for the date to be made to fit his own con-venience, presumably his business convenience. This was done, and he came in style, on May 2, with a number of companions, all on horses which numbered twenty altogether—and with a

---

[1] Rupp, R.G., p. 86, issues an important warning against thinking that the historical evidence which survives provides us with precisely the most significant events. It is not likely to be the case. 'There is a great temptation to forget the haphazard and accidental quality of historical evidence, and to suppose that because we seek to solve certain questions, what evidence there is must speak to their condition.' All the same the incidents on the day of the first Mass do seem to be of special import.

gift of twenty gulden, which, as we have seen, was possibly as much as £110. He is the same rather overbearing, hearty, self-assertive father we have already seen.

Many a new priest probably finds the intrusion of 'the world' threatening to disorientate him at a time when he is to exercise his priesthood in offering Mass for the first time. He is conscious of a certain practical difficulty in completing the rite correctly for the first time; in Luther's day to make a mistake in the ritual was considered a serious matter. He perhaps experiences a natural anxiety at this spiritual climax in his life. His parents bring echoes of the past, of childhood and adolescence which distract as well as rejoice the mind and heart. For Luther his growing obsession with the justice of God and his own futility, worthlessness and guilt also laid a certain small shadow over everything. It was not enough, so far as we know, to cause anyone to worry unduly about the outcome, but that it was there we have Luther's own evidence. And in the event it caused him a moment of extreme anguish, when a wave of conviction about his own inability, sincerely or satisfactorily, to do what a priest has to do, swept over him.

Luther tells us that it was at the start of the silent part of the Canon of the Mass that this occurred. The Canon starts aloud with the 'Preface', said or sung, a solemn paragraph of thanksgiving and praise, concluding with the *Sanctus* ('Holy, Holy, Holy, Lord God of Hosts, heaven and earth are full of thy glory. Hosanna in the highest. Blessed is he that cometh in the name of the Lord. Hosanna in the highest'). From then onwards the celebrant says in a very low voice (according to the rubrics prescribed by Roman Canon Law of Luther's time and at the moment of writing) the long prayer which asks God to accept the 'gifts', the bread and the wine, offered for the benefit of all men, of the Pope, of the local Bishop—and in particular of various named people, and to accept the 'oblation' so that it may become the body and blood of Jesus Christ, recalling the way in which this was first done by Christ himself on the night of the Last Supper. This prayer begins with the words *Te igitur, clementissime Pater*, 'Therefore, O most merciful Father, . . .' It was then that Luther was overcome:

At these words I was utterly stupefied and terror-stricken. I thought to myself, 'With what tongue shall I address such Majesty, seeing that all men ought to tremble in the presence of even an earthly prince? Who am I, that I should lift up my eyes or raise my hands to the divine Majesty? The angels surround him. At his nod the earth trembles. And shall I, a miserable little pygmy, say I want this, I ask for that? For I am dust and ashes and full of sin and I am speaking to the living, eternal and true God.'[2]

Luther was stupefied, even terror-stricken, at the idea of addressing the Creator and Lord of all. He must have read the words often before, and had presumably practised them a number of times before he said them now. But it is a different matter to say them for the first time, officially, as a priest, conscious of their immense import, a prayer from the creature to the Creator. It is no doubt a common experience for a new priest to find a fuller meaning in prayers when he says them for the first time as the celebrant at Mass, and it is typical of Luther's temperament that he should have such an experience particularly strongly. No doubt the solemnity of the occasion also often bids fair to overwhelm the new priest, and to make him very sensible of his own littleness; this Luther had in common with many a new priest. But he added to all this his own special sense of terror, and almost of futility. These are the elements which are important for the future, and which distinguish Luther from other new priests who felt no such terror or futility, or not in such a decisive way.

After the words *clementissime Pater* follow the words *per Jesum Christum, Filium tuum, Dominum nostrum* ('through Jesus Christ, your Son, our Lord'). The priest addresses God, God the Father, through God's Son, the God-man, Jesus Christ; he says the prayers not simply on his own account, but in association with Christ, whose priesthood he shares. This would seem to shelter a priest somewhat from the feeling of terror which attacked Luther. Luther's description, however, implies that man faces God quite alone. His reaction is that of the Jews in the Old Testament, who turned away from any vision, who dared not look where they thought God might be, who would not speak the divine name.

[2] Translated by Bainton.

Christian theology maintains that the abyss has been bridged by the incarnation of the Word of God in Jesus Christ, and that this bridge is continued for all time through his Church in which his presence is perpetuated both sacramentally and dynamically. But for Luther there is an existential sense in which every Christian is still alone with God. And in the Bible there are many Judaic, Gospel and Pauline references to man's personal predicament before God, a predicament which for Paul is still something to be reckoned with even though its solution lies in Christ. And Christ himself speaks of man guilty before a judge as well as forgiven and loved by the Father. This is to anticipate the later development of Luther's theology, but the source of that theology lies in his own personal experience (and its special appeal for his age, and others, is related to this fact of its root in personal experience), and the earliest recorded occasion of such experience is this moment at his first Mass at the age of twenty-three.

Luther's failure to advert to the mediation of Christ in the opening words of this part of the Canon is highly significant. He often spoke later of his vision of Christ as a judge, as the great God who would punish him for his wrong-doing—Christ on the cross was in some rather horrible way a threatening Christ for him. It is true that in spite of the great humanization of Christ in popular art, he remained more of a 'god' than a brother to the pious, and theology often enough equated him simply with God; the emphasis of the phrase 'Word Incarnate' was all on the divine. The authoritarian fideist approach of the Nominalists to theology was a further potent factor in evacuating human warmth and incarnational theology from the Gospels.[3]

On Luther's description of his stupefaction have been built all sorts of stories about an attempt to run away from the altar, for which there is no historical evidence. Perhaps Luther paused, and to anyone close by it was possibly clear that he was overcome by the thoughts and experience he then had. It seems very unlikely that there was more to it than that, but it remained for Luther a milestone in the building of his own spiritual outlook, his religious life.

---

[3] See pp. 45–59 for more detailed discussion of the Nominalist influence.

It is right to add a reminder here of the interior force which this experience would have had if it was indeed related psychologically to a strong emotional relationship between father and son, liable to be projected into the priest's relationship to God.

After Mass there was a meal, which naturally had a certain festive character to it (two letters of Luther's survive, inviting the Franciscan Vicar John Braun and other friends from Eisenach to be present on this special occasion), and it must have been dominated by the presence of Herr Luther and his rather numerous companions from the home-town, probably small-town business men, maybe some farming relations, their jollification justified materially by Herr Luther's handsome cash gift. Martin began to talk, and turned to the occasion which was the origin of his decision to enter the priory, his vow at Stotternheim. His father interrupted: 'Let's hope it wasn't an illusion of the devil'[4]—it was typically ham-handed, poking rough and ready German fun at his son, father perhaps on his mettle in the priory and in the presence of his comrades, putting everything beyond the visible realities into the category of things 'peculiar', spooks to be laughed at or feared, or God to be respected. What if all Martin's spiritual life was due to the pixies who had been the cause of his panic in the storm and made him utter that vow, or, worse still, the devil? Martin made some reply, to smooth things over or to justify himself, something of both perhaps. But his father had never liked being answered back and was roused to verbal irritation and pomposity, quoting the ten commandments as a parent speaking to his child—perhaps as a layman reminding this community of priests of the fundamental laws which they, maybe, sometimes overlooked amidst their more advanced studies. 'Have you not read: "Honour thy father and thy mother"?' It was crude. What could his hosts reply? Even in Germany where this kind of eruption is more easily tolerated and outspokenness is perhaps expected, this sudden eruption of Herr Luther must have caused embarrassment.

It is tempting to make a lot of this, for it is indeed clear to the end of his life that there was a tension between father and son, and the father's question would probably have specially hurt Martin

[4] Rupp's translation, *R.G.*, p. 85.

who does seem precisely to have honoured his father, always thinking the best of him, and wishing, so far as he could, to do what his father wanted. One with a taste in irony, or in a variety of poetic justice, or simply in a satisfying dramatic pattern, can set beside this incident the fact that Luther himself did eventually leave the priory, and did eventually marry as Herr Luther had wished, and did at the time of his marriage comment on the pleasure that this event gave to his father.

The incidents of the ordination did not, so far as we know, make any great impression on Luther's superior or brethren. His life continued without special incident for some years. His subsequent promotion at an early age to teaching posts, and then to other responsibilities, seems to imply that he was not considered unbalanced, but rather the opposite, a young friar of unusual promise.

7. *Student and Lecturer at Wittenberg*

AFTER ordination, Luther continued his study of theology in the priory at Erfurt. Father John Nathin was the professor in the priory and lectured there on the principal text book, the *Sentences* of Peter Lombard. We know that Luther also studied the *Collectiones* of Biel (whose book on the Mass he had studied before ordination), and the *Quaestiones* of d'Ailly and Occam. It is not known whether he studied Aquinas, but it seems improbable, since if he had done so he would hardly have failed to mention it and, we may surmise, Luther's theology would hardly have remained so untouched by Aquinas. Nathin had himself been a pupil of Biel, and the tradition in which Luther studied now, as previously both as an undergraduate at Erfurt and a novice and student in the priory, was in general Nominalist and Occamist. We discuss this in greater detail in the following chapter.

For seventeen months till October 1508, Luther devoted to these studies all the time which could be spared from attendance in choir and other monastic chores. It was his first long uninter-

rupted stretch of theological study; no doubt he would have been
surprised if he had been told that it would be his last, that he would
soon receive promotion to a teaching post, and thereafter to other
posts, and that ten years later his would be a notorious public
name. There seems no doubt that he spent this year and a half
well and laid the basis of his theological knowledge during it. In
October 1508 his studies were partially interrupted by promotion
to a teaching post which also involved moving to another priory.
He was appointed to be lecturer in philosophy in the University
of Wittenberg. This was rapid promotion indeed. But Wittenberg University was only six years old, founded by the Elector
Frederick ('the wise') who resided at Wittenberg, as a rival university, so Böhmer says, to that in the ducal (Duke George) town
of Leipzig, forty miles away. In making this foundation the reputation of Wittenberg and of Saxony was perhaps Frederick's
principal concern rather than consideration of the problem of how
to fill all the academic posts. Most of these posts were farmed out
as the responsibility of various other bodies and religious orders.
The Augustinians had to supply two posts, one the chair of
philosophy, and the other that of lecturer on the Bible. This latter had been held by John Staupitz since the founding of the
University; he was by this time superior of the Saxon Congregation of the Augustinians, and seems to have been absent a great
deal; so much so that Luther probably saw little of him.

The Augustinians, no doubt, had to appoint someone of real
intellectual ability to the philosophy lectureship, and young
Luther was regarded as an exceedingly promising young friar. But
his appointment was possibly due to the relatively small number
of students at Wittenberg—about 150 enrolling each year. Perhaps
the Prior was killing two birds with one stone—Luther both
lectured and continued his own studies which would eventually
enable him to lecture in the priory at Erfurt.

Perhaps the senior friars were unwilling to leave traditional
Erfurt for upstart Wittenberg—a city which in any case seems to
have had a poor reputation, as a rather specially smelly little
market town. Its principal claim to fame was that the Elector
Frederick resided there in his castle. This, together with the

Chapter House of All Saints, the new University lecture hall, and the parish church of St Mary were the only notable buildings. As capital of the electorate, it had some privileges, including that of supplying salt to the whole region. The castle had a reliquary, the contents of which could hardly be rivalled if any twentieth-century dramatist wished to invent a really shocking list of bogus relics.[1]

In travelling the hundred miles to Wittenberg from Erfurt, Luther would have had to go close to his home, and perhaps he called in. Arriving at Wittenberg in November shortly before his twenty-fifth birthday, he began to lecture on Aristotle's Nichomachean Ethics, on the first four days of each week at 2 o'clock in the afternoon, so Böhmer thinks. In undertaking this he was no doubt well served by his previous hard work in the University of Erfurt, and the experience of taking part, there, in disputations. This was not a full-time post and Luther was told to continue his own studies. This he did and five months after his arrival at Wittenberg he gained the title of *Baccalaureus Biblicus*. The result of this was that he was given the responsibility of giving a further course of lectures himself—on the Bible, presumably to make up for the absence of lectures from Staupitz, the official lecturer on this subject, who was so frequently absent on the business of the Order. But Luther was still able to continue with his own studies, and by the autumn of 1509 he had been declared *Sententiarius*, a degree entitling a man to lecture on the *Sentences* of Peter Lombard. One of his principal teachers during these studies was Jodocus Trutvetter, a renowned interpreter of Occam, previously at Erfurt, and a native of Eisenach, the town of Luther's old school.

We know that Luther found his work very heavy during the year at Wittenberg. He wrote to Father John Braun in Eisenach,

---

[1] Böhmer speaks of 5,005 of them, including a piece of the Burning Bush of Moses, nine thorns from the Crown of Thorns, thirty-five fragments of Christ's Cross, some stalks of hay and straw on which the Christ Child lay, remnants of the manger, cradle, and swaddling clothes of Jesus, bits of the hair, camisole, coat, girdle, veil and milk of the Blessed Virgin, and 204 parts of bodies and one whole body of the innocent babies of Bethlehem. These relics might perhaps have appeared in the chapter which referred to 'superstitions'. But bad as the absence of a historical sense is, the mentality that permitted Christians to believe in these relics is less radical in its weakness than the superstitions to which we referred there. An absence of a sense of historical time as we understand it today was still practically universal.

in March, about the hardness of the philosophical work and his preference for theology, using the oft-quoted phrase, 'I mean that theology which searches out the nut from the shell, the grain from the husk, the marrow from the bone'. The foundations of Luther's lifelong devotion to theology are now being laid. What the Gospel of Jesus really meant, what his message really is, what St Paul was really saying, what God really does for us, what our relation to him really is—these, the great questions of theology, were now gripping his mind, and he was enthralled by the argumentation of those whose work he read, and increasingly dissatisfied.

As soon as he had passed his exam, as *Sententiarius*, Luther's superior at Erfurt decided that he must return to take the theology classes in the priory. The Wittenberg *Sententiarius* was looked on somewhat askance by the senior academics at Erfurt University when the priory asked them to recognize Father Luther's degree. However Father Nathin persuaded them; it was he apparently who had had Luther recalled in order to relieve him somewhat. Luther now settled down to teaching theology to the student friars, a task which he took seriously, making copious annotations in the margins of the books he read. These have survived. We are able to examine Luther's own writing in the text-books which were in the priory library.

8. *Theology at Erfurt*

I. THE 'JUSTICE OF GOD' AND THE HUMAN PREDICAMENT

UP to this point in his life biographers have to rely on Luther's recollections much later in life, tested out against what other evidence can be found. The result may be some such picture as I have drawn, fairly reliable but not much more than an outline. With his first lectures in the priory at Erfurt in the autumn of 1509 we come to events which can be interpreted in the light of what Luther was himself writing. And the writing itself is of

major importance for Luther's own story. Although we do not
have an actual text of the lectures which he gave to the little group
of junior friars, we have Luther's own notes, made, according to
the tradition of the time, in the margins of the great pages of the
text-books on which he was lecturing. We have then a very
reliable witness to that which was in Luther's mind.

The books in which Luther wrote were *The Sentences* of Peter
Lombard and several volumes of St Augustine. The former was a
twelfth-century conflation of biblical texts and quotations from
the Fathers, the standard theological text-book which Luther himself had been studying only recently as a student. In these books,
in Luther's hand, are his copious comments, his frequent *nota
bene*, his '*please underline*'. The comments are twofold, on the
one hand affirmations and positive opinions, on the other
criticism.

First, emphatic attention is drawn to Christ and Faith, and to
the opposing Sin and Concupiscence—and generally there is 'a
doctrine which treats seriously the depth and tragedy of the
human predicament because it considers man and his world in the
presence of the Living God'.[1] Rupp places the whole of Luther's
early theology, brilliantly, under the summary phrase *coram Deo*—
'in God's presence', 'before God'—a phrase which Luther frequently repeats in the early lectures. The distinguishing mark of
Luther's comments in these first available writings, these marginalia, is a directness, an economy of interpretation which may well
owe something to Occam's razor (his principle of logical economy),
but which is already notably original in its forceful personal
application, its dominant biblical awareness of 'man and God'.
His treatment of the 'act of love', man's love of God, in the
marginal notes, shows his preference for saying in a simple
biblical fashion that the Holy Spirit dwells and works actively in
us, rather than speaking of 'habitus', the Aristotelian psychological category. And Luther appeals to Augustine to support
him.[2]

Again Luther appeals, in original fashion, against *multi inclyti
doctores*, to Scripture, for his opinion that the soul is an 'image of

[1] Rupp, R.G., p. 101.　　　　　[2] Rupp, R.G., p. 94.

God' (*quod anima sit imago Dei*).[3] It is interesting to know that these marginal writings occurred at a time when Luther had experienced a great new intellectual excitement, in reading Augustine for the first time. 'Before I fell in with his books I had very little room for him'—'In the beginning I devoured Augustine'.[4] Generally his new vision led Luther to approve what Peter Lombard said, to approve even more St Augustine, and to ponder with personal intensity on the text of the Bible. We must remember that he had come straight from lecturing on the Bible at Wittenberg where (either by himself or conceivably with a hint from Staupitz, the Bible lecturer for the previous six years or so—but Luther probably saw nothing or little of him) he must have begun to understand the value of studying the biblical text itself. And about this time it is important that he began to study Hebrew with a view to understanding the text better. It was a new thing to study the Bible in the original languages. Luther was following a trail blazed by the early humanists, in resorting to Hebrew as he now did; later the Greek text of the New Testament produced by Erasmus contributed greatly to the ever-increasing influence on him of the Bible. It was only in 1518 that he discovered that '*Poenitentia*', 'penance', a word full of 'penal' and 'culpable' associations was in Greek 'metanoia', change of heart, a dynamic and more optimistic word.

The affirmations, inspired by Scripture, which appeared in the marginalia, are thrown into sharp perspective by the negative comments; fierce criticism of the philosophers, and harsh comments on the theologians of recent times for allowing theology to be invaded by philosophical terms, categories and methods.

The force which Luther put into his opposition to Aristotle, to Scotus, to Occam, and to Biel, and the force he gives his own affirmations, using Scripture and praising Augustine and Peter Lombard, is remarkable. It seems certain that the vehemence, the distinctively Lutheran power, derives from his spiritual predicament to which we have already referred. His own spiritual crisis, his *Anfechtung,* was beginning to have a primary influence on his

---

[3] Rupp, *R.G.*, p. 94, footnote 5.   [4] Rupp, *R.G.*, p. 92, footnote 4.

exposition of Scripture and theology; a discussion of redemption
was not just a matter of balancing one argument about the different kinds of grace with another, it was becoming a crucial personal concern. It seems very improbable that Luther had yet
formulated for himself his own definitive answer. But he had
possibly glimpsed something of it. His rejection of the rational
categories of late medieval philosophy as adequate linguistic
vehicles for the Good News, his acceptance of Peter Lombard and
more notably of Augustine, and the growing tendency to quote
Scripture as the final argument are setting the scene for a theology
which concerns itself in existential fashion with what God in
Christ does for man, here and now—a dynamic scheme very
different from the received scheme in which man worked his way
through to merit, even perfection. Attention has been drawn to a
text in Peter Lombard, significantly a quotation from St Augustine, which may have been the precise point that set Luther thinking out his own special key doctrine—even though it was probably
another two years, perhaps more, before the solution became
fully explicit:

> The love of God is said to be shed abroad in our hearts, not
> because he loves us, but because he makes us his lovers: just as the
> justice of God (Justitia Dei) is that by which we are made just by
> his gift: and 'salvation of the Lord' by which he saves us: and 'faith
> of Jesus Christ' that which makes us believers.[5]

This involves a contradiction of the sense in which Biel
normally used *justitia*, that of the retributive justice of God which
punishes sinners. Luther tells us of the effect which this word
had had on him. 'Wherefore, if I may speak personally, the word
"Justitia" so nauseated me to hear, that I would hardly have been
sorry if somebody had made away with me.'[6] This he said in
1515, speaking with the memory of very recent suffering. In
1509 and 1510 the anguish must have been great and provided
vehemence for Luther's denunciation of those rational arguers
who gave no comfort to one acutely conscious of the abyss
between man and God, and who seemed to debase the Gospel

[5] Rupp, *R.G.*, p. 124.   [6] Rupp, *R.G.*, p. 126.

to a purely human level and religion to merely human effort.

It seems likely that already at this time Luther was making the very frequent use, daily or oftener, of the sacrament of confession which he certainly did two years later. Unable to escape from the mental perspective of the merit-theology, he was perpetually conscious of his own failure to merit, of his guilt before God. So he takes the way the Church recommended and goes frequently to confession. He suffers intensely, seeing Christ as an angry judge, both the creator of this sinful creature and his judge. He is obliged by the Church and by his own faith to plead for mercy and to try to merit what he feels he could never merit. 'I knew Christ as none other than a stern judge, from whose face I wanted to flee, and yet could not.' 'Christ was for me, not a mediator, but a judge.' 'I used to turn pale, when I heard the name Christ'. 'I have often been terrified by the name of Christ, and when I saw him on the Cross, it was like a lightning stroke to me.'[7] His confessions seem likely to have included references to sexual temptations and sexual thoughts, not unusual in a young friar. He also perhaps confessed to petty rages. The really troublesome thing, however, was his inner resentment, his 'anger' with God.

An autobiographical fragment written in 1545 refers to his anguish, and something of what he there describes must have been present in his life in 1509–10: 'I hated this word *Justitia Dei* which by the use and consent of all doctors I was taught to understand philosophically of that formal or active justice (as they call it) with which God is just and punishes unjust sinners.' Exegetes, biblical scholars, had not commonly spoken of 'justitia' in this retributive sense, but the theologians which Luther read did so.

For, however irreproachably I lived as a religious, I felt myself in the presence of God to be a sinner with a most unquiet conscience nor could I trust that I had pleased him with my satisfaction. I did not love, nay, rather I hated this just God who punished sinners and if not with 'open blasphemy' certainly with huge murmurings I was

[7] Rupp, *R.G.*, p. 145.

angry [here Luther uses John von Grefenstein's criticism of him] with God, saying: 'As though it really were not enough that miserable sinners should be eternally damned with original sin, and have all kinds of calamities laid upon them by the law of the ten commandments, God must go and add sorrow upon sorrow and even through the Gospel itself bring his Justice and his Wrath to bear!'

Luther here describes better than any third party can his own nightmare, the anger, frustration and bitterness which it caused. The Gospel, the Good News, was turned into an instrument of vengeance in his mind.[8]

We may see in Luther's situation a number of elements. We may see him, as his contemporaries did, and Luther himself sometimes did, as a 'scrupulant'—he seems to have caught the spiritual disease of scruples, one of the occupational diseases of religious, an obsession with the possible moral failing of one's every action, with degrees of unworthy motivation and intention, with the minutiae of ethics in the minute to minute daily life. We may see him as having an inherent tendency towards depressions, a tendency which may have some physiological basis. We may see him as having a certain neurosis in relation to authority, wanting to please his father, and acting towards God in the same way, frightened of him, and never successful in his attempts to please, committed to a certain degree of revolt, and still trying to please. Luther's attitude to God, in common with most of the rest of mankind, is clearly analogical with his attitude to his parents. All these factors no doubt contributed to, and were also themselves enflamed by, the specifically spiritual and religious elements which lie at the heart of Luther's struggle—the fact of man's separation from God and the inadequate solution provided by the merit-theology. All had their place in the structure both of criticism and of affirmative biblical theology which can be seen in embryo in the marginalia. Finally, Luther always remained an admirer of the logical rigour of Occam; to the end of his life his attempts to express Christian doctrine did not ignore logic or take refuge in any pseudo-mystical rejection of the intellect.

Erfurt University mirrored both the general complacency and

[8] Autobiographical fragment translated by Rupp, *R.G.*, pp. 121–122.

the atomization of society. A prosperous and closed civilization, lacking any fundamental challenge in spite of the Turkish threats (which were realities only to a few), and in spite of what seem to us the difficulties of physical survival, had grown fatally unable to criticize itself. The Christian tradition as such had become over-specialized and may be said perhaps to have suffered the corruption which follows on the disappearance of a unified tradition. Theology, private prayer, public ritual and liturgy, *lectio divina* (the reading of the Bible or Fathers or other spiritual books, at one time a regular part and almost a sacrament of Christian living) had become separate disciplines. Theology had cut loose from life and ceased to have a primary concern for the daily experience of the individual Christian. This personal experience was allowed for in a marginal fashion by the theory of 'private revelation' by which the occasional individual was supposed to be favoured with visits and specific messages from saints and angels.

2. SCHOLASTICISM

A return to the Bible, a determination to base theology exclusively on what can be found there, is liable to attract supporters who wish to discredit all intellectual activity. There is an impatience with all attempts to express the ultimate mysteries in any other than prophetic terms, or to erect any kind of intellectual or metaphysical development on the message of the New Testament. There was perhaps something of this, in the temperamental sense, in Luther. But he never went in for a purely simpliste anti-intellectualism. Luther always remained a theologian, was always prepared to argue. The method of dialectic in which he had been educated at Erfurt remained with him to the end. His opposition to the scholastics cannot be transformed into an anti-intellectual generalization, except at the cost of Luther lying under his own judgment. And the case cannot be made out.

However, Luther was certainly impatient with the late medieval reliance on 'reason' for the exposition of religious truth, and with the, at one time Thomist, attempt to integrate all things within a single system. His impatience embraced also the late medieval Nominalist reaction to this Thomist attempt. Luther dismissed

'Thomism' and natural theology as irrelevant and inadequate, defining his objection as an objection on principle to the use of Aristotelian categories for expounding Scripture.[9] For instance he wrote: 'The distinction between "person" and "essence" in "god" is a frivolous and useless confection of philosophy'. He disliked both the Thomist attempt, so far as he knew it, and the Nominalist reaction to it.

It is clear from his marginal notes that Luther had already reached a stage of intense irritation with the whole medieval system which his teachers and the great majority of lecturers and professors used. He was already calling Aristotle 'that rancid philosopher' and his and his followers' methods the 'rancid rules of the logicians'. This is what he wrote in the margins and it is clear that his mind was already working furiously in the direction of a return to sources in the hope of uncovering the truth, the Word of God, by removing, as Vignaux says, the 'envelope of philosophy'.

What Luther wrote in the margins he did not necessarily say to his students, or not with such force. Possibly his lectures were of the fire-eating kind; possibly not. Possibly, the excitement which they caused amongst his young student friars was discounted—it must have been common then as it is now for a young lecturer on theology in a religious house (himself only recently emerged from the schools) to excite his students with his own vibrant theological vision. It would not easily create anything more than immediate and patronizing pleasure amongst the other elder friars, a mixture of pleasure at the enthusiasm of one of their pupils, with a touch of concern that he might be teaching

[9] In *Let God be God*, Philip S. Watson posits an absolute contradiction between Luther's doctrine and that of Aquinas. Luther's existential theology implies that any natural theology is superfluous and sometimes misleading; but it seems irrelevant to try to recommend Luther by criticizing Aquinas, whom Luther had probably never read. Watson makes a mistake, very common in the past, of supposing that Aquinas's 'Five Ways' were intended as simple logical proofs of God's existence. Edward Sillem in *Ways of Thinking about God* (Darton, Longman & Todd, London; Newman Press, U.S.A., 1961) has shown conclusively that Aquinas was more concerned with God's revelation of himself than with logical proofs of his existence. In this sense his thought is much nearer to Luther's dynamic theology and further away from the later Nominalism than Watson realizes. His book involves a powerful attempt at systematizing Luther's theology; but no such attempt can expect to be fully successful, and it is liable to be misleading when it is set up as a contradiction of another system.

something peculiar or that he might even become a rival. But Luther may have turned his more controversial denunciations into hypotheses, or omitted them altogether. Finally it must be remembered that a measure of vituperation was common form.

Aquinas had used the Aristotelian categories with an awareness of their limitations; it was later, no doubt very much as a result of his triumphant experimental synthesis, that such categories tended to become canons regarded as virtually absolute, operating within a closed world. Aquinas wanted to provide a *Summa* or summary of all that could be understood about the world, man and God, on the basis both of common sense and of revelation; *Summae* were also written by other men in a similar spirit. Reason would enable faith to penetrate the nature of revelation, and of the world which God had created and to which he had brought salvation. The difficulty was to use the same language both for the everyday world of the senses, and for the world of doctrine. Ordinary logic could not cope with the world of doctrine; it forbids one to say that there could be three persons in one being. So a system of analogy was invented, and the whole created world seen as in some sense pointers to God, and descriptions of it as able to provide analogies of him, who 'in the fullness of time sent his Son'. Although man was created by God 'in his image', and could only find his fullest satisfaction and final development in him, yet bound as he was by his senses in a finite world of space and time, the 'supernatural' world of God was always difficult for him—it demanded 'faith', and depended on God's gift of 'grace', prevenient and sacramental.

The Nominalists were not satisfied with the idea of analogy and preferred to make a radical distinction between the world of revelation for which 'faith' was required, and the world of the senses for which the reason was completely adequate. It is difficult to give a proper idea of these immensely proliferating philosophical systems in a paragraph or two. But one example may help to point up the seriousness of those who opposed the Thomist system, and its attempt to provide a rational view of nature and revelation, of man and God, within the same terms of reference.

The Nominalists considered that to guard the sovereignty of God, it was essential to avoid describing him. To attempt to describe or argue about God led inevitably to minimizing him, reducing him to human categories—God was a matter of faith not of reason. God's sovereignty and freedom could only be asserted and believed, not argued about. This was a capital point in the Nominalist system.

This is one example of the teaching of the modern philosophical and theological school in which Luther studied both as an undergraduate at Erfurt and then as a friar there, and subsequently at Wittenberg—he studied under Trutvetter, possibly at both places. The 'Nominalists' were so called because they said that 'universals', that is general concepts such as 'power', were no more than names, *nomina*, a mere convenience whose justification was logical, with no reality beyond this immediate functional justification. As a school, the Nominalists had been in existence almost as long as those whom they opposed, the *Realists*, who considered that concepts, universals, abstractions from objects were themselves 'real', in some sense, perhaps in the sense of being real products of, expressions produced by, the human intellect. Aquinas was in agreement with the Realists here. Luther affirmed that he himself was and always remained a Nominalist.

The Nominalists, especially since the time of Occam's 'razor' (in popular terms: 'Do not multiply, possibly imaginary, causes'), prided themselves on a special rigour not entirely dissimilar from the way in which the Logical Positivists of recent decades in Europe have prided themselves on their logical rigour. In both cases there has been an impatience with metaphysics. In the fifteenth century the philosophers were all Christian, and therefore committed in practice to a metaphysic of some kind. As we have seen, their solution was simply to abandon the hope of a 'reasonable' solution of this dilemma and to satisfy their anti-'universal' position by denying that the world of revelation was within the scope of reason. The result was, by reaction, to throw a great empirical emphasis on the authority of the Church, which meant, at that time, of the Pope and Councils. This emphasis was strongly present in Biel, the author of the standard text-books which Luther studied both in his preparation for the priesthood and in his subsequent theological study.[10]

Nominalism did not dominate all the theological and philosophical schools. While most of Luther's teachers were Occamists and Nominalists there were followers of other schools in his priory.[11] The precise influence on Luther of Nominalism is still a matter for discussion. But it has been said that the philosophy and theology which Luther learnt, predominantly Nominalist, were far short of the main Catholic tradition, and contributed in a dominant way to his own doctrine, partly by direct influence, partly by stimulating a diametrical opposite. This has been said to 'explain' Luther's ultimate rejection of Catholic authority—a thesis put forward by Louis Bouyer.[12] This seems to be too much of a simplification, but there are important elements of truth in it.

First, on the theology of grace it does seem that Catholics were notably ill-equipped. On the crucial question of 'free will', Erasmus in his later controversy with Luther[13] failed to do justice to the Catholic tradition to which in fact Luther himself was in some sense returning in his attempt to re-state the biblical doctrine—ironically parallel to Erasmus's own work in attempting to establish more reliable texts. Luther's existential statement of man's will as only good when 'freed' from the law and 'enslaved' by God's grace, and unable to do anything eternally valuable on its own is Catholic doctrine.

Second, as we have indicated, Luther's training in Occamist

[10] Francis Clark, S.J. in *Eucharistic Sacrifice and the Reformation*, quotes from the *Dictionnaire de Théologie Catholique*, the article of C. Ruch on Biel, and says: 'C. Ruch, after showing how for Biel the decisions of the Church and of the Pope "demand an entire and unreserved adherence", and that "what characterizes Biel above all is concern for doctrinal orthodoxy", makes the following comment: "It was Nominalism that dictated this attitude. It was a consequence of that system that the less one can rely on the power of human reason, the more one must take one's stand upon revelation, authentically interpreted. Biel's orthodoxy is ensured by the distinction to which he constantly refers, between what God has in fact ordained (potentia ordinata) and what he could have decreed (potentia absoluta). To know what is, what the Creator has in fact willed, Biel has recourse to revelation; to investigate what God could have done, he turns to speculation. The Catholic believes what is; the Nominalist theorizes on what could be. Faith and reason have their own proper domains and do not come into conflict. For Biel, to be orthodox was the only possible path."'

[11] A new text of Occam's works is being prepared at the moment, and the matter of his influence on early sixteenth-century thought can hardly be settled yet. For a brief reference to the various other philosophical schools of the time, Thomist, Scotist, Augustinian and others, see Clark and Schwiebert.

[12] See *The Spirit and Forms o Protestantism.*   [13] See pp. 247–58.

logic probably helped him to find his way towards a radically 'economical' theology, attributing all to God rather than to secondary causes. This fitted nicely with his own unique initiative in being content with biblical terms, rather than looking for an explanation of them in traditional abstractions. It may be objected that the sovereignty of God as expressed by the Occamists was a severely abstract concept and as such not welcome to Luther's doctrine. True, but we are dealing not with two sets of propositions but with the influencing and growth of Luther's thought over a decade and more. Luther's biblical theology was not simply a spontaneous growth. His mind would not have thrown off entirely and in every respect the influence of his teachers in favour of the Bible all at once, nor would he have formulated his thoughts outside the long training in disputations of the Nominalist kind. It seems reasonable at least to see some transitory, perhaps more permanent, influence on him in this matter, and even in the dichotomy between faith and reason. As Luther struggled towards an expression in conformity with the Bible many aspects of what he had learnt could have helped. This is not to trace the pedigree of a word such as 'imputation' or 'justification' and make it due simply and solely to its use by his teachers, when its primary significance for Luther is clearly biblical.[14] It is simply to admit some continuity in Luther's thought and to understand as fully as possible part of the historical provenance of some factors in it. There is a real analogy between the faith/reason division in Occamism and that in Luther's thought.

Finally, the attitude of extreme reliance on and almost adulation of the authority of the Pope was taken up by Luther from his educators, and this of course he kept for another nine years from the time of which we are writing. His ultimate rejection of this was a diametrical reversal not entirely surprising when one considers the exaggerated terms of the original statements.

[14] See Rupp's rejection of attempts to trace the pedigree of words or phrases used by Luther to Nominalist sources; Luther's use of them is itself a refutation of such parentage, being biblical and actual rather than scholastic and theoretical. However, it would be foolish to posit a virtual 'revelation' to Luther. His teachers were Occamists; it was from their lips and their books that Luther learnt methods of intellectual activity. Their words and ideas, as well as those derived from the Bible and St Augustine, were in his mind and formed the grist from which he ground out his own new uses of them.

We must add to the historical context another fact which must have encouraged Luther in the early days of his opposition to conventional scholastic doctrine. Dissatisfaction with scholasticism, indeed with the whole body of theologians and philosophers, was becoming widespread. Their bitter arguments raging within the closed world of Aristotelian canons aroused impatience amongst free-lance intellectuals widely from radical conservative lawyers like Sir Thomas More, through Catholic biblical scholars, with a certain professional neutrality, like Erasmus, to the new Protestant biblical scholars like Tyndale. Amongst them the Renaissance flowered in the 'new learning', a determination to seek out a more reliable theology from the original New Testament texts by learning Greek. The extent of the influence which More and Erasmus could have had on Luther's is doubtful. But Luther was not ignorant of the humanist movement as a whole and shared its desire for greater accuracy.

Luther would not have had the influence he did if his thought was no more than a developed amalgam of what he had been taught, with some fierce reactions from it. Like every good student Luther made intense use of the material fed to him. But it remains that his theology cannot be sufficiently analyzed merely by way of these antecedents and influences. St Augustine, and much more the Bible itself, were bigger influences; and finally there emerged an individual interpretation, a personal exposition of the Gospel radically 'new'—and a return in method to a dynamic approach, perhaps nearer to that of the Fathers, but living in a world so different from theirs, that Luther's work cannot be properly compared, in the concrete, with their commentaries. This theology will have its place in a later chapter. For the moment the marginal comments of 1509–10 show a determination to fall back on Scripture, quite unusual at Erfurt, and a pleasure with Augustine which fitted naturally with a strong dislike for the philosophical and theological schools in which he had been brought up, an impatience with them, for which in the end one can only account at a personal and spiritual level. Of a deeply religious temperament, Luther has become worried, almost obsessed with his personal relation to Christ. He has become

impatient, at a deep spiritual level, with merely abstract distinctions.
The Nominalist distinction made between what God could have
done (*potestas absoluta*) and what he has actually done (*potestas
ordinata*) is not relevant. What interests Luther is what Christ
does at this moment for 'me'.

It is this application to the immediate human problem, 'my'
problem, at this moment, which gives the clue to Luther's eventually enormous practical influence. His theology is concerned
with the individual. And to the solution of the individual's
problem he brought impatience and courage, a somewhat unusual combination in the theological world. Many were impatient
with the Church but had neither the vision nor the courage to do
anything about it. Very many had seen something of what
needed to be done—they turned to some such 'reform' as that of
the Brothers of the Common life, seeking a simpler life, or they
turned to unravelling the text of the Bible, or they initiated
reforms of the Roman Curia. But either their projects were
insufficient for the Church's predicament, or else like the many
projected reforms they were never put into effect. In the delicately
penned annotations on the margins of the theology teacher's
text-books at Erfurt lay the qualities which would elicit a response
from many, not only those who were impatient with the scholastic formulas but those who were impatient with religious autocracy, the personal and financial domination by Italy, and more
widely those whose impatience is commonly general at all times,
throughout society, with the existing civil order. The measure of
Luther's initiative, its originality and influence, can be taken
when we remember not only this Europe-wide response, but
that the Council of Trent formulated the Catholic doctrine of
justification with careful consideration of his views, and is, within
certain bounds, in substantial agreement with him if we look
behind the words to the certain meaning of both parties. Its full
measure perhaps is taken when we see that one of the most
important books in the current twentieth-century theological
scene is entitled *Rechtfertigung* (Justification),[15] and centres its

---

[15] *Rechtfertigung; die Lehre Karl Barths und eine katholisches Besinnung*, by Hans Küng
(Einsiedeln, Johannes Verlag, 1957).

theme on a comparison of the contemporary Protestant Barthian interpretation of Luther's theory of Justification with Catholic doctrine.

9. *Visit to Rome*

YOUNG Father Luther continued to lecture to the student friars, and to write his marginal notes in the monastic copies of the text-books through the winter of 1509, and the spring and summer of 1510. The latter was Erfurt's 'mad' year; in January there was a violent revolt of apprentices and small craftsmen against high taxation and other things. In June the head of the Town Council (of four) was executed. In August the great hall of the university was wrecked. Luther, himself the son of a member of another town council, was on the side of law and order and very critical of the violence used, but the troubles in the city did not apparently hinder his theology lectures which he was still bound to prepare and to give to the student friars.

In October a five months' interruption of work intervened in · the form of a visit to Rome. The purpose of the journey was an appeal to Rome on behalf of the priory against the intentions of the Superior of the Saxon Congregation, Staupitz. The latter, who was also Vicar-General of the Order, had been trying to improve the general standard of observance in the Augustinian priories and to spread more widely the effects of a previous reform. The priory at Erfurt was not trying to resist being reformed—for they had been reformed—but were jealous of their reform, and did not want to have some other, at present unreformed, priories amalgamated with their Saxon Congregation. Staupitz's purpose in trying to effect an amalgamation was to reform the remaining priories in the district. Erfurt's viewpoint seems not to have stretched much beyond its own boundaries, very conscious of its own status, its privileges, its individuality, and no doubt its 'reformed' nature. The friars wished to be left to continue in their own group of reformed priories and not to have it enlarged with a further group of 'undesirables'—a situation typical of the contemporary muddy religious scene, complex, confusing, and often unworthy.

Why Luther was chosen for the journey, and how he could be spared from lecturing, we do not know; but a religious house will commonly put its own communal good before other considerations—also it could be that the numbers of student friars had declined. Luther's status for the journey was that of *socius*, travelling companion to the older friar, who was actually responsible for the business. The first part of the journey was only to Halle, with Father Nathin, to the Archbishop of Magdeburg, who could give the priory the necessary permission to appeal. They failed to obtain permission, and went on to their immediate destination, Nuremberg, where a group of reformed priories were meeting (there was a total of twenty-nine reformed priories; the meeting at Nuremberg was of seven only, who were resisting the amalgamation). The meeting determined to proceed with an appeal in spite of the prohibition on any appeal against the bull with which Staupitz was trying to effect the reform. Father Nathin returned to Erfurt. Some other older friar, probably from Nuremberg, went on to Rome, with Luther as *socius*.

The visit to Rome was a shock, but the full effect only finally worked itself out after 1517 when Luther began to add up all the different shocks he had had at many levels. For the moment his surprise at many apparently unworthy aspects of the Church in Christendom's capital city was no doubt tempered by thoughts of his own youth, and of the strangeness with which unaccustomed places and people always strike one. Rome seems to have been a mixture of squalor and magnificence, a condition to be found in most big cities throughout most of history, but possibly magnified in the Italian capital of the Catholic Church. The magnificence was perhaps difficult to find and largely absent, in the sense of public display, if the Pope was away from Rome. Julius II (who had accepted Bramante's design for St Peter's, and put Michelangelo to work in the Sistine Chapel) was frequently occupied with wars, and was out of Rome throughout Luther's time there, during mid-winter 1510–11. It can be damp and cold

in Rome at such time and it rained for most of Luther's visit.
Altogether Rome must have presented a drab aspect. As a city,
from the economic point of view, it was probably a poorer town
than many in Germany. Tourism, then as now, must have been
its principal source of income.

Roman 'tourism' covers and covered a wide range of activities
from the pious pilgrimages of Roman Catholics, intensely religious, deeply moved by their first visit to the capital of Christendom, the place of the martyrdom of St Peter and St Paul, to the
visits of historians, artists, aesthetes, philosophers or of the avow-
edly 'worldly'. The Renaissance accounted for some of the tourism
of Luther's time; for Luther this meant nothing—we have no
comment of his on artistic achievement in Rome, or on work in
progress, even that of the building of St Peter's. For Luther
Rome was Holy Rome and he spent a great deal of his time
earning the accepted indulgences by performing the necessary
pious activities. He visited the catacombs and the shrines. He
offered Mass at altars where a plenary indulgence could be gained
and transferred by an intention to do so to the souls of the dead
in purgatory—an action which he believed at the time automatically released a soul from purgatory.[1] He said he wished his father
and mother were dead so that he could effect their release from
purgatory by means of the plenary indulgences he was earning.
For all of this activity he had a number of weeks to spare, for the
Roman authorities delayed in giving their inevitable refusal to
the appeal. When he first saw Rome at his approach Luther knelt
down on the road. 'I threw myself on the ground and said:
"Blessed art thou, Holy Rome!"' To him as to many before
and since Rome was the one great tangible symbol, Rome with
the Pope in it, of the Church of Christ.

But holy Rome was also unholy Rome, and if Luther had no
eye for the Renaissance he could not help seeing the prostitutes,
and hearing the gossip and being astonished at the off-hand
behaviour of the Italian priests, very much at home in the great
capital. Perhaps the most devastating factor, underlying all else,
was the complacency of Rome, a specially sophisticated type of

[1] See Appendix I.

complacency; it involved a real awareness of the unworthiness of the city, of the need for reform on a wide front—the papal court and administration (the Curia), the personal lives of the cardinals, the Church in general. The need for reform had been recognized for a century. Indeed *ecclesia semper reformanda* (the church always in need of reformation) was a specially appropriate definition then. The last century had shown a special awareness of the need for a thorough Church-wide attention to reform. A number of reforms had been drawn up and agreed, but they had not got beyond that stage.[2]

The recent denunciations of Savonarola in Florence hung over the town. Murder was common. The historian can look back and see this state of affairs very clearly. But Luther was in the middle of it, surrounded by the complex and the detailed. He was himself a member of a 'reformed' priory; he must often have heard talk of 'reform'. A religious person grew up with the idea of 'reform' in the air—it was a powerful inoculation against the possibility that a radical reform might ever be successful. The state of the city of Rome and the behaviour of the priests there and of the Church's officials must simply have bewildered Luther at first.

Luther was never an ingenuous idealist. He did not suppose that men can live universally up to some specified standard. And he saw the good points of the Italians—he understood something of their distaste for German boorishness, he realized the presence of a major temperamental factor. He liked the Italian tailors, and found the people generally more polite, and less drunken. It was not till later that he became really shocked, when his theology and later the experience of his own personal treatment by Roman authority, high-lighted the memory of what he had seen. It was only then that his experiences at Rome fused into a kind of horror at what came to seem a radical degradation, as he remembered the almost blasphemy with which the priests had seemed to juggle so casually with the sacraments and remembered the worldly lives of themselves and others: the hurried Masses (he

---

[2] See *The Council of Trent* by Hubert Jedin (Nelson, 1957), and see pp. 98–101 of this book.

tells of the whispers of a priest at an altar next to him as he finished his Mass when Luther was only a third of the way through his own: '*Passa, passa . . .*', 'Hurry up, for goodness sake, there are others waiting . . .'), and the atmosphere of relaxation and self-satisfaction combined with a putrefying legalism, implying an idea of God far distant from anything to be found in the New Testament, a mess from which others had reacted by instituting one reform or another, but which eventually helped to prompt the whole massive Protestant reaction.

Luther spoke later in some detail of his journey. His comments were those of an intelligent observer. He noted fertile soil and was impressed by the valley of the Po when staying at the great Benedictine monastery there on the way to Rome. He noted a well-organized town and a friendly people. He saw a striking clock at Nuremberg, he liked the Bavarians, also the Swiss though he was worried by the lack of productive soil in their mountainous land. He was impressed by the size of the figs and grapes in Italy. These five months, mostly occupied in journeying on foot, perhaps a total of 1,500 miles, partly at Rome itself, must have 'broadened' Luther a bit in whatever sense it is true that 'foreign travel broadens the mind'—he must have heard a deal of ecclesiastical gossip in the monasteries at which he stopped. He must have seen the pleasant, pious lives of the Bavarians. By the end he would have a better idea of 'the Church' as it really was, and the degree to which it could present a different face in one place and another.

The five months had no special significance in Luther's immediate spiritual development, or in the development of his theology. But they are an important factor in the accumulation of practical pressures which, in the next seven years, helped to convince Luther first that the Church was in need of radical reform, and then a little later that the papacy and the Catholic Church in communion with Rome could not claim to call itself alone, as a human entity, the Church established by Christ to preach the Gospel.

Luther and his companion were back in Nuremberg by March and delivered the news of their failure. But the seven priories were not prepared to accept failure and believed that by constant attrition they might wear down the Superior-General in Rome; two more messengers were dispatched immediately to Rome. Luther returned to Erfurt and probably resumed his lectures. Staupitz called a meeting at Jena in July where he offered a number of concessions if the seven would agree to the amalgamation. The proposals were taken back to the priories and discussed. At Erfurt the majority remained determinedly against amalgamation at any price; but two friars (possibly more) were for agreeing with Staupitz on the grounds that further opposition was improper and would endanger authority—the two were John Lang and Martin Luther. We find Luther, interestingly, on the side of the higher authority against the local authority, and prepared to express his opinion against an overwhelming majority of older men in his own community, an attitude at the same time orthodox, authoritarian, against the majority, and courageous.

There seems to have been such irritation in the community at the attitude of Lang and Luther that they had to go to another priory. Staupitz had them sent to his own house at Wittenberg. Lang matriculated at the university there shortly afterwards, in August. The move was important for Luther in that to return to Wittenberg brought him into immediate personal contact with Staupitz who set him thinking and living (helping him in his personal spiritual difficulties) along the lines which would take him to his full reformation doctrine. Staupitz was to give him promotion and the encouragement to develop and deepen his studies.

In the autumn of 1511 we are now only six years from the cataclysm which will follow the nailing of the Ninety-five Theses. There was as yet little or nothing foreshadowing those events. Staupitz saw latent talent in the young intellectual of twenty-eight, with his sincerity and his deep religious drive, and his youthful 'anti' attitudes, his clean driven face and his sharp eyes. He was glad to welcome him permanently to Wittenberg.

This was the importance of the campaign for amalgamation for Luther—to bring him to Wittenberg and Staupitz. As for the amalgamation campaign, the big priory at Nuremberg continued to be obstructive, as also Erfurt, and Staupitz eventually gave up defeated. In 1514 Luther wrote a letter to Erfurt which implies that his departure from the priory there in 1511 had been accompanied by strife. In the same year he defended himself against Nathin who had turned against him after his departure from Erfurt. However the rift between Erfurt and those who departed does not seem to have remained. In 1516 Lang was recalled to Erfurt; and Luther, by then the District Vicar, made him their prior, and this seemingly without opposition. Later his old priory was on Luther's side, along with Wittenberg, against his enemies.

10. Dr Luther

SOON after Luther's arrival at Wittenberg in the late summer of 1511 there occurred the ceremonies at which four Augustinians were given the degree of doctor of theology, in the University of Wittenberg. The doctorate was the highest honour that could be conferred on a theologian. Staupitz, the Vicar-General of the order, and the Provincial Superior, conferred the doctor's cap in the course of the ceremony; he had probably been largely instrumental in selecting the men who received the doctorate. About this time he suggested to Luther that he too should be made a doctor of theology—the suggestion was probably unusual in that Luther was not yet twenty-eight, and had not had much time in which to show himself worthy of the honour. But Staupitz, kind, quiet and plump, was also a man of perception. He had evidently kept an eye on Luther from his first appearance at Wittenberg three years previously; he had been at least partly responsible for Luther's appointment to his first lecturing task there, and certainly for the appointment to the second course on the Bible. He had heard of Luther's success with his theology lectures to the young friars at Erfurt, and he knew of, and could hardly help being pleased by, Luther's final stand against the majority at Erfurt on the amalgamation issue, after his selection as *socius on* the appeal journey. And it seems that he recognized in Luther a powerful driving force that needed canalizing and using:

'You must become a doctor and a preacher, then you will have something to do' (Perhaps he meant 'a chance to say what you want').

The occasion when Staupitz spoke these words to him was described in detail by Luther—it was during the time of 'recreation', a time prescribed, after meals, for relaxation during which the religious, then as now, commonly talk together either in a common-room or walking round the grounds or court yards attached to the house. At Wittenberg there was only a little ground available outside. In the courtyard which faced on to the street, there was a large pear tree and it was during conversation under this tree that Staupitz made his proposal to Luther, who was perhaps too astonished to say much. It seems to have been a day or two later when Staupitz repeated his suggestion that Luther presented a detailed opposition to the scheme which he had evidently been thinking over, for he had fifteen precise reasons, prepared in the academic fashion, why he should not become a doctor of theology. Staupitz fell back on reproaching Luther with wilfulness in face of the wishes of authority. Luther's response to that was straight from the heart, he really felt he could not take on such responsibility: 'You will kill me. I shall never stick it out longer than three months.' The answer was somewhat facetious; a classic European Catholic remark, encouraging, whilst also patronizing and indeed commanding. 'Well, you know that the Lord has many great matters to attend to. He needs clever people to advise him. If you die, you will be taken into his council in heaven, for he needs doctors too.' And that was clearly the end of that.

The status of doctor involved the obligation of preaching, and whilst it was going to take some time to arrange for Luther to be made a doctor (primarily it seems on account of the difficulty of finding the fifty guldens to be paid to the University), there was no need to wait at all before Father Luther could start preaching. So he began to preach, apparently to the friars. This was in the autumn of 1511, and it seems that apart from preaching Luther was free to study on his own account for a year, though he may have been instructing young friars. He seems to have learnt Greek during this time and to have continued his study of Hebrew and his reading of St Augustine. And this time of relative freedom from commitment allowed him to continue his study of the Bible—above all to ponder his own problem, which was now both a matter of only too familiar and acute worry and an objective theological problem. There was a previous occasion when some free time brought depression to a head—after Luther had taken his degree as a graduate at Erfurt. That time it led to Luther's entry into religion. This time it was followed eventually by Luther's lectures, as doctor of theology, in the university at Wittenberg, in which he unfolded a series of theological insights that were gradually to excite the support first of others in the Faculty there, and eventually to form the basis of Protestant theology. These insights, from a strictly dogmatic point of view, were not absolutely novel, but the young doctor propounded them in such an individual and personal way, gradually making of them a practically complete corpus of theology, that this was in effect a new thing, something of the new era, the era of the self-conscious individual, and sharply differentiated from all the existing schools of theology, in content, method and temper. The germ of them we have already glimpsed in the marginal comments on Peter Lombard and Augustine.

These first Wittenberg lectures cover the years 1513–18 and were devoted to the Psalms, and the Epistles to the Romans, Galatians and Hebrews. A brief treatment of each of the courses together with a chronology of events will be found in Chapters 16, 17, and 21. There follows here a more general description of Luther's life and thought between 1513 and 1517 (Chapters 12–15).

Part Three

DOCTOR AND PREACHER

II. *Anguish and the End of an Age*

LUTHER'S new insights drew their force ultimately from his own personal anguish and from the solvent of them which he found, through the Bible, in the person of Christ. The starting-point is the force with which Luther experienced the threatening face of Christ, the angry God ready to punish, the just Lord who was bound, so it seemed to him, to take vengeance on man in his inadequacy and futility, always failing, always less than the Christian man that he was called to be. The anguish arose from a fundamental religious weakness of the time, a widespread malaise. Historians have waxed eloquent about the 'birth-pangs of the new age', and so forth. Man and woman could no longer bear to be permanently relegated to a position of childish inferiority. The Christian and the citizen were no longer satisfied with a sometimes pious, but often impious paternalism; they were in revolt against both the threatening and the paternal side of the autocratic coin.

The phenomenon of Luther marked the birth of modern 'man', the birth of 'I' in the world of religion.[1] Until then the Church had resisted and protected itself from this psychological invasion. The inspiring doctrine of the body of Christ, of the Church—the Eucharistic unity of the first centuries—had been thoroughly institutionalized and built up into a vast juridical framework, highly articulated in libraries of abstract philosophy and theology, and practically applied in the Mass, the seven sacraments, the sacramentals, and many other pious activities and charitable works—a great machine within which every individual had his place. It gave scope for the expression of personal activity in the life of an occasional mystic, in the rather mechanical piety of the people at large, and in personal charity and good works.

But the community was all, and in practice a highly juridical

[1] This is not to imply that Jacques Maritain is right in his *Three Reformers* where he interprets the whole of Luther's achievement as perversely egocentric. He ends an eclectic study with an almost irrelevant disquisition on the priority of the intellect in the teaching of Aquinas. It is an unhappy example of a great scholar stepping far outside the bounds of his own speciality.

'all'. The Church in fact mirrored, as always, the political, social and craft-artist forms and institutions of society. But these institutions had already begun to burst their bonds. The nation states had arrived. Economic unions existed. The individual artist was flaming up in works of astonishing and utterly unprecedented virtuosity. The Church had succeeded so far in digesting every such phenomenon that arose within her midst, of which St Francis and his followers were one of the earlier examples—or else in repulsing and rejecting them so decisively that the resultant heretic was commonly physically destroyed as a danger to the whole order of society. Even Savonarola, only a decade or two previously, had been burnt at the stake for heresy by the secular arm.

In Luther the experience of common religious practice and thought produced a truly violent reaction, at first confined entirely to his own inner life. The inner struggle, the *Anfechtungen*, led in the end to something like a paroxysm of hate for God; and the more Luther hated, the more guilty he felt. In 1518 he wrote something in which he was surely describing himself:

> I knew a man, who said he had often suffered these pains [infernal torments] in the shortest possible compass of times, so great and infernal that 'nor tongue nor pen can show' nor can those believe who have not experienced, so that if they were completed, or lasted half an hour, or even the tenth part of an hour, he would utterly perish, and his bones be reduced to ashes. Then God appears horrifyingly angry, and like God so the whole creation. There can be no flight, no consolation, neither within nor without, but all is accusation. Then he laments: 'I am cast away from thy face: Lord accuse me not in thy Wrath'. In this moment, extraordinary to say, the soul cannot believe that it will even be redeemed, but believes that it is suffering a punishment not yet complete . . . but left only with the naked longing for help and terrifying trembling, but it knows not whence help can come. This is the soul stretched out with Christ, so that all his bones can be numbered, nor is there any corner not filled with the most bitter bitterness, horror, fear, grief—and all of it seems everlasting.[2]

[2] It would be worth while to examine Luther's spiritual life under the categories of progress in that life outlined by St John of the Cross. Valuable insights might be achieved into the 'nights' through which Luther surely went.
    The passage here quoted might also be usefully compared with passages in *Portrait of the Artist as a Young Man* by James Joyce, and his other works.

The anguish reached a special height when he considered the question of predestination and the 'elect'. When he considered the question, it seemed simply impossible that he could be saved. He reached a point of mental exhaustion and desperation where it seems hardly too much to say that it was inevitable either that his mind must give way so that he would be clearly deranged or take refuge in simpleness, or else that he would somehow refute or change the premises on which the desperation was based. No doubt desperation had some permanent foothold in Luther's constitution as a whole,[3] relating to his childhood, upbringing, and conceivably (though we have no evidence) to genetically inherited factors, and the *Anfechtungen* continued throughout his life. But a disposition to mental crises of this kind finds its application in particular situations. The problems are no less problems for being posed in the personal context of one who easily becomes desperate. Indeed many problems perhaps never are solved until they present themselves to someone whose make-up insists, in its desperation, on their solution. The intense personal experience of an *impasse* brings it to an apotheosis, a crisis, and a solution. At no time did his contemporaries provide any respectable evidence that Luther was unbalanced. The authority and status given to him at an early age seems to indicate on the contrary a special respect for his sensitivity and conscientiousness. And Staupitz, his Superior, was no 'enthusiast' and no fool.

Luther was not only 'man' superseding a ready-made theology, a ready-made piety, a ready-made religious life, complete with its assumptions and prejudices about the whole nature of life. He was not only 'man', the individual rejecting, in a psychologically compulsive way, something that was repulsively inadequate. He was also a Christian. He could not therefore do as others did

---

[3] Physical and mental predispositions are obviously of great importance. Luther had a number of physical ailments, many of which seem likely to have been connected with his very sensitive and jumpy disposition—no doubt 'nervous' in a general way. John Osborne's play high-lighted Luther's constipation. Erikson (*Young Man Luther*) mentions urine retention. Later there is insomnia, and other things. No doubt they all affected the process of events as these things commonly do, but the present writer finds it difficult to see that they have any special relevance beyond the general and important fact, noted in the text here, that the problems with which Luther grappled probably required someone of this particular disposition if they were to be tackled. A good character study has yet to be made in the present age.

in other spheres, marching forward exultantly, individually, into new political forms, new economic arrangements, wonderful artistic developments. He was concerned with a historical religion, tied to a revelation of ultimate truth; he was concerned with a historical fact which he believed to contain the whole of this truth in itself, the fact of the life of the man-God, Jesus Christ, and the fact of the Book which told of his revelation. Luther's advance had, then, also to be a renewal. He turned back to look at the credentials of his belief. So his insight occurred, and was expounded, in the context of an exposition of the Bible.

12. *Luther's Crisis*

DURING his first two or three years of permanent residence at Wittenberg, Luther's nervous anxiety must have been at its height. He was living a pious life, fasting more than he was bound to do, praying, sleeping probably less than he needed. He would go to confession frequently; he found the act of offering Mass a matter of acute anxiety—was he in a fit state? 'When I went up the altar after confession and contrition, I felt myself so fearful in conscience that I had to beckon to me another priest [to obtain absolution].' He could never be sure he had confessed everything or that he had not committed some new sin.

Horror of some sort of sexual impurity, common in Catholic moral tradition, led to a common opinion in medieval times that a priest should generally refrain from offering Mass on a morning after he had experienced a seminal emission during sleep— described, then as now, precisely as 'pollution'. In Luther's sensitive mind, always inclined to a certain morbidity, this sort of emphasis on the gross sinfulness or impurity of involuntary acts led to a fear of being in a state of sin which became a permanent dread, weighing him down. The Gospel became a 'law' condemning him to death. 'I said Mass with great dread.'

It is a historical fact that such scruples have been experienced by men and women within the Catholic Church over many centuries. The emphasis on precise canonical prescriptions in regard to the sacraments and on the relation between being in a state of grace and one's eternal destiny, has led to the regular danger, on the one hand of phariseeism, and on the other of scrupulosity. Means were sought and found of combating both evils, particularly the evil of scruples which was common amongst young men in religious orders.

So Luther's condition was nothing to surprise the man who had great hopes of him. Staupitz not only knew how to cope with a 'scrupulant', but he was genuinely sorry for young Father Martin. He prescribed activity—to distract him and give an outlet for his energies. He must become a doctor of theology and preach. And Staupitz knew the way in which to direct Luther spiritually. He must abandon the idea of Christ as a judge, and look to the God-man on the cross, and contemplate his wounds. 'One must contemplate that man who is called Christ.' He must relax and give up the idea of frequent confession; his so-called sins were not sins. Confession did not have for its purpose the mere setting of one's mind at rest. He let Luther into the secrets of his own life: 'I, too, once confessed daily, and daily resolved to be devout and remain devout. But every day I utterly failed. Then I decided that I could deceive God no longer; I could not have done it anyhow. I shall await an opportune hour that God may come to me with his Grace.'[1]

Staupitz did what probably many another wise spiritual director might have done for Luther, putting the sacrament of penance into a proper perspective for him. The tenor of his advice fits both with the simplifications of the *devotio moderna* and indeed with primitive Christian tradition. Staupitz told Luther that repentance begins with the love of God. This was a great moment for Luther—Biel had always said, in tune with the Occamist philosophy, that repentance begins with the love of self (one of those truisms whose validity is so general that if they are to be given any real meaning, they tend to be given a more precise connotation which is no longer valid). Of these words of

[1] Quoted by Böhmer, p. 104.

Staupitz, 'repentance begins with the love of God', Luther said in 1518:

> These words stuck in me like some sharp and mighty arrow and I began from that time onward to look up what the Scriptures teach about penitence. And then, what a game began. The words came up to me on every side jostling one another and smiling in agreement, so that, where before there was hardly any word in the whole of Scripture more bitter to me than *penitentia* (which I sought to feign in the presence of God—*coram Deo*—and tried to express with a fictitious and forced love), now nothing sounds sweeter or more gracious to me than *penitentia*. For thus the precepts of God become sweet to us when we understand them, not only by reading books, but in the wounds of the most sweet Saviour.[2]

It would not be too much to say that Staupitz saved Luther from what we would call a nervous breakdown. In addition he turned Luther's mind in a direction which was harmonious with the theology that was gradually forming there. Luther always recognized the sovereign part which Staupitz played in his life: 'If Dr Staupitz had not helped me out . . . I should have been swallowed up in hell.' 'I cannot forget or be ungrateful, for it was through you that the light of the Gospel began first to shine out of the darkness of my heart.' 'He was my very first father in this teaching, and he bore me in Christ.'

Staupitz seems to have been typical of a certain humanist and spiritual tradition in the medieval Church, the fruit of a thousand years of monastic life in the West. 'Wisdom' is perhaps the best characterization, in a single word, of the ripe fruit of this life which was Staupitz. He was a man of ideals and a reformer—he wanted to bring the priories under his authority to a higher standard of observance. He was not simply a man of rules. He knew that religion in the end is a matter of the spirit which needs great liberty. But also he was practical.

The initiative of Staupitz, his advice to Luther, seems to have affected Luther radically, both in calming his overwrought conscience, and in giving some support to the direction, and general orientation, which his theology was taking. His effect seems to

[2] Quoted by Rupp, R.G., p. 119.

1. Margaret Luther, *née* Ziegler, Martin's mother (c. 1463–1531)
From a painting by Cranach the Elder, c. 1527

2. Hans Luther, Martin's father (1459–1530)
From a tempera study by Cranach the Elder, 1527

have been rather similar to that of a good psychiatrist, relaxing the patient, freeing energy, turning it outwards, setting him off on a 'way of salvation' in the natural sense. Staupitz seems to have achieved all this, and perhaps to have been limited to this. Luther's fundamental struggle was not brought to an end, nor his problems solved. They no longer upset his life so fundamentally. But they remained—linked to the merit-theology, which itself stood as a rock of offence, dominating the Church's life, presenting to Luther a spiritual contradiction in terms, and fitted menacingly well to an image of God threatening retribution for those who failed. Merit was a meaningless word for Luther, in discussion of man's relationship with God, because he could not envisage any merit which could measure up to God's requirements. But Staupitz enabled Luther to relax, to look at Christ on the cross, not on the judgment-seat. It was an incentive to find an alternative to merit-theology, an alternative which would fit more harmoniously with this practical spiritual approach.

Staupitz himself eventually confessed that he was beaten. After he had applied all the cures he knew, and had in fact brought much relief to Luther, the patient continued to belly-ache. 'I do not understand you,' said Staupitz. 'Then', Luther wrote later, 'I thought I was the only one who had ever experienced these "spiritual temptations" and I felt like a dead man.' This is surely a highly significant sentence. In Luther were pinpointed, in one man experiencing them in the isolated intimacy of his own self-reflection, things which he found it impossible to share. He is like a dead man. His unique 'death' will eventually enable him to propound a unique solution, with exceptional force. Luther was thrown back on his own resources. If Staupitz who had helped him so much could go no further with him then he was truly alone and must somehow fight the battle out on his own. He returned to the Bible, to his anguish, to St Augustine, and to Christ —sufficiently relaxed by the reassurances of Staupitz not to be totally inhibited by the *impasse* of the man/God relationship, and finding some comfort in the Cross, in the Crucified.

13. The Solution: The Theology of Justification

THE battle was resolved into a purely personal affair, spiritual and theological. There was no question, no inkling of a possibility in Luther's mind, of any revolt or defection from the Church, or from the principles and conventions in which he had been educated as man and as friar. It was purely a matter of finding a meaning in Scripture, in theology, which was acceptable, which fitted man's condition, in other words, Martin Luther's condition, spiritually and intellectually.

Of the moment of insight Luther wrote with enlightening clarity in the last year of his life. It revolved round chapter one, verse seventeen of the Epistle to the Romans: 'The just shall live by faith.' Luther wrote:

> At last, God being merciful, as I meditated day and night on the connection of the words, namely, 'the Justice of God is revealed in it, as it is written "the just shall live by faith"' there I began to understand the justice of God as that by which the just live, by the gift of God, namely by faith, and this sentence, 'the justice of God is revealed in the Gospel' to be that passive justice, with which the merciful God justifies us, by faith, as it is written 'The just man lives by faith'.
>
> This immediately made me feel as if I was reborn, and as though I had entered through open gates into paradise itself. From then on, the whole face of Scripture appeared different. I ran through the Scriptures then, as my memory enabled me to, and found the same analogy in other words, as the Work of God (*opus*) that which God works in us, Power of God (*virtus Dei*) with which he makes us strong, wisdom of God (*sapientia Dei*) with which he makes us wise, fortitude of God, salvation of God, glory of God.
>
> And now, as much as I had hated this word 'Justice of God' before, so much the more sweetly I extolled this word to myself now, so that this place in Paul was to me as a real gate of paradise. Afterwards, I read Augustine, 'On the Spirit and the Letter', where beyond hope I found that he also similarly interpreted the Justice of God: that with which God endues us, when he justifies us. And

although this were said imperfectly, and he does not clearly explain
about 'imputation', yet it pleased that he should teach a Justice of
God with which we are justified.[1]

Simply seen as an isolated dogma, Luther's proposition is
identical, not only in principle, but in detail, in relation to the
particular matter of the exposition of *Justitia*, with the teaching of
the Catholic Church, as St Augustine had expounded it,[2] and as
many others had done so subsequently. But Luther had been
taught a retributive conception of *Justitia* in Biel. On rediscover-
ing the proper interpretation of it, Luther gives it a new context,
in fact he makes this the leading theme and the context for the
whole of the Christian revelation. He makes of this revelation a
doctrine of the pure generosity of God, a statement of the total
acceptance of man by God, a justification of man by God's act of
redemption, by the life, death and resurrection of Jesus. All man
has to do is to believe, to receive the gift. From this will flow a
life in which good works will come naturally and are in a sense
even obligatory; but they are subsequent and never prior to the
gift of God, which cannot be earned, and is never due to any
merit on man's part. Man has been redeemed, righteousness has
been given, and by this alone, by the faith which receives it, man
is saved. It is not a purely spiritual (in the sense of being intangible)
affair. God has left us his Word. His Word is Christ, once on earth
and now speaking to us in Scripture. Through Scripture we know
of and receive God's gift.

*Sola Scriptura, sola Gratia, sola Fides; Justitia; Homo semper
peccator, semper penitens, semper justus.* We might represent Luther's
thought as shown by these words thus: From Scripture alone,
which is the Word of God, man, always a sinner but always penitent, receives by faith alone the unique grace of God, and is
justified. Here, in so far as it can be summarized, is a summary of
Luther's theology. 'In so far as it can be summarized', because the

[1] This is the essence of Luther's 'discovery'. It is sometimes called the 'tower theology'
or the 'tower-discovery' because in a passage in the *Table Talk* Luther refers to the room
in the tower in which the idea came to him. A whole Lutheran 'myth' has grown up
around the phrase 'tower-theology'. The precise room to which Luther was referring
is not known for certain. It has been identified by some with a lavatory in that part of
the building, to the delight of some and the dismay of others.

[2] See p. 48.

whole point of this theology is that it is an attempt to describe something which is happening at this moment, the dynamic relation between God and the individual man. The summary provides a key, but we should add to it Luther's most typical illustration of justification, the parable of the Good Samaritan—Luther sees Christ as the Good Samaritan who takes man into the Inn of the Church and justifies him. Also frequent is the 'thought of the Saviour as the hen under whose covering wings the chicks gather together.'[3]

They were crucial years from 1513 to 1518 when Luther was first propounding the lineaments of this theology in his lectures in the University of Wittenberg—lectures on the Psalms (p. 87), on Romans (p. 90), on Galatians (p. 105), on Hebrews (p. 107). The doctrines did not spring fully articulated from his mind. They grew, bit by bit, from the inner necessity which he had experienced, the necessity of being certain that Jesus Christ had really and effectively lifted him up, made him free of the ruin of sin which threatens every man, a certainty to which he had previously been able to find no way. To receive the Gospel of Christ in a fully effective way, to believe in it, Luther re-deployed all the theology he had learnt, he transformed it. He went behind the whole framework of sacraments, Mass, sacramentals, indulgences and pious works and good works. He re-stated this one radical fact which had always been at the centre of theology in some form or other, man's justification by God, an act done once and for all, regardless of man's sin or of good works. Man was saved, redeemed, put on the road to a new life, a supernatural life, a life of commune with Christ, of charity with all men, leading to eternal life after death. Only believe and you shall live.

[3] Rupp, R.G., p. 140.

14. Justification—a Catholic Doctrine

CRUCIAL years indeed. Luther was not accused of heresy when he propounded this theology. He carried the Faculty of Theology at Wittenberg with him, and then the University as a whole by 1517. Luther had proposed what amounted to a biblical and existential re-statement of traditional theology, em- phasizing all that had of recent years been played down, trans- forming it into a kerygma, a preaching, a message. It is important at this point to have some idea of the immense wealth, depth and breadth of traditional Catholic theology. Luther was an inheritor of it and in one sense remained always simply a very great medieval theologian. It is essential to remember that from the be- ginning his writing has in it the compass of a rich, well articulated theology.[1] As with all theology, one must not look for the solution of problems which were not problems to men and women of those days, nor dismiss as foolish the whole system because parts of it are obviously defective. The religious faith of pagans, the secular man of good will, hell—none of these were 'problems' in the sense that they now are. Their problematical aspects were not envisaged.

What Luther called, and what we have called the merit- theology was a metaphorical description[2] of a theoretical mechanism by which the free gift of grace was available and might in practice be effective. It was also elaborated as a means of encouraging the faithful to pray, or to do works useful to the Church of one kind and another, such as going on a crusade or helping to build a church. The essential purpose of Indulgences was related in theory not to anything essential in theology, not to the redemption but merely to the curtailment of punishment in

[1] The whole of the exposition in Rupp's *The Righteousness of God* is the fruit of long and careful study of Luther's enormous work and cannot be recommended too highly to anyone who wants to have an insight into Luther's mind in English. Other books have been described as 'allowing Luther to speak for himself', but in no other English book is there such a quantity of direct translation from Luther himself. One might cite, for a piece of exposition of Luther's theology, not cited elsewhere in this book, Rupp's pages 253–5.

[2] See Appendix 1.

purgatory. Indulgences were an inessential superstructure, but they had come to occupy the forefront of the religious life of the common people, and to have a greatly exaggerated emphasis doctrinally in the theory of merit-theology as well. But the fact that it was, essentially, only superstructure, and that it was recognized as such, is demonstrated very clearly by the reception given both immediately and later to Luther's theology. It was not branded as heretical. Luther thought, at first, in terms of putting back into their place in the Church the priorities of the Gospel and of the sacraments. He and his companions in the academic life at Wittenberg saw no essential discrepancy between Luther's theology and Catholic tradition, nothing of the sort that would lead immediately and automatically to a clash with authority. They supposed that it was a possible basis on which to erect a reforming programme—a programme of the sort that had been outlined so often before by so many different people in the last hundred years.

In the ensuing pages we shall refer very briefly to the particular stages in which Luther outlined his theology, in his courses of university lectures, in university disputations, and in parochial sermons, stages in the course of which he began to criticize more and more severely the many disreputable aspects of Church life at the time. It was forthright and animated criticism; paralleled by though more methodical than the ridicule and scorn used by Erasmus in his *Encomium Moriae*. It grew gradually into what amounted to a programme of reform which in this case had behind it the dynamic of a fresh preaching of the Christian Gospel.[*]

Luther's new theology was neither propounded outside the Church, nor was it immediately called in question by ecclesiastical authority. To the witness of Wittenberg at the time, of Cajetan at a later date, and of the Council of Trent later again, we may add the twentieth-century witness of Roman Catholic theologians that Luther's essential theology of justification and grace is not incompatible with, not absolutely contradictory of Catholic dogmatic tradition.[3]

[3] This is the essential theme of Bouyer's book some of whose historical statements about Luther have been refuted but whose essential theological theme of the orthodoxy of the theology of justification remains intact. A more detailed theological work is that of Hans Küng, another Roman Catholic, on justification in the theology of Karl Barth, establishing the orthodox Catholic character of Barth's protestantism. See note on p. 58.

The crucial and often ambivalent point concerns the part assigned to ecclesiastical authority, the pope and the bishops, in Luther's theology. So long as Luther was propounding his doctrine from within the Roman Catholic Church he was assuming that the traditional sacraments and discipline were to play their part. Scripture was the Word of God, Christ speaking to man, and it did so within the Church; it was in the context of her liturgy and her discipline that the Word spoke. At the time of which we are speaking it seems certain that it never occurred to Luther that he might be called to oppose the whole authority of the Catholic Church as such. He said Mass, he made use of the sacraments and administered them to others. He believed that a great deal of grossly superstitious practice had grown up and that the whole machinery of Massing priests, saying Masses for the souls of the dead as their main occupation, of indulgences and the general emphasis on man's work, the gaining of merits, and the virtual omission, very often, of reference to faith and to God's gift, God's work of grace, was in need of radical reform. His own spiritual scruples continued to make his own celebration of Mass a trial. But he was in no mind to attempt anything like a transformation of the sacramental and eucharistic framework, as though this must follow naturally on from the theology he was propounding.

His temper is on the whole conservative; his most natural reaction is to side with authority, as he had done against the Erfurt rioters, and as he had done against the Erfurt anti-amalgamation friars; he is indeed himself, by this time, an ecclesiastical authority in his order. But it is not only a matter of temper. His new theology of justification was not itself such as to require automatically the suppression or transformation of the sacraments, or of Catholic ecclesiastical authority. In practice, Luther's programme of reform, subsequent to 1517, did gradually move from advocating reforms which were not contradictory of traditional doctrine to reforms which were partially so. The stages by which this occurred, the motives and doctrinal issues involved, we discuss in later chapters. For the moment there are a classic five years in which Luther stands, as prophet and reformer, doctor and preacher, within the Catholic Church.

It is a point at which it is tempting to speculate what would have happened if. . . .[4] We have already moved a short way into such speculation by referring to opinions about the compatibility of Luther's essential theological doctrines up to 1518 with Catholic dogma, both then and now. But we are concerned here simply with the historical record. The historical facts are that Luther propounded his theology within the Catholic Church, and that he did this for about five years, without any thought that he must eventually take his theology and his own life outside the existing ecclesiastical framework and oppose the authority and some of the theological traditions of the Catholic Church. In a strictly theological and historical sense what he was teaching till 1518 was not in fact incompatible with Catholic doctrine. This is not to deny that Luther had conservative-minded opponents. But the life of the theological schools had lived on opposition and dialogue, often very bitter dialogue, and indeed accusations of heresy, for many centuries.

The facts remain. In the lectures and disputations of 1513-1518 Luther was propounding a radically new presentation of theology, which contains the germ of his essential teaching on Justification, Grace, and Scripture, and he was doing it as a good Catholic, from a position of ecclesiastical and academic authority. This doctrine can still be understood today in a Catholic sense. To this statement must be added the rider that Luther was spiritually uncomfortable all this time, and that the whole practical connotation of 'justification' was rooted in the atmosphere of Luther's experience of this discomfort.[5]

[4] Mackinnon in his *Luther and the Reformation* poses the matter thus: 'On the clamant necessity of the reform of those glaring abuses he speaks with no uncertain voice. As to the institutions of the Church in themselves he is only at the stage of incipient doubt. Whether the doubt would increase or decrease would depend on the question whether the Pope and the hierarchy would come some way towards meeting his demand for a thorough reformation of the Church in a spiritual direction.'

[5] Radically mistaken interpretations and factually incorrect accounts of Luther's theology remain common amongst Roman Catholic historians. What seems to this author an indefensible account may be found on pages 166-9 of Vol. I of *The Council of Trent* by Hubert Jedin (Nelson, 1957).

15. *Lectures and Status, 1511–18*

LUTHER arrived at Wittenberg in the autumn of 1511. He became preacher in the priory shortly after, and was told to prepare himself to be made a doctor of theology. This did not involve any precise study, but Luther must have felt the need to prepare himself as thoroughly as possible for the lectures he would have to give in the University as a doctor. He was given the doctorate in the autumn of 1512. About the same time Staupitz made Luther sub-prior in the priory at Wittenberg and put him in charge of the studies of the young friars. The precise date and subject of his first lectures as doctor are in doubt. We know, however, that he began a series of lectures on the Psalms in the summer of 1513 (on Tuesday, August 16, at 6.0 a.m. says Böhmer). But this leaves a gap after his promotion to the doctorate from the autumn of 1512 till the late summer of 1513. Some believe that Luther lectured on Genesis at this time, but we do not know; he no doubt had some added work as sub-prior and as master of studies. But it is possible to leave the problem of this year aside and still have (as a result of the intense studies on existing manuscripts by scholars) a very good idea of what Luther was thinking, how his thought was developing, and some idea of what he actually taught in the lectures which began in 1513.

The lectures on the Psalms, starting in the summer of 1513, went on till the autumn of 1515. Luther seems to have gone almost straight on to lectures on the Epistle to the Romans, from November 1515 to September 1516. There was a University disputation of which we know, in that autumn. And again he started shortly after in October on the Epistle to the Galatians which went on till March 1517. Immediately again follow the lectures on the Epistle to the Hebrews, lasting from March 1517 till the end of March in 1518. We have then a great body of material, the last part of which coincides with the first months of the great public storm.

The manuscripts are in greatly varying, often very complicated condition, but they are there. The scholars sift and sift. Some idea of their difficulties is indicated by the lectures on the Psalms, lectures which are crucial for a judgment about the precise time when Luther had the experience related in the previous section of an insight into the proper meaning of *Justitia*. Three different manuscripts, the Wolfenbüttler Psalter, the Dresdener Psalter, and a copy of the Psalterium Quintuplex of Faber Stapulensis have Luther's annotations, made at differing times; and the annotations involve formal *Glossae* (exegetical glosses on the text), *Scholiae* (longer theological expositions), and various other notes and workings over and revisions. None of these documents give the text of the Lectures themselves but are Luther's private writing on the texts of the Psalms from which or with the help of which he was delivering his lectures. However, sufficient work has been done by a sufficient number of scholars for substantial and reliable conclusions to be drawn, and it is on syntheses of such conclusions drawn by the scholars that this present account is based.

Half-way through his course on the Psalms, Luther was appointed to be Preacher in the parish church at Wittenberg, in 1514. This enabled him to apply the theology he was working out in a pastoral and practical fashion. This post, which Luther held and treasured for most of his life, was important for the development of his theology and thought as a whole, giving it a thoroughly practical and immediate orientation. It was also important for the influence that he so suddenly began to have in 1517, making it more effective, and providing experience of speaking to ordinary people over a considerable period. Before the end of the crucial lectures on the Psalms, Luther was made Provincial or District Superior, having under him eleven priories which brought him a deal of routine business, disciplinary and financial. As we have seen, it was as 'Provincial' that he appointed John Lang to be Prior of Erfurt.

From 1512 to 1518 we have if not a meteoric ascent, at least the beginning of what promises to be a remarkable career. Shortly before his twenty-ninth birthday he had been made a doctor of theology, in the young, sometimes despised University of Wittenberg, also sub-Prior and Master of Studies in the small priory in the same town. This was already some achievement for so young a man, even though Wittenberg was obscure. Three years later he achieved a series of lectures which were something of a *tour de force*, and in the course of which he began to preach in the town and to take up a position of local responsibility in his religious order. In the following two years, from 1516 to 1518, his lectures continued and in the course of these two years he formulated quite precisely his fundamental objections to scholastic theology, his preference for the Bible as the primary text and its nature as the Word of God, the full outline and much detail of a complete new theology, based on the Bible, and finally a wide variety of criticisms of contemporary sacramental usage. During these years, disputations in the University served to win over the leading professors at Wittenberg to the new theology.

Towards the end of this period a purely routine procedure suddenly and entirely unexpectedly rocketed him to fame. The Ninety-five Theses were in many ways less fundamental than a previous ninety-seven theses. Their nailing to the door of the castle church was no act of defiance but a routine procedure for the holding of a University disputation. But their subject was one with practical interest for the ordinary people, verging on many more spheres than the purely religious. From a promising young doctor of theology, lecturer, preacher, provincial superior, confessor, reformer (of a type which was not uncommon), a theologian bidding fair to be the founder of a whole new school in the Church, Luther became a public figure, involved in the mass emotions roused by national controversies, and the extreme reactions of *amour propre* roused in churchmen when their authority and eventually that of the Church itself is challenged.

16. *The Psalms, 1513–15*

THE notes on the Psalms seem to show that it was in the course of preparing these lectures that Luther came to his fundamental insight—in particular whilst preparing for the lecture on Psalms 70 and 71. There is a close resemblance between the words used, and those in the autobiographical piece,[1] and again a resemblance with the quotation from Augustine which speaks in a similar way of *justitia*. It is from Augustine that Luther quotes most frequently in the commentary on the Psalms, regularly using St Augustine's own commentary on them. But he also quotes, and returns several times to St Augustine's *Confessions*, Book 8, where St Augustine speaks of his own conversion. The passage obviously had a deep effect on Luther, and its highly personal introverted spiritual note is significant. Luther's comment is harmoniously profound and sincere. He tells his listeners that Scripture can only be properly spoken and heard by someone whose feelings are conformed to them. Luther is speaking of 'compunction', and says that because he cannot speak practically out of an experience of compunction, therefore he sets forth instead the example and practice of St Augustine.

A constant theme in these notes is that of 'humility', which is often referred to in the typically dynamic form of *humiliatio*. And this is connected with the humility and the humiliation of Christ. The notes are full of the 'wrath' of God, of the humiliation of Christ on the Cross. 'This work of God in Christ which took place in history is reproduced when Christ lives in us.'[2] That the Cross is the crown and climax of Christ's identification with us is a major theme of Luther's: 'For the Cross of Christ runs through the whole of Scripture'; 'You see, therefore, the passion and the Cross of Christ is everywhere depicted, so that we can very well say with St Paul: "We will know nothing save Christ, and him crucified".' The cry of dereliction on the Cross was central in Luther's mind then—a cry of dereliction which was unplumbable but which is echoed in each of us. Luther was already describing his 'theology of the Cross' which he opposed to the traditional Catholic theology, with its reliance first on 'nature' on which grace will build, a 'theology of glory'.

Luther solved his own inner problem some time in the course of these lectures (though he continued, as through all his life, to experience his *Anfechtungen*). And it is surely as a result of this

[1] Rupp, R.G., pp. 135–6.
[2] Rupp, R. G., p. 145. The following quotations are also derived from the same work.

that we find in his notes the first criticisms of the Church's life; from a personal problem he is able to begin, occasionally, to turn to an outward public problem. Once in the course of these notes he writes: 'The state of the Church has never been so unhappy as it is in these days'. In addition to a critique of theologians and philosophers, and to bitterness at the eminence given to Aristotle, there is criticism of daily devotional practice. Böhmer summarizes Luther: 'The sacraments are administered in the most frivolous and profane fashion, and prayer has become lukewarm, dry and spiritless. Lukewarmness is prevalent everywhere, as a matter of fact, and connected with it is the attempt "to make the way to heaven as easy as possible for the people by means of indulgences and false teachings". Moreover, the administration of the judicial and the executive power in the Church is very poorly managed. "And who can count up the abuses which take place in the bestowal of benefices?"'

On the whole the picture painted is as yet not much worse than might be expected in practice to exist somewhere in the Church at any time in history. And the reaction is typical of the reaction of many conscientious people at that time and for centuries past— indeed so far it is less bitter than that of Erasmus. The significant thing is that not only has Luther joined the band of those who make no bones about speaking their opinions freely and frankly, but that he makes these criticisms on the same pages which contain theological exposition of a profound and spiritual nature. The criticisms thus take on a much greater seriousness than those in the pages of Erasmus where the whole treatment is a mixture of high sophistication and simpliste spirituality. This combination of practicality with intense personal spirituality was to lift Luther above his contemporaries, other scholars and other reformers.

17. *The Epistle to the Romans. Tauler*

IN the autumn of 1515, Luther began his second series of lectures on Scripture in the University of Wittenberg. He was now at the climax of his new theological understanding. He chose that Epistle in the words of the first chapter of which he had found a clue to his new understanding. For a year he proceeded to expound in detail his conception of the whole man, sinful, unable of himself to do good, completely dependent on God, on God's grace, and then bound by faith in Christ. Man is always in need of justification, and always destined to justification in Christ. Good works, righteousness, are not something of concern in relation to man, but in relation to God.[1] In all his denunciation of 'good works' and his insistence on the unavoidably sinful nature of man (sinful tendencies, egoistic tendencies always menacing) Luther was not envisaging the modern problem of the good pagan but the problem of the complacent hypocritical Christian. 'Faith is life and the living word abbreviated', 'Unless faith illumines and love frees, no man is able to will or possess, or work, anything good'.

The scope of these lectures and Luther's notes for them is immense. It is the outline of a complete theology. Luther is concerned first and last with 'man as he stands in the presence of the Holy and Living God, who is of purer eyes than to behold iniquity, yet who of His pure mercy receives sinners in His Son Jesus Christ'.[2] Luther outlines the traditional theology of grace. 'It is the work of grace, to make it [the will] willing and cheerful (*libentem ac hilarem*) towards the law. So I rightly said that all our good is outside us (*extrinsecum nobis*)—that is, Christ.'[3] 'They can never fulfil the law, while they do not obey from the heart.' The unregenerate 'do good works wholly from fear, or from love of reward'. All

[1] Rupp, *R.G.*, p. 161.
[2] Rupp, *R.G.*, p. 161. Rupp gives a very numerous collection of references in Luther's works for the fundamental conception of *coram Deo*, 'in God's presence', in opposition to *coram nobis*, 'in the perspective of creation' or 'in the eyes of our fellow men'.
[3] Rupp, *R.G.*, p. 163, also the following quotations.

this is normal enough, though it had possibly not been put down so forthrightly, in such an Augustinian fashion, for some time. But the rub comes when Luther opposes this to the current philosophy and declares: 'Where is "Free Will" now? Where are those who try to make out that, from our own natural strength we can make an act of love to God above all things. . . . This philosophy stinks in our nostrils, as though reason always seeks the best things, and we chatter about the Law of Nature.'

Luther's conception of man as always sinful (the legacy of 'original sin', in the traditional formulation), whilst at the same time penitent and justified, relates to his understanding of the Hebraic meaning of flesh (*sarx*) and spirit (*pneuma*): 'For the same person is "spirit" and "flesh": thus what the "flesh" does the whole man is said to do. And yet what resists is not the whole man but is rightly called a part of him.'[4] 'He is concerned with the persistence of sin in the believer, not as a mere tinder (*fomes peccati*), but as that ferment of egoism for which man is accountable since his whole personal existence is involved in it, but which in the redeemed is restrained by God, until it is finally driven out by grace, a work growingly fulfilled but never perfectly achieved in this present life.'[5] The common idea of Luther's doctrine as antinomian, with Christ's righteousness as a purely outward legal cloak thrown over a man chained willy nilly to sin, is false. Grace for him, as in Catholic doctrine, works interiorly, giving man full strength but never compelling him, nor freeing him from temptation or weakness of will. Luther wrote: 'For all this life is a time of wanting righteousness, but never having it perfectly, for that is for the future life. But to want it is to show with all our strength, our studies, prayers, works, sufferings, that we desire righteousness but that we have not attained it perfectly.'[6]

[4] Rupp, *R.G.*, pp. 166–7.
[5] Rupp, *R.G.*, p. 174.
[6] The theology described in this paragraph with its insistence on the dominance of sin might be seen as a contradiction of the Catholic doctrine that the grace of a sacrament offers a man, for the moment, the perfect life of Christ. But when the full context of such an abstract, scholastic statement of the Christ-life offered to man sacramentally is examined and the context of Luther's dynamic description of the actual (and eschatological) state of affairs in the individual is taken into consideration, the contradiction is no longer obvious, and can be argued not to exist. This is beyond the scope of the present work. Küng's *Rechtfertigung* is probably the best detailed guide to the theological problem.

Resignation even to damnation is necessary for full self-purification:

> For even Christ was damned and abandoned more than all the saints. And his sufferings were not, as some imagine, light and easy. For really and truly he offered himself to eternal damnation to God the Father for us. And in his human nature he behaved in no other way than as a man eternally damned to hell. On account of such love to God, God at once raised him from the dead and hell and thus devoured hell. . . .
>
> Our good is hidden, and that so deeply that it is hidden under its contrary. Thus our life is hidden under death, our joy under our hatred, glory under shame, salvation under perdition, the kingdom under exile, heaven under hell, wisdom under foolishness, righteousness under sin, strength under infirmity.[7]

Probably about half-way through these lectures, in May 1516, Luther began to read the works of Tauler, the German Dominican mystic. Tauler's thought he found very sympathetic. At one time it was supposed that Tauler had had a fundamental influence on Luther so similar was Luther's personal expression of the love of Christ, of the sharing with Christ crucified, of love of the Cross. But in fact Tauler confirmed rather than initiated the theology that Luther was working out, strengthening his conviction of its rightness. He had some influence on Luther's vocabulary, and in general his influence is another such as those we discussed in Chapter 7. But the German mystics had given something to the whole ambience of German devotion. Something of their influence must have been apparent in the lives of the more seriously devout friars and monks whom Luther had met as man and boy. His own intensely personal attitude to Christ has about it a family likeness to that of the German mystics, notwithstanding their radical differences.

There is an ambiguity about the word 'mysticism'. In the past it has often been used in a semi-popular fashion to describe unusual spiritual phenomena; or it has been thought of as referring only to those Catholic spiritual masters who have a highly schematized idea of individual progress in spiritual life. Recently

7 Rupp, R.G., p. 190.

3. Spalatin (1484–1545)
From a painting by Cranach the Elder, 1537

4. Frederick the Wise (1463–1525), Elector of Saxony
From a painting by Cranach the Elder

a more sober, and generalizing, interpretation has been favoured amongst Catholics. Abbot Cuthbert Butler's *Western Mysticism* was the classical modern exposition of this sober view, mysticism being properly seen as Pauline, Augustinian, Gregorian and Bernardine. It has recently been succinctly re-defined by his successor and namesake, Abbot Christopher Butler: 'All souls are called to the mystical life and to some form of mystical prayer'.[8]

For Luther and for many Protestants the word 'mystic' was used to describe those who had in common an idea of the possibility of taking steps to make steady progress towards perfection, and who spoke of subjective experiences connected with this progress. As Luther was increasingly convinced that these ideas were contradictory of the Gospel he was increasingly unwilling to be guided by anyone who could be called a mystic. But Tauler's influence on his *Theologia Crucis* was lasting.

Tauler helped Luther personally a great deal by his emphasis on the value for the individual of turning always to Christ crucified (advice similar to that of Staupitz and with obviously biblical inspiration), and by his recognition that souls must all pass through a period of great suffering. His witness added confidence to Luther's own convictions about the reality of Christ's personal message.[9] And for four years he escapes Luther's anti-mystic diatribes. Luther ceased to praise Tauler after 1520 and he always looked on the mystics, thereafter, as heavily tainted with the merit-theology and with 'works'—on account of their penitential practices.

[8] *Prayer, An Adventure in Living*, by B. C. Butler, Darton, Longman and Todd, London, and Helicon Press, Baltimore, 1961, p. 117.

[9] See the pages on Tauler listed in the index of Böhmer. Böhmer thinks that Luther always reinterpreted Tauler and that the two men never really mean the same thing at all. There is obviously some truth in this, but pushed to an extreme it becomes eventually merely the truism that every man interprets everything he reads in his own individual way, and if two centuries separate the reader and the author the discrepancy is liable to be considerable. Böhmer recognizes the influence which Tauler had on Luther in inspiring him and keeping the divine impulse strong. But he wants to insist that in every objective doctrinal respect there is a contradiction between the two. He strains the evidence, going beyond it when he repeats, uncriticized and unexplained, the generalization about the 'dominantly pantheistic mood' of the mystics. As usual Rupp seems to be nearer the mark. He distinguishes the different schools of mystics, of which the Victorines influenced Luther not at all, the Bernardines a little (Luther always had a great love of St Bernard simply because of St Bernard's own so palpable love of God), and the German mystics rather more. This latter influence is perhaps best expressed by saying that Luther had much in common with it and shared this native German tradition.

In fact the mystics did not commonly regard extreme ascetic practices as essential; their concern was with God. But for Luther their frequently penitential *methods* were redolent of all that he came to reject eventually. Their doctrine of a programme to achieve progressive 'detachment' from the 'things of this world' he regarded as a pointless attempt on man's part to reach God— God who had already given himself to man, and in whom it was necessary simply to believe and to trust. The material objects of the world were for Luther *larvae*, masks or signs of God, rather than things from which we need to be 'detached'.

Here, in a sense, the argument is on the way to coming full circle, for such an attitude is also that of St Thomas and of a 'theology of glory', which sees in everything the good things of God's creation, ripe for glory. Christian tradition has always had both faces—the negative theology and the affirmative theology— they are not mutually contradictory. However, the point here is simply the radical opposition in temper between Luther and virtually all his teachers: (1) The emphasis given by Luther to man's sinfulness, his absolute need of God, and the importance of complete faith and reliance simply on grace. (2) The practical emphasis, in contradiction of this, in the daily piety of most people on an assertion that man could obtain merit in God's eyes, an assertion which did also assume man's hopelessly sinful nature (see Tetzel's sermon, pp. 114–7), but which saw the remedy for it in the canonical sacraments and sacramentals, without much emphasis being laid on faith, greater emphasis being put on the authority of the Church as it mediated grace to man when he took part in the sacraments. The disposition of the individual, his personal relationship to God, is assumed to need little attention beyond the external observances—he must have the right dispositions for the sacrament of confession, but the assumption is that this is virtually a part of the data.

The manuscripts of the notes for these lectures on Romans are sufficient for the actual content of the lectures to be more easily surmised, than in the case of those on the Psalms. The lectures, so far as can be seen, make a more easily manageable whole, articulating a single theme. The notes reveal the tenor of Luther's inner thought. We can go a little way towards comparing his increasingly critical private concern for the whole state of the Church with what he thought it prudent to say to his students—and to the parishioners of Wittenberg in his sermons of which there is also some record. He picks out what seem to be clear and flagrant cases of abuse, without, however, involving himself in too much detail, or personalities, or in too extreme generalizations. Both the latter are kept for private notes. Indulgences, according to Böhmer, are one of the few things that we can be sure he was attacking in public by 1516—their abuse, but not the basic theory of them. Linked with this were some denunciations from the pulpit of what Luther considered to be abuses in the degree of confidence which the people reposed in wearing Christopher medals, and in praying to particular saints for special purposes when in fact the saints were able to help people in every way, and should be prayed to in all physical and spiritual needs.[10]

Luther was by this time getting extremely vehement in the notes he made for lectures and sermons. His vehemence is directly related to his own spiritual conviction of the depth of man's sinfulness and its horror. It is thought that most of this material was left on the paper when Luther spoke to his students and his parishioners; it hardly concerned his students to whom he was teaching theology; and his parishioners he possibly thought would do best with one subject at a time. The criticism runs the gamut of Church and State; we might not find it very difficult to parallel this criticism in various other ages, in one place or another, if allowance is made for language; the private notebooks of critically-minded but loyal Catholics at other times might contain similar material, since it is seldom difficult to compare the acts of officials of any body with an ideal and make telling criticisms. The difference, of course, is that Luther eventually changed his ecclesiastical allegiance and became famous. His private notes are the visible forerunners of his future public denunciations—and are available to historians.

'The Roman Curia is thoroughly corrupted and infected, a colossal chaos of all conceivable debaucheries, gluttonies, knaveries,

[10] Böhmer, pp. 155 ff for this and quotations following.

ambitions and sacrilegious outrages. Today Rome is carousing as much as in the time of the Caesars—if not more. Hence it has even more need of the apostles today than it did before.' He says that all a man's vices are overlooked so long as he defends the rights and liberties of the Church. Indulgences are an illustration of how the Church fails in its charity towards the poor and is indulgent only to the rich. Too much money is spent on outward show, at the expense of neighbourly love. Yet the liturgy is performed in a slovenly way. He considers obligatory fasting should be modified, and the number of holidays cut down. Public figures, Pope Julius II and his own secular ruler, Frederick the Wise, are criticized for their irresponsibility. And he has strictures to make on the drunkenness and laziness which is widespread in society.

He writes that he makes these criticisms 'in obedience to my duty and the burden resting on me. . . . Moreover by virtue of papal authority I hold a public teaching office. Accordingly, it is one of my official duties to strike out against all the wrong of which I become aware, even if the wrong is done by persons in high position.'

18. *Spalatin*

By the autumn of 1516 when Luther completed the lectures on Romans, he had achieved a certain stature, locally. We have seen the various appointments he held. In addition to these there was an important friendship with the private secretary, principal adviser and chaplain of Frederick the Wise, Spalatin, a thin-faced, intelligent-looking man, sensitive but firm, having also a prominent nose, according to the painting by Lucas Cranach the Elder.[1] Luther had met him probably about the time of his reception of the doctorate. Wittenberg being Frederick's residence, and the University being his own pet creation, it was natural that his principal adviser should be present at such a ceremony, and make it his business to know at least something about the University

[1] Reproduced facing p. 92.

doctors themselves. But Spalatin really fell for Luther in a big way.

Here was one more of the connections which put Luther into the position at which all roads met sooner or later. His personality and gifts attracted precisely that combination of people which would give him the maximum of influence at a later date. There must have been a special personal charm about him, and something to create confidence—a young friar who was learned and yet still very human, a religious whose religion had a new intensity about it and who was for ever quoting the Bible, chunks of it, a German who would speak to the people, and severely, yet remained very obviously conscious of his own shortcomings. Here was a man to follow—a leader who did not realize he was a leader, a master who had a vivid sense of service. The sombre side must have been enough to lend a certain excitement, but no more; a young man, he naturally had troubles of his own—in his early thirties, he must have lacked the signs of maturity. He overworked, and would shut himself up in his room to get through a whole back-log of the breviary he had had to leave unsaid, even a whole week's worth. Then he would be ill with headache and internal troubles. And he would be upset at the sight of the crowds with their herd-emotion stirred by some favourite festival, and their attention riveted not on the sacred liturgy and the sacraments, but on the exposition of some relic which they hoped might bring a miracle if enough prayers were said, or on the latest indulgence which might enable them to free souls from purgatory or shorten their own time there. The ascetic features of Luther's heavy face had on them the question: What is all this to do with the Gospel?—the Gospel which is 'a doctrine concerning Christ, who is assuredly neither law nor work, but our righteousness, wisdom, sanctification, and redemption'.[2] The sharp, piercing dark eyes looked with anxiety on these herds.

Spalatin found him irresistible. In 1513 Dr Martin is 'an excellent man and scholar, whose judgment I value very highly'. In March 1514 Spalatin wishes 'to become wholly his'. By 1515 Luther was being consulted very frequently on questions put to Spalatin by Frederick. Spalatin would consult him, above all,

[2] *Commentary on Galatians* (James Clarke, London, 1953).

about the University, and Luther would unfold to him his gradually developing idea of what a university should teach—a Christian university. In 1516 Luther must have become, as far as superficial appearances went, a recognizable, though highly independent, member of the humanists who throughout Europe were busy trying to reform the Church—for a short time now he affected a Greek form for his name and signed himself Eleutherius in letters to Spalatin.

'Reform' had been a familiar word to Luther all his life; it had now come to mean for him a reform of the method of teaching theology, a reform which had practical implications for the whole range of the Christian life, individual and ecclesiastical. And, already he meant more by this than the humanists did—and something different. For the humanists were concerned primarily with correcting objective intellectual errors, particularly with providing a more accurate text of the Bible, and reforming obvious abuses. Luther's wish was to return to what seemed to him to be the original dynamic Christian message, with all its Pauline impact.

Working in Wittenberg Luther perhaps knew only a little of the numerous attempts at 'reform' which had been made in recent times. Probably he was less well-informed than such a sophisticated scholar as Erasmus, or such a man of affairs as Sir Thomas More. But it is clear that he is now living and thinking in the European context of a Church which needed reformation. Although he was only just beginning to be heard of outside Wittenberg, we must see him now in this full historical context.

19. *The Church in Need of Reform*

A TIME of crisis for authority is a description that can be applied to most periods in European history. It can certainly be applied to the sixteenth century. The Church had been undergoing such a crisis for a long time—a crisis which involved argument about where sovereignty lay in the Church's organization, both centrally and locally. The argument became a disagreement between those who said the final authority should be a Council, and those who supported the papacy. This disagreement came into the forefront of Luther's history for a short time later when he appealed from the Pope to a future Council. But its importance is also central in the movement for reform during the fifteenth and sixteenth centuries, which must be understood if Luther's reform is to have its proper context. Numerous plans were drawn up, and many pieces written in the hope of inspiring a Council which would reform the Church.[1]

We may cite the suggestions put forward in France in 1403-4 by Matthew of Cracow in his *Concerning the Filth of the Roman Curia*, whose title will be a convenient reminder that language which appears brutal to us was normal.

> The granting of benefices by the Pope is at variance with the 'ancient code'. . . . His right of disposal is circumscribed by the canons, but above all by the very purpose of the benefices, which is the edification of the faithful. When he grants them against payment of money, as happens at this time, he incurs the guilt of simony. . . . All those who have anything to do with these practices are simoniacs and are in a state of mortal sin. . . . The wretched financial situation of the Apostolic See is the direct result of the neglect of Councils.

Matthew, who was later Bishop of Worms, had as a companion-in-arms Dietrich of Niem who had himself been a member of the Roman Curia and is no less critical.

In 1449 the Carthusian Jacob of Jüterbog wrote: 'The reform Councils have made it abundantly clear that the doctrine of the Pope's supremacy is only a shield behind which the Italians and their party shelter from reform. Even if the Pope were a man of good will, the resistance which the people around him offer to reform is such that one may boldly affirm that a reform of the Church cannot be brought about by the Pope alone; it needs an effort by the whole Church gathered in Council.' In describing the contemporary writing of another Carthusian, Jedin writes: 'There are passages which give the reader the impression that he

---

[1] The quotations in this chapter are all from Jedin, Volume I.

is listening to Savonarola or to Luther, so impassioned and revolutionary is the language.'

The Popes were pressed hard by such reform proposals. *Advisamenta* to them by their cardinals were drawn up more than once in the first half of the century. These flowered, during the reign of Nicholas V (1447–55), into the *Advisamenta super reformatione papae et romanae curiae* drawn up by Cardinal Capranica. Jedin writes: 'Capranica's memorial reads like a complete programme of the Catholic reformation. A century later it was actually carried out, but after what catastrophes! The Cardinal had a premonition of the approach of "scourges" and "straits"— partly divine punishment, partly simple consequences of neglect.'

Pius II's pontificate (1458–64) contains another programme of reform proposals and projects. He consulted Domenico Domenichi and Nicholas of Cusa. Their recommendations were similar to those of Capranica—'Obedience to the Holy See will only be restored on the day when the prelates of the Church, headed by the Pope and the Cardinals, begin to seek the kingdom of God instead of their personal advantage'. They preach a sermon, one no doubt much needed: the reform is to be a return to the *forma Christi*; 'its aim is to transform all Christians, beginning with the Pope, into the likeness of Christ'. The means: 'a reform of the members through three visitors whose action is determined by fourteen rules, the quintessence of which consists in the restoration in all ecclesiastical corporations of the primitive mode of life. . . .' Pius II drafted a bull, *Pastor aeternus*, which had a few pale reflections of these recommendations—but died before it became law. And so it went on. Even Alexander VI admitted that a reform was necessary and tried to institute one. But the will was never there. The facts were all known—that the Church was in a disgraceful state, that it was not worthy of the authority given it by Christ, that it deserved punishment. But the will failed. Oliviero Carafa to whom Alexander VI entrusted the responsibility for reform wrote: 'The first thing is that our hearts be cleansed within us'— and he repeats the words of St Bernard: 'Let the Pope realize that he is the successor of Peter, not of the Emperor Constantine, and that Peter was commissioned by our Lord to feed his sheep. The

most grievous danger for any Pope lies in the fact that, encom-
passed as he is by flatterers, he never hears the truth about his own
person and ends by not wishing to hear it.'[2]

Under Julius II (Pope at the time of Luther's visit to Rome) the
Fifth Lateran Council was the occasion for two Venetians to
present a memorial to the Pope, again right up to date, fully
aware of the problems:

> Pride of place is assigned to the missions in the recently discovered
> continent of America and to union with the Eastern Christians. . . .
> They ruthlessly expose the internal injuries of the Church: the
> ignorance of the clergy and religious, of whom only two per cent
> are said to understand the Latin of the liturgical books; ignorance
> among the laity, who should be instructed in the fundamental truths
> of the faith at least on all Sundays; superstition, which had infiltrated
> into every sphere of public and private life. Entangled as they are
> themselves in these and other miseries the clergy have forgotten
> that it is their duty to act as leaders. Responsibility for all this lies
> largely with the Popes, who have surrounded themselves with
> benefice-hunting flatterers and allowed Rome to become a shameful
> *lupanar*.

And the evils were spread out through all the Church. In every
town throughout Europe there were houses of the numerous
religious orders. The life lived in many of them, a majority in
some countries, appears to have been so mediocre, so far from
both the spirit and the letter of the Rule originally laid down by
their founders, that they were in effect little more than convenient
places for those who preferred such a life to family life, and hoped
to gain their place in heaven thereby.[3] There were some fervent
houses where nothing could have been much improved. There
were a few gravely scandalous places. But many were merely
mediocre, lacking in fervour to such a degree that it was difficult
to see how they could be reformed.

[2] An expression which has been repeated frequently by *avant-garde* Catholics in Europe in
the years since the accession of Pope John XXIII is similarly phrased and motivated: 'The
Constantinian era is ended'.

[3] This is the opinion expressed by the authors of the *Consilium de emendanda ecclesia* in
1537; it is also the opinion of the present-day historian Professor David Knowles as far
as the religious houses in England are concerned. See the closing pages of Volume III
of *The Religious Orders in England*.

20. *Luther and Reform*

LUTHER could not have known all the detail, some examples of which were given in the previous chapter. But there must have been some general recognition by him that reforming movements came and went, and that the contemporary Fifth Lateran Council on the one hand and his contemporaries the humanists on the other were achieving as little as similar councils and movements in the past. His strength lay in his deep personal experience of spiritual shock and disaster—he was not simply objectively scandalized, rather he had suffered, deeply, and then recognized the cause of his suffering in a defective presentation of the Gospel. He was concerned not simply with abuse but with theology. The special power of his sermons lay in their combination of deeply personal spirituality with trenchant reform proposals. Luther had not been involved in any official reform programme; he had not suffered the inevitable inoculation against action which is almost unavoidable for those in official positions for any length of time— if their proposals are rejected, direct action becomes almost impossibly difficult, and in any case to challenge Rome with actions, as distinct from words, was to risk a process for heresy.

Luther was still the small-town friar, the doctor of theology in an upstart university. Within a few years he surrounded himself, though in no sense deliberately, first by a faculty, then by a whole university, who admired him and were convinced by his teaching. Its existence became, in 1518, a challenge to Rome herself. It was a David and Goliath situation. David's simplicity was a great help. Goliath was enraged. An upstart friar, at a provincial university, a German doctor of theology still in his early thirties. He should be squashed—swiftly. If he would not lie down he must be excommunicated for disobedience, and his teachings shown to be heretical, which they must be if they challenged Rome's authority on an official matter such as the issue of indulgences. As far as any wide generalization of this sort is justified, this is the picture. And it is important to catch some understanding of the general temper of events before entering on the detail which is complex.

It is impossible to identify a particular point at which Luther finally developed his own doctrine to the point where it contradicted Catholic tradition irretrievably, and established a new independent tradition. The theses on which the Bull of Excommunication would be based were never debated or examined with full academic care, one by one at Rome, where the judgment of Louvain University on them was accepted as sufficient justification for a blanket condemnation with a few points emphasized. Cajetan disagreed with this procedure, preferring a comment on each thesis, and in any case apparently considered that the theses involved 'errors' rather than 'heresies'. Luther's distinctive theology of justification was not involved in them except in so far as the 'errors' were connected with his growing distrust of the Church's traditional sacramental teaching. But even here the picture is not simple. It seems almost certain that Luther's sacramental doctrine was in essentials at first simply a judgment on contemporary sacramental practice rather than on traditional Catholic theory—a practice which did often make something very like magic of the doctrine of sacramental efficacy, that a sacrament, *ex opere operato*, automatically conferred grace on the man who receives the sacrament 'validly', reducing the element of faith, the interior disposition, almost to vanishing point.

Aquinas had in fact taught that faith was essential to the man who receives a sacrament, and this has remained Catholic teaching.[1] A man, who receives grace, has to correspond to it; but in Luther's time the emphasis on this had become minimal. Luther went to the other extreme, emphasizing faith as the first essential

---

[1] The traditional Catholic doctrine that a sacrament confers grace unavoidably, *ex opere operato*, has been very widely misunderstood both by Catholics and Protestants. If no disposition of any sort were required in the recipient it would be difficult to distinguish such a doctrine from magic. In fact the Catholic Church's authoritative teaching has always been that whilst grace is conferred by the sacrament by virtue of Christ's redemptive act and the intention of the one conferring it in Christ's name, yet the grace of the sacrament remains dormant in the recipient who lacks the proper dispositions, faith and the will to respond to the grace. The recipient must have faith. Böhmer is one of many authors who fail to make this distinction, and by doing so make the Catholic situation against which Luther revolted absurd and unhistorical. The whole religious complex becomes something so akin to superstition that the twentieth-century historian is sometimes reluctant to take it seriously.

—finally giving it priority in a sense which probably reduced the sacraments to something radically incompatible with Catholic tradition, denying the efficacy which Catholic tradition had always taught.

Luther himself never planned a separate ecclesiastical body. He believed in the one 'Church', established by Christ. He believed he was reforming it. He came to believe that the Roman authority had de-formed it. The extent of general support from other people both for his activities and his theory confirmed him in this belief. Large numbers of people of all classes supported his virtually schismatic actions. Following from their support he was faced with the practical problem of advising and organizing them —how much of their traditional ecclesiastical life to leave intact, to what extent he should encourage new forms. He solved the problems as they came along.

Particular pastoral problems pointed Luther's way. In the autumn of 1516 the evil of indulgences had already stirred him and he was attacking the use of them in sermons at the same time as he was starting on a further course of University lectures. The following two chapters are concerned with these University lectures 1516–18. Then follows the indulgence controversy.

21. Galatians and Hebrews

LUTHER probably completed his lectures on Romans on September 7, 1516. Before starting on his next series he instigated an academic disputation in the University. His pupil Bartholomew Bernhardi had to defend a thesis, for his degree of sententiarius. The thesis chosen was that man can do nothing pleasing to God without grace. In other words it was an attack on the Occamist doctrine of man's ability to do things pleasing to God by his own will, and it developed a further attack on the corpus of medieval philosophy and the Aristotelian methods. Augustine was quoted in defence of the thesis. The marginalia of 1512-13 had been developed into a full thesis.

It seems to have been considered likely that the thesis would not be sustained, but when the thesis was defended publicly the conclusion was, for the moment anyhow, in its favour. It caused sufficient concern in the mind of Dr Carlstadt of the University and of Luther's priory, an academic senior there since Luther's arrival, to impel him to travel to Leipzig the following January to buy a complete set of St Augustine's works—with a view to controverting Luther. In the event he was himself converted and became convinced that Luther was right and the Occamists wrong. In another 151 theses, published in April 1517, Carlstadt made clear his own position in support of Luther. On these occasions Nicholas von Amsdorf, of similar seniority to Carlstadt, was also deeply impressed and eventually won over as a life-long supporter of Luther's teaching.

In February 1517 Luther sent some anti-Aristotelian propositions to Trutvetter and Lang at Erfurt. In May he wrote to Lang: 'Our theology and that of St Augustine are going ahead, and they reign in our University, and it is the Lord's doing. Aristotle is gradually going down, perhaps into permanent ruin. It is wonderful how out of favour are the lectures on the Sentences. Nobody can hope for an audience unless he professes this theology, i.e. the Bible or St Augustine or some doctor of real authority in the Church.' Luther has become a popular lecturer and an academic leader at Wittenberg, corresponding with other university men on the burning topics.

In October 1516 Luther had started lecturing again, this time on Galatians. The only manuscript which remains is that of a student who was taking the lecture down, and the version which Luther published in 1519. The valuable preparatory notes which might have shown what was in Luther's mind though not suitable for the actual lecture have not been found. The exposition which is available continues with Luther's distinctive theology, much of it concerned with the contrast between the 'Law' and the 'Gospel'. 'Every imperative which stands over and against men as a commandment, including the decalogue itself, is the Law, and . . . .

it brings condemnation when men attempt to fulfil it in their own strength, and according to the inward motive.'[1] Faith is the only way, and in it are summed up all the virtues. In case it should be concluded that he is recommending an unchristian quietism, Luther poses the problem: 'Then are we not free? Are there no more good things to be done, or bad things to be left undone, because faith in Christ and his righteousness are sufficient?' He replies:

> They are sufficient indeed, but no one's faith is so great that it cannot or ought not to be increased. Thus for its increase good works are to be done, and bad ones avoided. For faith is a thing of the widest extent and differing with many degrees, until all things are perfectly despised save Christ. Which even if it were perfectly accomplished, which rarely happens, there would still be good works to be done, not that anything should be sought by them, but that the Lord might be served with the utmost freedom, that Christ might be his sufficiency, and there should be no obedience save the will of Christ his Lord.[2]

As in all the lectures there are continual references to a relationship with Christ, in a personal or mystical sense, although this is not to suggest that it is vague, or subjective. It was in December of 1516 that Luther wrote to Spalatin: 'If you take delight in pure and solid theology in the German language—a theology very similar to that of the ancients—get the sermons of John Tauler, of the Order of Preachers, of whose teaching I send you herewith an epitome. For I have not found in Latin or German a more wholesome theology or one more consonant with the Gospel. Taste, therefore, and see how sweet is the Lord, where formerly you have seen how bitter is whatever is of ourselves.' Luther can be sententious, and Spalatin enjoyed it.

Although his sermons are usually informal, Tauler's teaching runs a very wide gamut of Christian life and reflects the synthesis of Aquinas who as a Dominican influenced all subsequent members of the order including Eckhart whose speculations also occasionally have a place in Tauler. The Thomist tradition flowered in the high but simple and practical advice of

---

[1] Rupp, R.G., p. 195.　　　　[2] Rupp, R.G., p. 198.

Tauler's sermons, with their deep spirituality. Perhaps this simple German mysticism was the nearest Luther ever came to Aquinas. Commenting on Galatians (4. 19) on 'Christ being formed in us', Luther wrote:

> For the life of the Christian is not of himself, but of Christ living in him . . . it is to be noted that it is true that Christ is not exactly 'formed' in anybody 'personaliter', and thus the gloss is correct which says that faith in Christ or the knowledge of Christ should be taken here for 'Christ' . . . but beware most carefully lest this be taken as a kind of speculative knowledge, with which Christ is known as a kind of object . . . for this is dead and even the demons have this . . . but it is to be taken practically, as life, essence and experience of the example and image of Christ, that Christ may be no longer an object of our knowledge, but rather we are the object of his knowledge.[3]

It is probable that the lectures on Galatians ended in March and that Luther immediately began the next lectures on Hebrews. These ran for a year, and, from November, 1517, were given at a time first of anxiety for Luther and then of increasing publicity and controversy. After Scripture, to which there are over a thousand references, the most frequent reference in these lectures is to St Chrysostom's Homilies on Hebrews.

The mystical vein continues in these lectures:

> The hardest of all things is faith in Christ, which is being rapt and translated from all things of sense, within and without, into those things beyond sense within and without, namely into the invisible, most high and incomprehensible God.
>
> For faith causes the heart to be fixed and to adhere to celestial things, and thoroughly to be rapt and turned towards invisible things . . .;
>
> . . . to adhere to God means to be deprived of the world and of all creatures, as to carry the image of Christ is to live after the affection and example of Christ . . . but all these goods, as they are invisible, incomprehensible and entirely hidden, nature cannot attain to or love, unless it be raised by the grace of God. For the same reason, the spiritual man can be judged, known, seen, by none, not

[3] Rupp, R.G., p. 200.

even by himself, since he dwells in the most high darknesses of God . . . and this begins in this life, but is made perfect in the next . . .;

. . . oh, it is a great thing to be a Christian man, and have a hidden life, hidden not in some cell, like the hermits, or even in the human heart, which is an unsearchable abyss, but in the invisible God himself, and thus to live in the things of this world, but to feed on him who never appears except in the only vehicle of the hearing of the Word.[4]

There are strong echoes here of Tauler, indeed of Aquinas, and even of the culmination of Aquinas's teaching in St John of the Cross. Luther is saying just what Tauler was saying, both of them dependent on St Paul and the Gospels. But in Luther's commentary such sequences have only a relatively small importance historically. They play their part as a minor theme within an over-riding polemic against the canonical minimizers, and the philosophical 'humanists' of various kinds, and as part of a new personal dynamic theology. The latter part of the lectures were given in the winter 1517–18 in circumstances which clearly played their part in producing a strongly felt and argued text, Luther beginning to be faced with public controversy. On Noah he wrote: 'The whole ways of the world were vehemently embattled against the faith of this one man.' Again:

This is the glory of faith: not to know where you go, what you do, what you are to suffer, and with all things made captive (sense and intellect and virtue and will) to follow the naked voice of God and rather to be led than to go . . . and so it is plain that Abraham with this obedience of faith shows the highest example of the evangelical life, who left all to follow the Lord, preferring the Word of God to everything else and loving it beyond all things, and willingly becoming a pilgrim and was subject at all hours to perils of life and death.

[4] Rupp, R.G., p. 212. Rupp is also the authority for the previous paragraph, and the following quotation.

22. *All Saints' Eve 1516–October 1517*

ONE of the earliest examples of Luther's public expression of his opinion about indulgences[1] occurs in the text of a sermon which he preached on the eve of All Saints' Day, October 31, 1516, in the parish church at Wittenberg. It was the eve of the day on which a plenary indulgence could be gained by those reverencing the great collection of relics; it and many other indulgences could be transferred to the souls in purgatory. It was a great annual event. It seems to be certain that the vast majority of the ordinary people rejoiced in this occasion, the Feast of All Saints' Day, not primarily as one on which they had the opportunity to praise God in the liturgy, to offer thanks in their participation in the Eucharist, and to pray to him and to Mary and the other saints for their needs, a glorious festival of Christ's Kingdom, but primarily as one on which they could obtain certain 'goods', spiritual 'goods', and do this not primarily by the grace of Christ affecting their inner dispositions, their purity of heart and their exercise of charity, but primarily by performing certain ritual acts.

On this occasion at Wittenberg, and on many other similar occasions throughout Europe at the time and for many decades past, the order of things as preached by Jesus Christ, and as maintained by every serious and authoritative theorist of the Church, including and pre-eminently Aquinas, had been to some extent reversed in practice. Instead of a man purifying his heart and his intention, giving himself to God in prayer, coming to church to signify his purpose and his membership of Christ by solemn ritual acts, which he understood as acts of participation in the life of Christ, of God, of the whole Church, sacraments, signs of his intention and means of grace to him; instead of this, a man came to perform these same acts in the belief that by performing them he would obtain for himself, and for the dead, certain goods, the condition for this being sorrow for his sins. A secondary result of

[1] See Appendix 1 for a detailed explanation of indulgences.

this was perhaps understood to be union with Christ, but this was rather a matter of special 'piety' and 'devotion' and thought of as something for those specially favoured by mystical graces. Sacraments had in practice lost much of their truly sacramental character and become straight 'means'; the 'sacramental presence' of Christ had become simply the 'presence'.

Daily practice contradicted theology at many points. For three centuries theology had been increasingly engrossed in finding rationalizations and justifications, of popular practice. Aquinas had made out a *rationale* for indulgences,[2] and it is a highly representative key to the situation. The *rationale* ended with a warning: 'other works of satisfaction are more meritorious with respect to our essential reward, which is infinitely better than the remission of temporal punishment'. Aquinas had felt obliged to treat the practice and to provide an apologetic for it. This he did with his customary learning, logic and impact. But the practice itself, though logically defensible, permissible and tolerable, when considered as the extra practice of a Christian who lived by the sacraments, tended by itself to militate against the ultimate principles of the Gospel as defined elsewhere and predominantly in Aquinas's theology. Hence his final terse rider to what had gone before. That rider implies that concentration on the gaining of indulgences is hardly worthy of a Christian, since what he should concentrate on as regards the future life is not avoidance of punishment but the life he will live with God in Christ, his 'reward', and that the best way to prepare for this is by the direct exercise of charity. It was not the purpose of Aquinas to draw out such practical implications in detail. They were already clear, for those who could read, by the dominant content of his writing. But the absence of anyone to draw out the correct practical implications for the people at large resulted in the fall of standards in daily Catholic practice, ever lower and lower, in spite of many notable exceptions. The lower they fell the more difficult (and scandalous to many) would be an attempt to change them. The more therefore theologians were busy trying to adapt their theories, to make the low-level practices tolerable.

[2] See p. 277.

At the same time it is important to remember that Christianity poses an ideal of perfection; the perennial failure to reach it is always shocking. The sublimity of the motive, the absolute nature of the purpose, the overtly sacred nature of the whole profession of Christianity, its worship and all the lives of all its members makes failure all the more dreadful, all the more scandalous. A proper historical assessment of the failure in a particular age must recognize these things and recall, at the same time, the relative success achieved in even the most degenerate times. Scandal makes its effect, achieves its shock, by contrast with an ideal, always sufficiently attempted and realized to be still in view. If the attempt ceased or failed altogether, and the ideal died, Christianity itself would have ceased to exist, and with it the scandals. Even at this time of such extraordinary perversion of the Gospel, many people lived lives which were good by the standards of the Gospel, exercised great charity towards one another, and lived a life of prayer. The evidence for this is strictly historical. This was still a great religious age, able also to inspire astonishing works of religious art, and lives of great integrity. The crowds running for indulgences ran because they first believed, because they had some understanding of Christianity, and wanted to follow it. A picture of total 'superstition' is unhistorical and absurd, reducing the whole religious aspect to myth and in the process falsifying all interpretations of other aspects of the history of the time.

In his sermon of October 31, 1516, Luther spoke of his fear that an indulgence often militated against true repentance even though officially it could only be gained by one who is truly repentant; he feared that 'the inner penitence of the heart which should pervade the whole life of the believer' would be lacking—for 'one who feels remorse for his sins does not try to evade punishment, but rather actually longs for punishment'.[3] In other words, as in Aquinas's rider, man's life should be orientated not to the avoidance of punishment but to Christ. Luther and Aquinas are concerned with the same ultimates but there is a difference. Aquinas spoke of the next life as the 'reward', Luther expresses

[3] See Böhmer, p. 176.

his concern explicitly in terms of man's relationship with Christ here and now. He hammers his point home by insisting that a man who is really sorry will be glad to be punished—a dynamic presentation of traditional asceticism, penitence and penance, not the working out of a programme of penances, but the acceptance of whatever God may send. Thus Luther came to a fresh and personal preaching of the traditional ascetic Gospel.

As well as his fresh treatment of punishment for sin, Luther proposed a new interpretation of indulgences themselves. This was one of the early occasions on which Luther put forward the view, to be repeated a year later in the Ninety-five Theses, and eventually condemned as heretical, that an indulgence is no more than the remission of canonical penalties, the penance which the priest may have actually imposed on the penitent, and not a remission of punishment due to be suffered in purgatory. Soon he would be claiming that when God forgives a sinner, all punishment is remitted, and that the sacrament of penance involves complete release to one who is really penitent. For the moment he proposed the theory of indulgences as no more than an announcement of forgiveness, but qualified all he said by a statement of adherence to the Pope's teaching: 'Nevertheless, I affirm emphatically that the purpose which the pope has in view is good—at least as far as it can be ascertained from the wording of the indulgence Bulls.'

The Elector Frederick was not pleased with Luther's sermon. His astonishing collection of relics, heavily indulgenced, reflected a pet hobby and was also a paying concern. He provided himself with an income and his people with objects of devotion. He expressed his displeasure, but Spalatin's advice protected Luther and in any case Frederick by nature preferred to sit on the fence.

Four months later, February 24, 1517, St Matthew's day, Luther returned to the subject more fiercely. The pace was increasing—he had recently sent his anti-Aristotelian theses to the Erfurt academics. He had nearly finished his Galatians lectures and would soon start with Hebrews. In his sermons he applied the theology worked out in his lectures, and preached the implications of his approach from the Bible. He said that indulgences were well named—they simply indulge. They may be of some use for the weak in faith. For the rest they simply have the effect of preventing people from receiving the true absolution, divine forgiveness of sins, and such people never truly come to Christ: 'Oh how great are the perils of our times! How fast asleep are the priests! Oh what worse than Egyptian darkness we are in! How safely and securely we go on living in the midst of the most grievous sins!' Luther spoke from his own experience as a confessor. He found the people not really repentant. Abuse of the sacrament was already leading Luther to emphasize the fundamental importance of the interior act and disposition—an emphasis which would gradually increase until there was little place left at all for the objective value of the sacrament itself.

Through it all Luther is very busy—but a sense of humour is visible: 'I could use two secretaries. I do little during the day but write lectures. I am a conventual preacher, reader at meals, parochial preacher, director of studies, overseer of eleven priories, superintendent of the fishpond at Litzkau, referee of the squabble at Torgau, lecturer on Paul, collector of material for a commentary on the Psalms. . . .'

In September Luther took another step in the academic world. His pupil Francis Gunther had to defend a thesis, and this he did with Luther's help. It comprised ninety-seven theses against the teaching of Scotus and Occam, d'Ailly and Biel. He sent copies off to the universities at Erfurt and Nuremberg, offering to debate them in those cities—and eagerly awaited some reaction. None came. Theses were two a penny then as now. And Luther was young—even upstart. However outrageous or fundamental, it was difficult for anyone to take theses as more than an intellectual exercise. These theses did express Luther's position forcefully in the intellectual sense. They helped to consolidate his position in Wittenberg University and to prepare individual academies elsewhere for the storms to come. But it needed something of a more practical nature to rouse people.

On October 31, the anniversary of his sermon against indulgences, he did something more than preach against them, he proposed an academic debate on them, and posted the famous Ninety-five Theses. This action was intended simply as another step in the promotion of what he saw as the true theology, another step in his opposition to practices which militated against it, and which in any case were riddled with abuses. Preaching to the populace about indulgences had achieved little or nothing except their respect, sometimes a little opposition and fear—and the goodwill of other academics who having heard of the sermons knew that Luther was voicing something that had been felt for centuries both about the practice itself, and the abuses connected with them. The particular indulgence with which the Ninety-five Theses were concerned was a classic on both counts, high-lighting both the abuses and the doctrinally unsatisfactory methods used in preaching it.

23. The St. Peter's Indulgence

POPE JULIUS II issued the bull *Liquet omnibus* in 1510 establishing an indulgence the income from which would help to pay for the building of St Peter's. In return for a contribution towards this good work, anyone who went to confession in the normal way could gain several plenary indulgences. In 1515 Leo X commissioned the Elector, Archbishop of Mainz, Albert, to conduct the indulgence in the dioceses of Mainz and Magdeburg. The Archbishop gave the Dominican friar John Tetzel the task of preaching the indulgence, and the friar drew up specimen sermons.[1]

The bull gives a good idea of the deliberately financial nature of the operation. One section runs: 'Moreover all Christians of either sex, secular as well as regular, . . . who shall effectively place a pious alms in the chest for the above-mentioned building [St Peter's], may gain the fullest remission of their sins . . .' The whole text does not permit one to suppose that sins are forgiven by an indulgence. But the wording seems deliberately loose in places. The preachers commonly referred to the ease of rescuing a soul

---

[1] A sample sermon and part of the Indulgence bull can be consulted in 'The Sources of Christian Theology', Volume II, *Sacraments and Forgiveness*, edited by Paul F. Palmer, S.J. (England: Darton, Longman & Todd; U.S.A.: Newman Press, 1960).

from purgatory, by transferring the indulgence, if one wished, to such a soul. The minute the coin drops into the money chest, the soul would jump from purgatory into heaven. There was a little jingle for this:

As soon as coin in coffer rings
The soul from purgatory springs.

Illustrations survive showing the great money chest and the issuing of indulgences.

One of Tetzel's simple sermons gives a further idea of the overt 'legalism' both of the underlying 'moral theology', and of the whole conception of the relation between God and man—Christ (and the saints) having provided a fund, and man being able to call on it. This operation was apparently as easily accomplished and as disconnected from a man's inner spiritual life as the commission of mortal sins. To judge from Tetzel's sermon these would be committed frequently and inevitably.[2] And the sermon, like the bull itself, shows the extent to which the indulgence was deliberately associated with the very matter of salvation itself. The preaching of the indulgence was regarded as an 'occasion of grace', an occasion on which to encourage the people to go to the sacrament of confession because without that the indulgence could not be gained. The emotional atmosphere generated by the whole operation went along with the idea that the visit of the preacher was a time of salvation.

Let them know that in these letters [of indulgence] all the ministries of Christ's passion are engraved and etched. Let them be aware that for any mortal sin there is need to do penance for seven years after confession and contrition, either in this life or in purgatory. They are all but infinite, and they have to undergo an infinite penalty in the flaming punishment of purgatory. And yet in virtue of these confessional letters, you shall be able to gain, once in life, full pardon of the penalties due up to that time. . . . Again, through

[2] A mortal sin, briefly, is a deliberate and fully intended offence against God in a serious matter. 'Full knowledge' and 'full consent' must be present, so moral theologians have commonly said. Preaching which assumes that people commonly commit 'mortal sins', as Tetzel's did, and as has that of many other popular preachers at many times, implicitly contradicts this.

the whole of life you may, wherever you are willing to confess, gain as well a similar remission in cases not reserved to the Pope, and, finally, at the moment of death, a plenary indulgence of all penalties and sins, and a share in all the spiritual good works which are performed in the Church militant and in her members.

It was the summit of an era which had subordinated moral theology to Canon Law, and had schematized the whole divine economy in mechanical and anthropocentric terms. It is a truism, in religion, that man is always tempted to make God in his own image. Another historian[3] in fact, sees the theological argument in an exactly contrary 'anthropocentric' sense, calling Luther's theology anthropocentric, because he concentrated on the human predicament, and man's personal relationship with God, implying that such concentration, in the minimization of the objective sacramental order, also undermines recognition of the 'supernatural' as the only final reality. But practice rather than theory is the acid test, and the practice concentrated obsessively on man's avoidance of punishment, not on God's grace.

Luther said that he knew from his own personal contact with people as a confessor that inner penitence was only marginally present, and that the virtue of religion, a fully willed assent to the Christ-life, was practically absent for all the effect that it could be seen to have in their lives, for all the spiritual or moral improvement to be seen. He found, many a time apparently, little intention in a penitent of avoiding a sinful life in the future. Sometimes he had people coming to confession who believed that a confessor must grant them absolution unconditionally, regardless of their intentions, because they had an indulgence along with its accompanying letter of confession. His conscience impelled him to speak, and it was not the outburst of a lone neurotic individual. He had, immediately, the congratulations and assent of others who had felt the same way about indulgences but had seen no way of making a protest that would lead anywhere except to their own defeat.

[3] 'Anthropomorphism' and 'anthropocentric' are sometimes used in religious controversy rather loosely. See Jedin, p. 169, for the contrary view.

It is interesting that Luther did not give great prominence to a denunciation of the financial abuses connected with the St Peter's indulgence. He concerned himself primarily with the effect that its preaching had on the lives of Christians, and thence with the doctrinal basis of them. He had been denouncing abuses in the Church for some years, he knew they could not be solved in a day and that in any case the human factors would always muddy ecclesiastical waters. He had preached the general need for a reform and discussed abuses on other occasions. However, a few of the theses were devoted to practical abuses, and though few they are of importance—the populace knew or guessed something of the abuses connected with the financial arrangements and the sort of lives lived by some of the principal protagonists.

The collection of the cash and its transference to Rome was a major financial operation. The Fuggers, German bankers, received a commission for performing this useful service, a necessary service justly paid for. But the fact that part of the money which had been paid in order to secure release from the pains of purgatory actually ended up in the pocket of a man performing the task of the transference of credit, a job almost without risks for which he was well paid, cannot have failed to lower the general atmosphere. In the case of the St Peter's indulgence no less than half of all the money collected went into the Fugger coffers. The Archbishop of Mainz owed them a very large sum, and had bargained with Rome to be allowed to keep half what was contributed for the indulgence in order to be able to pay off his debt. His debt to them was on account of a loan from the Fuggers to him, a few years previously, when he wished to become Archbishop of Mainz. He was already Bishop of the sees of Halberstadt and Magdeburg, and Canon Law forbade pluralism. Furthermore he was too young according to the Canon Law regulating the age at which a priest might be made an archbishop. So Albert had had to borrow a heavy sum to convince Rome that these two hurdles might be surmounted—in common language, he had to bribe the Curia, the normal procedure.

Princely sums were also paid to Tetzel himself and his servant—the latter's pay was higher than that paid to the chief official of the town of Leipzig.[4] In the end something substantially under half the proceeds went to Rome and helped to pay the architect and his office, the quarrymen, the builders, and all engaged on the building of the Basilica of St Peter's which now stands in Rome.

From inside, from a background of daily contact with this late medieval set-up, it probably looked less despicable than it does to the historian. But there must have been some spontaneous reaction, an 'instinctive' though not fully informed reaction amongst people generally and this would inevitably reach the active stage eventually—at any rate so long as something of the biblical Christian ideal continued to be preached, and the Church to sponsor that preaching.

24. *The Ninety-five Theses*

TETZEL was preaching the indulgence in the district of Magdeburg about the month of April, 1517. He was unable to come to Wittenberg because the Elector Frederick would not give him permission to preach in his territories—the motives for this refusal being probably a mixture on the one hand of political antagonism to the house of Hohenzollern who had achieved a substantial victory when the Elector Albert was appointed Archbishop of Mainz, and on the other concern about possible competition with the indulgences already available, and very remunerative to Frederick, at Wittenberg. Frederick did not want a rival ruler, the Elector-Archbishop, collecting money to pay his own personal debts by means of preaching indulgence in his, Frederick's, territories and thereby diminishing the return to be expected from Frederick's own native indulgence income. But the populace were enthusiastic for the indulgence, what with its origin in Rome, the promises of release from purgatorial punishment, the impressive written document handed to everybody who earned one, and the whole sacred circus accompanying Tetzel's

[4] Böhmer, p. 182.

preaching.[1] They travelled and crossed the boundary to obtain it. Tetzel had been preaching indulgences for ten years and knew how to attract the people, with processions, banners on which the indulgences hung, and a mixture of promises and threats in his sermons, and finally a theatrical gesture as he walked himself to the chest and put a coin in it thereby gaining an indulgence for his own father.[2]

Luther seems to have discussed his anxiety about indulgences with colleagues, and to have continued to voice his own deep concern about the ultimate effect of such preaching: the lowering of the standards of Christian life, and the risks of a practical evacuation of the essential personal response.

Luther was stung into further action by the *Instructio Summaria* which had been issued by the Archbishop of Mainz for the guidance of the indulgence sellers. This apparently came into Luther's hands in the autumn (1517). The way in which this Instruction suggested that indulgences should be recommended as a means of reconciliation between man and God, and its reference to the ease with which a soul might be released automatically from purgatory, persuaded Luther that he must take some further public action. And so he had the idea of a disputation, an academic discussion based on theses drawn up with the customary provocation of the dialectical form, in academic language, giving a long series of arguments which showed why indulgences should be strictly limited in their definition and should not play an important part in daily life. The content was easy for him to draw up since his mind had been much occupied for some time with the way in which indulgences tended to obscure the Gospel, and to hinder

---

[1] In Osborne's play the indulgence-preaching scene (as indeed much of the rest of the play) owes much of its dramatic force to the material which he uses—historically accurate, virtually to the exclusion of invention—for Tetzel's sermon. It includes some elements not in the sample sermons, and a modified form of one at least of the reported 'exaggerations' which Tetzel later swore he had never indulged in when it was widely reported (that even one who violated the Blessed Virgin would be forgiven on paying up; though Osborne uses the phrase: 'offer violence to'). But the speech as a whole is a brilliant construction of just what a preacher might have done with the sample sermons set down by Tetzel. The cross and the banners used have a great dramatic effect, and were copied from the work of sixteenth-century artists who provided a visual report of what occurred.

[2] Anyone who has taken part in one of the old-fashioned Catholic parish 'missions' in England will know something of the psychological power of a mixture of 'Gospel' teaching on salvation, deliberately emotive, and a highly legalistic presentation of the sacraments and grace.

good living. And he had already made the essence of the material public in the sermons to which we have referred, and had written a dissertation on the subject.

Luther nailed the theses up, in routine fashion, on the door of the castle church, accompanied at the time by his servant, Agricola. The theses invited those interested to discuss the matter, either at a meeting or by letter. The operation was one of normal academic sobriety. Luther did not even send a copy of the theses to Spalatin—a prudent reservation this in that although the Elector Frederick had not liked Luther preaching against indulgences, he would be pleased with this gesture against the indulgence preached in his rival's territories, and Luther did not want any suggestion of political motivation, or of Frederick's patronage. Furthermore, Luther sent a copy privately to the Archbishop of Mainz and to his own diocesan Bishop of Brandenburg, and he did not want Frederick to have the theses until the ecclesiastics had looked at them. The theses were printed on a placard, the printing having been done by John Grünenberg of Wittenberg. The copies sent to the Archbishop and Bishop were accompanied by explanatory letters in traditional form. All was as it ought to be.

A fully satisfactory summary of the theses would indicate their relevance, at considerable length, to the whole historical situation, both political and religious.[3] An adequate theological discussion of them would involve a book on its own. However, a summary of their contents will make clear something of their practical and theological significance in the light of preceding chapters. Luther was still a fully loyal Catholic, knowing well what could and what could not be properly challenged—virtually every theological statement in the theses was patient at least of the kind of dialectical defence that a serious theologian could not reject out of hand. Cajetan was to state his opinion that the theses involved only 'errors', but not 'heresies'.

---

[3] The matter is brilliantly summarized by Bainton, p. 63: 'Luther's *Ninety-five Theses* ranged all the way from the complaints of aggrieved Germans to the cries of a wrestler in the night watches. One portion demanded financial relief, the other called for the crucifixion of the self. The masses could grasp the first. Only a few elect spirits would ever comprehend the full import of the second, and yet in the second lay all the power to create a popular revolution. Complaints of financial extortion had been voiced for over a century without visible effect. Men were stirred to deeds only by one who regarded indulgences not merely as venal but as blasphemy against the holiness and mercy of God.'

Theses 1-4 concerned the basic theory of repentance. 'Our Lord and Master Jesus Christ, when he said *poenitentiam agite*, willed that the whole life of the faithful should be repentance.'[4] *Poenitentia* must be related to *poena*, penalty; Luther turns here to his basic objection to the selfish nature of the practice of indulgences by pointing out that if one is truly repentant one should not try to evade punishment.

Theses 5-7 put forward Luther's innovating thesis that the Pope can only be intending to remit punishment imposed by the Church, canonical not purgatorial penalties—innovating though it had been proposed, less publicly, before. Indulgences also asserted that guilt itself is removed only by God, in association with the sacrament of penance.

Theses 8-29 denied the power of the Pope over souls in purgatory and asserted that he can only help them through prayer. This was an attempt to solve a matter which was implicitly in dispute. Highly technical in the doctrinal and devotional sense, yet it symbolizes exactly the fundamental gravamen of Luther's case, and does relate back to an important theological point. In the appendix on indulgences it is clear that the official teaching of the Catholic Church has always favoured the view that it is a good thing to pray for the dead and that the prayers of the faithful are *effective* in the same way that all prayer is effective, made in obedience to the command of Jesus that man should pray for what he wants for himself or others, but also *limited* by God's wisdom, 'thy will be done'. The gap between teaching which is officially promulgated and guaranteed at the highest level and that which appears in sermons or may be readily inferred from devotional practices tolerated by the Church is clearly present on the matter of plenary indulgences for the souls in purgatory, both in Luther's day and up to the present time. In Luther's day, however, this matter still seems to have allowed of a difference of opinion whether the souls in purgatory could be released only by prayer, *suffragium* (including an application of a plenary indulgence to them), and therefore not in a way which could be absolutely

---

[4] A year later, in line with the Greek which he had just read, Luther preferred to speak of change of heart, rather than acts of penance.

assured, or whether these souls really could be actually released, because the Church exercised jurisdiction in purgatory, through the power of the keys. Official documents[5] only support the first contention. Yet common practice and opinions and sermons went the other way.[6] It is proper to notice that although at the time of writing the teaching of the Church can only be adduced to support the former thesis, yet the common practice of the faithful seems to assume an almost magical efficacy, implying a real power over the souls in purgatory. The only official Catholic clarification in the last three centuries presents the matter deviously. The souls of the dead are entirely and exclusively in God's hands, but plenary indulgences may be applied to them with the intention of the Church that they should be released from purgatory.[7] Luther wanted the teaching of the Church to be absolutely clear that whilst it is good to pray for the dead the Church has no direct power in purgatory; his intention was quite clear that the Church should concern herself more with urgent matters on earth, the true place of her life and jurisdiction and mission.

In theses 30–40 Luther adds a doctrine of his own, that all penalties, canonical or not, are effaced with the death of the penitent. Those who think they can be sure of salvation simply through buying an indulgence will fall into damnation. But indulgences are not to be despised since 'they are a declaration' of divine forgiveness; Luther is driven to find *some* justification of a practice so widespread and common, and he does it by approving the extra comfort an indulgence might give to someone weak in faith after confessing.

Theses 41–52 emphasize the subordinate place such actions as the buying of an indulgence should take in a Christian life—'it is not the Pope's intention that the purchases of indulgences is in any way comparable with works of mercy'—and then a thesis

---

[5] See the first bull which contained an 'authentic application of an indulgence in the strict sense to the souls in purgatory', by Pope Sixtus IV, 1476. Palmer, p. 350.

[6] Tetzel's counter-theses definitely stated the proposition that the dead were released automatically, though attempting to retain at the same time the proposition that this was effected by prayer, *suffragium*. It was not the power of the keys over purgatory but it was the power to apply indulgences to the dead so that instantaneous release was achieved—this was in fact in his view 'a Christian dogma'. .

[7] See Palmer, note 1, page 351, giving part of the answer of the Congregation of Indulgences, July 28, 1840.

against abuses: 'If the Pope knew the demands made by the pardon-Preachers he would prefer to have St Peter's basilica reduced to ashes than built with the skin, flesh and bones of his sheep'.

Theses 53–80 in general compare the small value of preaching indulgences with the great value of preaching the Gospel, but also reiterate a defence of 'pardons' in principle whilst defending those who work against the abuses connected with them.

Theses 81–90 deal with various questions, including some important theological matters and some practical political matters. Why do prayers continue for the dead when plenary indulgences are preached in a fashion which implies the release of the dead from purgatory? Why should the faithful have to pay for St Peter's when the Pope is so wealthy—and this question has its background in the great wave of nationalistic feeling against Italian domination.[8]

The last five theses sum up the difference between 'indulgence religion' and true faith in Christ. Böhmer summarizes (p. 188): 'The true Christian yearns to follow his Master through penalties, death and hell (Thesis 94). He does not rely upon the security that the indulgence certificate promises him. He sees the sure way to the kingdom of heaven in present tribulations.'

The theses were prefaced in the usual way: '. . . the following subjoined theses will be discussed at Wittenberg under the presidency of the Reverend Father Martin Luther . . . he asks that those who cannot be present to engage in personal debate will do so in absence and in writing.'

[8] The Roman Curia, the cardinals resident in Rome having executive responsibility, who advise the Pope and govern the Church under the Pope remained almost exclusively Italian for the following four hundred years. In recent decades some attempt has been made to recruit a more international Curia, and this has been declared to be public policy by Pope Paul VI. However, it has not gone very far yet. Many archbishops resident in other countries have been raised to the rank of cardinal. But the cardinals in the Curia are still by a large majority Italian. The Roman Catholic Church remains, in this sense, the Italian body which Luther came to resent so bitterly. The Second Vatican Council will probably achieve a change in this matter.

25. The Reaction

No one came to the debate. No replies came from the archiepiscopal see of Mainz or the episcopal see of Brandenburg. The thing seemed to have fallen flat. That was by November 11. In view of the silence Luther decided to send some copies of the theses out to academic friends. Then, suddenly, the thing caught on. A mere academic thesis, and no request, or indeed permission to reprint it, or spread it abroad—but before the end of November it was reprinted in Leipzig and Magdeburg. By December it had been translated from Latin into German and published in Nuremberg, and in Basle in the form of a little book. In the following months all the intellectuals of Europe saw copies and took sides—or sat on the fence. On March 5, 1518, Erasmus in Louvain sent a copy to Sir Thomas More in England. Even those who should have known better did not treat the theses as theses for a university debate, theses not necessarily firmly held by their proposer, matters rather which he would like to see debated for the purpose of clarification: 'A disputation of Master Martin Luther, Theologian, for the purpose of making known the efficacy (*virtutis*) of Indulgences'. On the contrary the theses began to be treated as a manifesto—at last a manifesto on a subject on which many felt strongly for a wide variety of reasons. And those who were on Luther's side took the theses as his own definite opinion, and equally those against him opposed them in the same sense. The translation into German opened their meaning to all who could read and were able to understand. Dürer was amongst those who wrote in gratitude, sending Luther, of whom he had not heard before, some of his books of woodcuts.

But Luther's supporters were in high places as well. The Bishop of Mersburg said to a councillor of Saxony that he would be glad if the theses were posted in many places so that people generally would be warned against the fraudulent Tetzel. Motives were mixed. The opposition to money being collected for the Roman basilica by a German friar and to an operation organized by the Elector-Archbishop of Mainz aroused many variously motivated reactions. Some of these were frankly sectional and political; others perhaps more generally irresponsible, glad to see a storm raised—'Ho, ho!' said the old Franciscan Fleck, seeing the theses posted in his friary at Steinlausig in Muldenstein, 'here is a man who is going to do something'. Others, whilst being friendly, foresaw where such widespread publication of these opinions must lead for Luther himself: 'You speak the truth, dear Brother, but you will accomplish nothing. Go into your cell and say, "God have mercy upon me".' In Wittenberg University Carlstadt was enthusiastically for Luther. In the priory, however, the prior was frightened and asked Luther not to bring disgrace on the order. Böhmer suggests he was remembering that only eight years ago four Dominicans had been burnt to death as blasphemers.

Apparently the theses were soon in Tetzel's hands, sent on from the Bishop of Brandenburg before the year was out. Tetzel's reaction was typical—mere boastfulness: the heretic would be in the flames within three weeks, he said. Here was the standard opposition to an enemy: say he threatens the Church and challenges authority, call him a heretic, and defeat him with the destruction, the dramatic destruction of fire, public fire. The conservative academics in many places began to shake their heads, some because as Occamists (Trutvetter at Erfurt) they were and always had been radically opposed to Luther's theology, others for prudential reasons. Many must have realized that in attacking Tetzel Luther had engaged Goliath. Tetzel was a Dominican. The Dominicans, who directed the Inquisition, were all-powerful in the Curia at Rome, and again in Saxony. A request from the Saxon congregation for a proceeding against heresy (which was soon to come), in particular heresy which involved a personal attack on a member of the Dominican Order (Tetzel), would inevitably set giant wheels turning. Luther did not appreciate the particular effects likely to proceed from the status and allegiance of Tetzel—he was concerned with other things. It might well not have occurred to him at first that there would be an attempt to start a process for heresy, considering that he had merely proposed a university discussion on indulgences based on academic theses, that the content of these theses he had preached several times in Wittenberg, and hardly went beyond similar suggestions made by other orthodox reformers in the past on this subject, and that his position was supported by a well-articulated theology which he had been propounding as a doctor of theology for the last four years, day in, day out.

At Magdeburg, where the counsellors of the Archbishop of Mainz resided, there seems to have been no attempt to take Luther seriously. Luther wrote in his accompanying letter:

> . . . Christ did not command the preaching of indulgences but of the Gospel, and what a horror it is, what a peril to a bishop, if he never gives the Gospel to his people except along with the racket of indulgences. . . . What shall I do, Illustrious Prince, if not to beseech your Paternity through Jesus Christ our Lord to suppress utterly these instructions. . . . May your Paternity accept my faithful admonition. I, too, am one of your sheep. May the Lord Jesus guard you forever. Amen.

What did the Archbishop think? He and his counsellors seem to have had purely political thoughts. The pastoral and theological concern which Luther expressed passed them by entirely. The Archbishop's thoughts were those of an Elector, a civil ruler, an enemy of Frederick the Wise, a debtor of the Fugger to the extent of a very large sum which he was to pay back from the income from the indulgences. By December it was probably already clear that income from the indulgences was being adversely affected by the publication of Luther's theses. The Archbishop took advice. Religion was not his forte. For that he looked to advisers and to the final ecclesiastical authority in Rome. He had, to help him, lawyers, canon lawyers, further afield theologians, and in Rome a Pope and the Roman Curia. Tiresome religious affairs were not really his business. His advisers suggested sending Luther's letter and theses on to Rome and meanwhile take a step which would protect himself and throw some preliminary mud at the young doctor at Wittenberg: prohibit him from speaking further on the subject. But the Archbishop and his secretariat wanted no possibility of local trouble. The first step was taken, not the second. The first step, however, was given a little extra punch; in the communication to Rome Luther was denounced for spreading 'new doctrines'; the theses against scholastic philosophy were sent on along with the indulgence theses. Heresy itself was not mentioned, but 'new doctrines' would prepare the ground. This action, taken privately, was not known to Luther and seemingly not to his other opponents in Germany. No letter was sent to Luther himself.

The year ended with news for Luther of the varied reactions of private people already described, of Tetzel's reaction, but also of an impending Dominican chapter meeting at Frankfurt. The first public reaction was at the chapter of the Saxon Province of the Dominican Order at Frankfurt in January 1518, two and a half months after the posting of the theses. Tetzel, himself a Dominican, had been hard at work and had persuaded Dr Conrad Koch of the local university, commonly known as Wimpina, to prepare some theses for him to debate, against Luther's theses. The public debate of Wimpina's theses was on January 20, 1518. These 106 theses are substantially a confirmation of all that Luther was opposing; they offer a defence precisely of the things which Luther considered intolerable, in the parts where argument is used. Much of these theses, however, is simple contradiction, statement, or condemnation.

The theses correctly impute to Luther a distinction between true repentance and the sacrament of penance; in opposition to this they declare that without sacramental confession and satisfaction, internal repentance is of no avail. But Luther had not suggested that internal repentance was alone sufficient: he had said it was the fundamental and primary thing without which sacramental confession was of no avail. Wimpina's counter-theses were near to formal heresy, being a virtual statement that the sacraments are magic. Some of their other points are of equally doubtful theological validity, considered as interpretations of traditional Catholic doctrine; they have the air of theses thought up in a great hurry and very inadequately supported. Canonical penalties, they declared, do apply to the dead; purgatory can be reached by indulgences, and this was astonishingly argued from the fact that the Church excommunicates heretics, schismatics and traitors after their death and exhumes and burns their remains.

Then they stated that the mere purchase of the indulgence apart from the spiritual condition of the purchaser is sufficient to ensure the desired spiritual effects and it takes effect even before the money clinks on the bottom of the money box (one better than Tetzel's original sermon)—again the quasi-magical attitude. Indulgences are given a speciously argued status:

> whilst giving or lending to the poor may be better from the point of view of augmenting merit, buying an indulgence is preferable from the point of view of satisfaction. It is also a work of mercy and certainly makes a better man if done in a pious spirit. Spiritual alms of this kind are more excellent than material ones, and whoever is in need of this benefit does far better in thinking of his own salvation than in giving to the poor except in a case of extreme necessity.[1]

Luther was being handed here, not the careful distinctions of an academic debate in his home university, but the precise transformation of the Gospel into formalized canonical activities, which his spiritual experience and his reading of the Bible text had led him to reject—all closely resembling the pharisaical hypocrisy so frequently pilloried by Jesus himself in the Gospel.

Luther's opponents were unable to take him seriously because for them the Church was simply 'God's Church' possessing an authority almost identical with that of God himself, and the Bible something secondary, a mine of texts, which could be taken directly or allegorically, or in any way that would harmonize with the Church's traditional practice; a practice must be defensible, indeed must be in a sense divine, if the Church had sanctioned it, and the Church's actions *ipso facto* received God's approbation.

When Luther read these theses, if he had not already begun to be deeply apprehensive about the whole situation, he must have begun to be so then. The men with power were coming out against him, and stating against him, in a new and blatantly empirical fashion, the very perversions of the Gospel against

---

[1] Mackinnon, p. 23.

which he had been building his theology for the last four years. After the Dominican chapter at Frankfurt Luther received Tetzel's counter-theses—and a message of refusal to come to Wittenberg; Luther, still essentially an innocent abroad and green as only a small-town German friar could be, had invited Tetzel to come and debate his, Luther's theses, at Wittenberg. Instead Tetzel simply sent his own (Wimpina's) theses, and then sent them also publicly and offered them for sale, 800 copies of them. Luther's second shock, on the public level, followed. The undergraduates started to rag Tetzel's messenger, a bookseller from Halle; they pushed him about, pulled at his papers, his bag full of Tetzel's 800 counter-theses—and very soon their minds turned in the usual direction, to violence, which in those days commonly meant fire. All the man's copies of the counter-theses were taken from him and publicly burnt. Luther found himself with an active following. The controversy was being transformed into an active public affair, expressed in terms of social actions of the kind which must gradually force others to take one side or the other.

Meanwhile to the private action of the Archbishop of Mainz, another private action had been added—much more fatal and ominous. The Dominican chapter had sent a denunciation of Luther to Rome for suspicion of heresy. The denunciation would quickly reach the ears of Cardinal Cajetan, and would have to be taken seriously. Along with the communication from Mainz it probably gave an impression to the Curia that there was another heretic brewing a revolt.

During these days Luther was continuing with his normal work in the University and continued to be as busy as ever with his other occupations. His lectures on Hebrews were, inevitably, beginning to have an apocalyptic note.[2] The manuscript breaks off in the course of Luther's comment on the tale of Moses and his contradictions from his brethren:

> Not on account of visible things which were greater than, or equal with them, but on account of the Cross, and those things which are only calamities; and he chose the wisdom or rather the foolishness of the Cross that he might reprove the wisdom with

[2] See p. 107.

which he had been endowed . . . but greatest of all, he was repudiated by the very brethren on account of whom he despised all
these things, and underwent these dangers, as Acts 7, 'Who made
you a ruler over us?' . . . and so he was forced to flee into Midian.

Luther himself had now to make a journey.

Part Four

THE PUBLIC FIGURE

26. *Into the Arena*

LUTHER had now to go to Heidelberg; for the Augustinians were holding their chapter, and Luther as a provincial superior had to attend it. He had already raised enmities sufficiently strong for his friends to be worried about the journey. There was felt to be a real danger that the Dominicans, or someone in the pay of the Pope, might kidnap him, whether to remove him from the public scene or to take him to Rome. But in Wittenberg and district Luther was already half a hero. Spalatin and Frederick the Wise did not want to risk trouble. When it was clear that Luther was not interested in declining to go to Heidelberg, where as Provincial Superior it was his duty to go and to take his proper part in the affairs of the order, they took steps to make his journey safe. He was provided with introductions to the eminent along his route.

This is a crucial point in Luther's career. He had in the ordinary course of affairs to break off his lectures and to go to Heidelberg. But he could have been excused and might have been praised if he had requested permission to be absent. So it was that to break off and to go meant taking a determined step into the public arena. For Luther himself it must have seemed something of a step into the unknown. Within six months a set of academic theses had brought him strong statements of friendship and enmity, and of many varying positions in between, from people he had never met. From a merely local reputation, as a brilliant young lecturer and preacher, he found himself of importance to enormous interests in Church and State. Tactically speaking he was not ready for it. He had not thought in terms of massive movements. He had simply been determined to preach what he understood to be the Gospel of Christ, and to denounce what seemed to be perversions of it. Much less than many other reformers of the past century had he intended a precise programme—his programme was primarily personal and spiritual, and his public statements about the necessity of reform of the Church's organization, though forth-right, did not verge on the spiked sarcasm or the sophisticated irony of Erasmus and others; when Luther denounced, it was straightforward Gospel stuff firmly tied in to theology and the Bible. He had nothing to regret except that the theses, couched in academic language, had been made widely public. He still ex-pected that sometime the matter of the theses would be properly debated and examined.

Heidelberg was a triumph for Luther—his last in the old world of his early monastic and university life. His journey there and back turned out quite pleasantly, with hospitality from old friends newly met, and from those in civil authority. At Heidelberg itself Staupitz put him in charge of the disputation, with his *socius* Leonard Beier from Wittenberg as his opposite number. Luther gave a series of academic lectures, in line with those he had been delivering at Wittenberg for four years, indeed something like a summary of them and a conclusion to them. He was defending his 'new theology' for the first time outside his own university and was evidently determined to use the best of all he had.

It was the last time that he was to debate a matter of theology or philosophy as an equal with his academic and religious con-freres in a relatively calm atmosphere. His enemies had hoped to bring pressure to bear on Staupitz to make this a moment of dis-grace for Luther. Instead he had an important opportunity to vindicate his teaching. The lectures and the occasion are of par-ticular importance for the historian. The wheels were already turning, on the one hand at Rome, and on the other amongst the populace at Wittenberg, and further afield, which would bring in the arguments of *force majeure*, political and ultimately physical force based on a determination by the one to maintain, by the other to change the *status quo—force majeure* which would render honest argument often null, or pervert it to the prejudiced sup-port of this or that public policy. At Heidelberg these forces were still in the background. In the published version of the theses which Luther defended in public, before his brethren and others, including Dominicans who had come on this important occasion, we can read his own carefully argued, now mature, reasons for rejecting scholastic theology, and his exposition of the Gospel as he understood it. And in the record of the meeting we can read how Luther's arguments and exposition apparently triumphed, winning new disciples for him.

The triumph was not one of bluster or denunciation. On the contrary, 'though our chief men refuted him with all their might, their wiles were not able to make him move an inch from his propositions. His charm in responding is amazing, his patience in listening is incomparable. His acuteness reminds one of the method of St Paul. With answers that are as brief as they are acute, drawn from the Holy Scriptures, he overcomes everyone with admiration.'[1] So Martin Bucer, a young Dominican from Alsace (writing to a friend), destined to be one of the major disciples of Luther in the Reform.

Luther's key phrase about this time was *theologia crucis*— theology of the cross. It is the heart of the Heidelberg theses, and likewise of his second set of lectures on the Psalms which he had recently been preparing for publication. We have referred already to the influence on Luther of Tauler; his influence and that of the author of *Ein Theologia Deutsch*, which Luther later republished, can be seen at this time. In his edition of Tauler Luther scored all the passages which were concerned with anguish and tension, inner distress, 'the birth of God in the soul'. It all fitted well with what Luther believed to be the proper basis of all theology, the faith which supersedes all man's own attempts at putting himself and the world to rights, faith in Christ's work on the cross— scandal and foolishness to man.

The whole movement by which a man is brought to awareness of his sin, to the accusation of himself, to acceptance of the divine judgment, to humility, and so to the abandonment of his own righteousness, and to embrace the mercy of God, is now summed up in the dialectic of the Law and Gospel, the tension between God's 'strange' and God's 'proper work'. Faith, so closely linked with the Word, and with Christ, becomes the secret of the whole approach of men to the invisible God. All these find a new focus in the theme 'theology of the Cross'.[2]

[1] Böhmer, p. 208.   [2] Rupp, R.G., p. 218.

It is a theology of crisis—and it was opposed to the late scholastic scheme as Luther knew it, on the one hand fideist, on the other an institution.

On his way to Heidelberg Luther had four hard days of foot-slogging and then came up with John Lang, in a waggon, bound for the same place and the same meeting. He had been entertained by the Bishop of Wurzburg and again royally treated at Heidelberg itself. The way back was pleasant too, with the brethren. Touching at Erfurt he tried and failed to convince Trutvetter that he must abandon the teaching of a lifetime; it was the three days of fast before Ascension Day and a public disputation was not to be thought of.

Luther arrived back at Wittenberg *'habitior et corpulentior'*—fatter perhaps in the face, and looking altogether more healthy. Part of his charm until now had been the ascetic appearance and it continues to be so for the next three years; but he begins slowly to put on weight. A physical and psychological climacteric seems to occur at this crisis time in Luther's life. Public events now begin to provide the context, the challenge, the opportunity for an intense activity, until now applied only to tasks at Wittenberg, an intense activity which inevitably had its own reactive effect on the subject. For the next twenty years Luther was averaging something like a writing a fortnight.[3] The sheer energy is astonishing. He must surely have had to eat more. In fact his theology gradually persuaded him to abandon the more negative ascetical practices, primarily rigid fasts. 'Not the suffering which you devise for youself, but the sorrow which comes upon you against your choosing, thinking or desiring—this is the way of the cross'. He was writing that in the lectures on the Psalms about this time—a version made by him for publication. But still at Worms three years later his ascetic appearance greatly impressed people.

It is sometimes said that with a growth in his public importance a man may experience a physical enlargement. It would not be surprising. He will usually be offered richer food. He will often have a sense of achievement, and perhaps a lessening of anxiety. Luther, however, was the anxious type, and on the face of it it is

[3] Rupp, R.G., p. 225.

perhaps suprising that he grew in bulk. He never stopped worry-
ing. But inevitably he came to have a sense of the activity of
providence in his regard; he could not fail to see as the years went
on that much, in the public sense, depended on his choice at one
time or another. With his growth in size came also more frequent
internal troubles—and with the increasing responsibility and
anxiety came more devastating periods of despair on several
occasions.

There is no case for making Luther out as a simple 'revolutionary'—other things being equal he always came out on the side of
established order; it caused him periods of horror and despair
when he saw, quite clearly, that the results of his actions and his
stand were sometimes chaotic socially and morally. He had
wanted to preach the truth. That meant denouncing untruth.
Eventually that meant, so he saw in a way he could not avoid, the
denunciation of Rome. And along with it came inevitably an
examination, *de novo*, of all accepted religious and social practices.
Were they Christian? Were they scriptural? Such questions cannot be asked by one on whose word people are hanging, in a time
of unrest, without devastating results. Fatter he became but no
less anguished.

27. *Luther in relation to Church,*
State, and Society

FROM February 1518 onwards the events relevant to Luther's
life become so numerous that a biographer has great difficulty
in presenting them as a single readable narrative unless he is prepared to write at very great length. Numerous different 'fronts'
exist, and in a concise work of this present kind the strict chronological method must be modified.

An increasingly important factor is the relationship between the
papacy and the Holy Roman Empire. The Roman Curia wished
to forestall the election of Charles of Spain as Emperor on the

expected death of Maximilian, since this would unite Spain and most of Europe under one ruler and make the Emperor too powerful. In this situation the six imperial Electors were of crucial importance, but particularly Frederick of Saxony, the chief elector, who would be Reichsvikar in the interim, and who was the only likely alternative to Charles of Spain as Emperor. In the following two years Rome's action against Luther was considerably delayed for this and associated political reasons: fear of upsetting Frederick, whose chaplain Spalatin was so close a friend of Luther, set in the context of a more general fear of nationalistic anti-Italian emotions in Germany.

Frederick became convinced in some final sense towards the end of 1518 that Luther should be protected and supported; his support and protection continued to be exercised in the same prudent way as in the past but more assuredly and he never shifted from this policy, which seems to have been rooted in a simple desire to be a good Christian ruler, and in the conviction that Luther, doctor of theology in his own university, ought not to be put down unless he could be shown to be wrong from Scripture. Frederick has been a shadowy figure so far in this account, and in some sense he must remain so. He never received Luther into his personal presence all his life, though Luther often preached before him. Frederick always dealt with Luther through Spalatin. Rome found Frederick as helpful as a high and well-built stone wall. He had a calm, vast, swarthy expressionless face. No one ever knew which direction he would go in—and he often managed to go in none. But he seems to have been genuinely pious, and genuinely won over by Luther. In practice his attitude amounted to opportunism of a very prudent kind and it was markedly successful. Rome had to balance Frederick's displeasure against other interests when proceeding against Luther.

The international political factor was fundamental as an influence on the practical outcome of Luther's protest, though in a variety of complicated ways. The most important of these is simply that at Rome a pastoral or theological consideration of Luther's theses was subordinated to the political factor. Neither Luther's intention, the promotion of Christian living, nor his doctrine, involving an attempt to reform the practice and doctrine on sacraments and indulgences, was considered with the seriousness which the carefully argued theses of a doctor of theology might had been expected to deserve—particularly considering the status, reputation and good life of Luther himself.

Rome's method of proceeding was essentially legalistic, and this related very closely throughout the proceedings to political considerations, and to the prestige and power of the Roman See. This is not necessarily to imply insincerity; it is simply to state the evident truth. Indeed it seems certain that the Roman Curia and the Pope really believed that the kind of quasi-absolute autocracy which they exercised was what the Church had been founded to exercise. They had a guilty conscience about many abuses; the numerous attempts at reform are witness to this. Pope Leo can hardly have been absolutely happy about the extent to which his hunting interfered with his responsibility, a responsibility that sometimes actually forced its way into the enjoyable events of the hunt itself, a notable example being the bull which condemned Luther's writings, *Exsurge Domine*, with its famous reference to the 'wild boar' in the vineyard. But on the matter of authority it seems improbable that he and his courtiers, the cardinals and other advisers, were aware of the travesty of 'Christian ministry' for which they were responsible.

The facts seem to suggest that their lax spiritual lives, their complacency with what they must have deemed a moderate response to the Gospel, blinded them to fundamental theological issues. Probably inattentive to prayer, and seldom making a thorough attempt to examine their own consciences, it seems that they were unable to believe that a critical theologian in Germany was really trying to work for the good of the Church. They accepted, easily and without qualm, the obvious solution, proffered to them, that a maliciously motivated German friar was trying to corrupt the true sovereignty which Christ had invested in the head of his Church. They turned naturally to these more or less political, canonical, categories—and then looked to traditional theological formulas to discover the theological 'error' in the position of their enemy.

Caught up into this highly complex world, Luther saw, in some senses much (that others only glimpsed), in other senses little (which yet was obvious enough to others). He seldom seems to have been fully aware of the political dimension in the sense that it dominated Roman decisions, even though the consistency of his relationship with Spalatin and Frederick the Wise in the local scene was a remarkable and permanent factor. He was unable, perhaps unwilling, to achieve an adequate understanding of the religious and doctrinal motives of those in authority. It may have been precisely this inability or unwillingness which pushed him into the leadership. He did not make any allowances for his enemies. When they failed to respond to the ideals and motives which he assumed in his missives to them, he turned to something approaching denunciation. To the Archbishop of Mainz, Luther's letter with the Ninety-five Theses read: 'God on high, is this the way the souls entrusted to your care are prepared for death? It is high time you looked into this matter. I can be silent no longer . . . what a peril to a Bishop if he never gives the Gospel to his people except along with the racket of indulgences.' To the Pope, Luther's *Resolutiones* read: 'Matters have already gone to such a length that the preachers have come to think they possess every licence, owing to the authority attached to your name; they have openly dared to teach very impious heresies. . . . They act as if the decretal *De Abusionibus* in no way applied to them.'

Luther suffered the disadvantages (or advantages) accompanying any attempt to understand the Gospel anew and to work out theology afresh. Increasingly shocked by the failure of traditional theology, the failure of the Church, priests and people, to achieve an exposition or understanding of the Gospel, at all adequate, increasingly caught up in his own vision of the Word, of Faith, of the *theologia crucis*, his viewpoint was increasingly single. He became a leader, an 'authority' to whom people turn. His psychological and physical make-up enabled powerful emotions to be thrown in—sometimes great fear, sometimes great exultation, filial, sullen, prophetic, desperate, and then as a contrast he could also be the blunt practical German. Always scrupulously responding to everything said or done in his regard, in him the religious dimension was dominant, almost obliterating all other considerations. The 'advantages' (or disadvantages) of this fact were then simply the difficulty of seeing the enemy's point of view; in Luther's case it meant that he took virtually no account of the political merry-go-round. He had never been very good at seeing the other man's point of view. The failure was exaggerated when he himself moved to the centre of the stage—and was in some sense a popular 'victim'. A certain personal and obsessive aspect was heightened, rather than allayed, by its public projection.

Men were glad to be obsessed, the way Martin put it, with their relationship with God, with their shortcomings, then with their faith, and so with revelation, justification and the all-solving gift. At first perhaps all seemed near enough in temper to the emotions which had been aroused by the old legalism. Yet it had a new authenticity about it. And it was in the easy yet moving and symbolical language of the Scripture. Eventually of course even the ecclesiastics caught the biblical fever, and in the 'thirties there was yet another reform movement, reaching to curial circles—for instance the experimental new breviary, Holy Cross breviary, in which practically everything without a biblical origin was suppressed. 'All over Europe during the fifteen-thirties theologians and laymen threw themselves into the study of Holy Writ and the Fathers—especially St Paul and St Augustine. . . . The German schism had roused men's minds.'[1]

28. The Literary Spate begins: January–August 1518

IN the three years preceding the Diet of Worms this reforming and scriptural impulse was running at high speed through the narrowest funnel in a pure Lutheran jet. From Martin's room began in 1518 to shoot the spate of writings which never dried up.

[1] Jedin, pp. 364–5, who says on p. 366: 'St Thomas Aquinas's Commentary on the Epistles of St Paul, printed three times between 1522 and 1532, rivalled the popularity of a romance of chivalry. It had become fashionable to study the Bible and to attend lectures on the Scripture.'

The targets, or partners or questioners, or occasions which elicited these writings, were numerous. His aim and his doctrine were misunderstood—so he must explain them further. Ecclesiastical authority might be upset by the public circulation of the theses—so they must be explained, and in the course of the explanation the interpretation was carried further. The *Resolutiones disputationum de indulgentiarum virtute* were submitted in February 1518 to his diocesan Bishop of Brandenburg, with the assurance that all this was provisional, 'disputable opinions'—'Nothing is so difficult to state as the true teachings of the Church, especially when one is so grievous a sinner'. But Luther also drew attention to the failure of the 'last Council' (Fifth Lateran, 1512–17) to reform the Church; so that reform becomes the concern not only of the Pope and cardinals but of everyone. Accusations in this document of the indulgence preachers we have already quoted. At the last moment he inserted some material answering, with vehemence, the Tetzel/Wimpina theses. The *Resolutiones* were rewritten again in May, at the request of Staupitz, for the Pope, and contained a reference to the fact that 'Do penance' (*poenitentiam agite*) does not translate properly the Greek text which uses the word *metanoia*, change of heart'. This was a result of Luther's study at this time of Erasmus's New Testament text.

The populace, those of it who could read or write or would listen to a friend who could do so, were having his theses retailed to them. He must, therefore, write something more down to their level. So he published the German 'Sermon on Indulgences and Grace' in March. Here things were stated much more than 'provisionally'. It was an attempt to put the statements from the theses in a form for popular consumption. In doing this Luther took a substantial step. The theses had been strictly academic material, hypotheses, and had been circulated against his will. Luther now implicitly put his own approval on the publicity they had received by issuing a clear popular version, and one that went further than the theses themselves had done.

Then the Tetzel/Wimpina theses must be formally answered, and Tetzel's further reply countered again (August 1518)—and this particular series of exchanges became coarse and personal in

the end. Luther allowed himself to write and publish this last reply in a day or two, and subsequently regretted doing so. Tetzel
had been rude from the beginning, and Luther himself lively.

Dr Eck of Ingolstadt, an intellectual friend of Luther, had written
his 'Obelisks' against Luther, so Luther must publish his 'asterisks'
in reply.

On his return from Heidelberg the populace needed sermons
and they must be acquainted with the limits of the Pope's power,
a subject already broached in the *Resolutiones* which had gone to
his diocesan bishop in February. In May then, on return from the
meeting of the Order, he preached on 'Excommunication' to the
people of Wittenberg. It might seem that Luther was here antici-
pating events in his own regard—but he was dealing primarily
with a matter of common abuse by which, for instance, when the
financial year was up if a debt to Rome had not been paid a ban
on the sacraments might be laid on a whole area, and the people
excommunicated for a time. Unjust excommunication was a common experience, sometimes corporate, sometimes personal. Like
Sir Thomas More when he advised Henry VIII against understanding papal sovereignty as based on an act of Christ himself,
Luther considered the Pope's power was a human not a divine
arrangement. A forged version of this sermon on excommunication was sent to Cajetan, and Spalatin said it did Luther much
harm. Eventually Spalatin persuaded Luther to publish the true
version.

More academic work was not ignored and Luther published a
commentary on the Psalms in the first months of 1518 and a
second edition of the 'German Theology' in June. Amongst other
pastoral works were one on the Ten Commandments, and another
on the Sacrament of Penance, and another on preparation for
Communion.

Poor Grünenberg, the printer, soon had more than he could
cope with and Luther started sending some material to Leipzig for
printing.

29. *The Man becomes Reformer and Prophet*

LUTHER was either unaware of, or determined to ignore, all political pressures. His position in relation to the Roman authorities was in some ways no doubt typical of the relation of any 'reformer', in any age or place, to any 'government'. The former is free to ignore, generally speaking, all the possible immediate practical results of what he proposes or does. He may not be 'irresponsible' but he does not in fact have many responsibilities. The 'government' is weighed down by secondary interests, and other factors, and a sure fear of what will result if such and such is done or made public. The reformer sees the principles, clear and uncompromised. The 'government' sees the world of affairs, and is hag-ridden by the need to make decisions which can be carried out—by the knowledge that politics is the art of the possible. Luther, indeed, was not the pure theorist—he had many local responsibilities, and it was just this, and his close relationship with the populace in Wittenberg partly through the pulpit, that enabled him to grow into a leader who had in the end to face the problems of 'government'. But at the present time he sometimes deliberately ignored, and sometimes was ignorant of, the political pressures in the international field. He was doing God's business. He had not started all this for some personal interest; and so he was able to find the courage to continue with what seemed to him right in spite of threats, and without the difficulty which someone with a closer knowledge of affairs would naturally have had.

When it came to the personal meetings, the confrontation with Cajetan at Augsburg (October 1518), with Eck at Leipzig (July 1519)—this was a lesser occasion but the presence of Duke George gave it the tincture of 'authority'—and with the Emperor at Worms (April 1521), Luther had none of the *savoir faire* which would have enabled him to speak to them man-to-man. He suffered the emotions of one about to meet important people for

the first time and with little or no diplomatic experience or resources of manners and upbringing to fall back on. He tended to
be very deferential at the start, somewhat overawed by the occasion, and subsequently to allow a certain resentment to appear and
then to forget himself when the heart of the controversy was
reached. He appeared very much in the role of prophet on such
occasions. He knew Scripture exceedingly well. He would bring
all doubtful matters back to the few guiding principles he had
found in Scripture, and above all he would put the test of Scripture itself directly. Where does the doctrine of the treasury of
merits occur in Scripture? he asked Cajetan when the latter wished
to make this a crucial matter, citing for his own opinion on it the
papal bull *Unigenitus* (1343).

His opponents always fell back in the end, even Cajetan, not on
theology strictly so called, not on the Gospel, but simply on
authority—what the Church has said, or the Church has done, is
the final test, and it was assumed that the meanings of the words
or the actions of a past age were crystal clear. From the start the
opposition fell back on authority; those strongly opposed to
Luther began at a very early stage to charge him with bringing
down the authority of the Pope and the Church, Tetzel being the
first of these.

For a year and a half from October 1517 Luther continued to
trust that, since what he was defending was the truth, or at least
an honest attempt to get at the truth, the Pope would not in the
end come out against him. He appealed, after his meeting with
Cajetan, from the 'Pope ill-informed' to the 'Pope better informed'—a common contemporary formula. But, as we have
seen, the Pope and the great majority of those surrounding him
were not in a position to take Luther seriously. In the end they
fell back on routine arguments, all relating to authority, declining to examine Luther's own arguments. The 'prophet' was increasingly isolated—not humanly, for great masses of people,
with many different motives, had gathered round him, but
spiritually and in the sense of a common doctrine and the traditional Christian community. And increasingly he had to explain
his position, and to do it almost solely from his own resources.

The debate on indulgences requested by him in his Ninety-five Theses never took place. Luther himself had to elucidate—and in the process had to respond to many needs, and, to elucidate his view on the sacraments and finally on the whole institutional aspect of the Church. As he developed his theory of the justification of the believing Christian, he more and more emphasized faith and opposed more and more violently all possibly superstitious use of the sacraments.

From an existential and personal theology which could take its place within the institutional framework of the Catholic Church, Luther moved gradually towards the development of this theology in a sense which was positively antagonistic to the traditional priority given to the sacramental and liturgical life in Catholic canonical prescriptions. From a theology which could be patient with the extremist views of the merit-theology he moved to a theology which must absolutely deny this priority. Yet it was not an extreme 'Protestant' theology; visible Church and sacrament remained, though much modified. And the movement was gradual, step by step, as Luther responded to this attack or that need. It was in no sense the ruly development of a foreseen, fore-known scheme.[1] And even when Luther finally reached the conclusion that the papacy must be 'Antichrist', he did not sit down to work out new Christian forms. He looked rather for the inner core of Christianity, to personal faith within the Church and continued to see himself simply as a 'reformer' of the Church.

30. Towards a Showdown

THE absolute impossibility of a non-schismatic conclusion to the whole controversy may perhaps be first glimpsed at Luther's interview with Cajetan at Augsburg in October. The great Cardinal told Luther that he required from him only the word *Revoco*. Here was the most intelligent and educated man in

---

[1] Jedin is in error when he speaks of Luther unfolding a programme (p. 176).

the Roman establishment treating Luther as a naughty schoolboy —in spite of the fact that Cajetan knew that Luther's theses were not mere child's play. The events leading up to the meeting are important.

In August Luther had received from Rome a citation requesting him to come to Rome within sixty days of receiving the document to answer charges of heresy. Accompanying the citation was the argument on the basis of which he was charged with heresy. This had been written by one Prierias (Sylvester Prierias Mazzolini), a Dominican and one-time Master of the Sacred Palace, at the request of the Roman Curia, and called *Dialogus* (an unsuitable title). Its content and tone are on the same level as the theses of Wimpina/Tetzel. Typical of the document is the statement that the Church universal is virtually present in the Roman Church, and the Roman Church is represented by the cardinals, but is virtually present in the Pope. This was in order to establish a degree of infallibility which would practically divinize whatever the Pope did—in particular what he granted about indulgences. Typical of his statements are: 'the Church's authority is greater than the authority of Scripture', 'the decretals of the Roman Church have to be added to Scripture', and 'in the New Law the Pope's judgment is the oracle of God'.[1] Included in this official document were the following phrases descriptive of Luther: 'a leper and a loathsome fellow', 'a false libeller and calumniator', 'a dog and the son of a bitch, born to bite and snap at the sky with his doggish mouth', having 'a brain of brass and a nose of iron'.[2] Prierias became the laughing-stock of the humanists who would not take him seriously. He is, however, of great importance. The fact that Rome took such a man as one of its principal spokesmen, based their first process against Luther on his writing and never disowned him was possibly the most important single factor in his

---

[1] Excerpted from a later writing of Prierias *Errata et argumenta Martini Lutheri* (similar statements occur in the *Dialogus*) cited in *Holy Writ or Holy Church* by George H. Tavard (Burns & Oates, London, and Harper, New York, 1959), pp. 116–17.

[2] Mackinnon, p. 64. We have already made the point that what seems to us rather foul language is not a matter of great import. But it is worth noting that well before Luther began to use denunciatory-prophetic and generally brutal language, an official Roman document, the first in fact in Luther's case, uses brutal language about Luther himself.

experiences which gradually convinced Luther that the traditional Catholic and papal structure must be disowned.

On receiving the document Luther replied to it and appealed to his University patron, and his civil ruler, the Elector Frederick, to ask that his case should be heard not in Rome but in Germany— the same appeal as Reuchlin had made, an appeal which implied that only in Germany could he be sure of a fair hearing, not an unreasonable supposition given the language of the *Dialogus*. Luther makes clear the central point of disagreement. Prierias had said the Roman Church is the rule of faith. Luther said on the contrary that faith derives from Scripture which is the rule of the Roman Church and all Churches. To the many threats which Prierias had included Luther replied:

> You threaten me with maledictions, invectives, censures. What and whereto? Spare your threats, my father, Christ lives. He not only lives, he also reigns, not only in heaven but even in Rome, however much she may rage. If I am cursed for the truth, I shall bless the Lord. The censures of the Church will not separate me from the Church if the truth joins me to the Church. I would rather be cursed and excommunicated by you and your like than blessed with you. I have nothing to lose. I am the Lord's. If I perish, I perish to the Lord, that is I am found by him. Seek, therefore, somebody else whom you may terrify.[3]

Meanwhile a further denunciation had gone to Rome. Some Dominicans had invited Luther to a supper party and introduced controversial subjects. Someone outside the door made a record of the conversation. A document was then drawn up purporting to be what Luther had said then. Added to it was a version, unauthenticated, of Luther's sermon on excommunication. The whole document was, in effect, little less than a forgery. The Dominicans sent it, via Cajetan their Cardinal Protector and Rome's legate in Germany, to Rome. Cajetan had recently received a letter from the Emperor requesting that Luther be excommunicated, and assuring the Pope that he the Emperor would carry out the papal sentence in so far as it was his task to do so. This was part of Emperor Maximilian's campaign against Elector Frederick who was opposed to the plan to elect Maximilian's grandson Charles

[3] Mackinnon, p. 67, Vol. II.

of Spain as his successor. This was sent on as well. Luther was then declared in Rome to be a notorious heretic and the Pope sent a breve (*Postquam ad Aures*) to Cajetan to arrest the heretic. Letters went also to the Elector of Saxony and to the General of the Order to make sure all the possible means of escape were dammed up.

If the political factor had not come into operation at this point it seems likely that Luther would have died the death of a heretic, perhaps by the end of the year.[4] But Luther had appealed to the Elector Frederick. Frederick liked Luther—and, it seems reasonable to say, was always genuinely wishful to do justice to all. His belief in Luther was no doubt allied to the support which Luther had from the whole Faculty at Wittenberg University. But Rome wanted Frederick kept sweet—in the hope that preventing the eventual election of Charles of Spain as Emperor, he would himself be elected. Frederick now sent a request to Cajetan to examine Luther in a kind and fatherly fashion. At this point Rome's previous orders were countermanded at the source. Frederick's wishes were to be indulged. The 'Golden Rose', highest honour, was to be offered to him. And the two and a half years of shilly-shallying over Luther's case began.

Papal legate in Germany, Cajetan had a number of different parts to play. He was a Thomist theologian of intellectual stature who had mastered the great logical and analogical systems. But he was also a man of affairs, and now in an awkward position as legate and Cardinal Protector of the Dominicans, between a degenerate papal court, his own religious order and a religiously-minded local ruler who was also a potential Emperor. He followed the accepted diplomatic tradition, a way which possibly seemed to him also the most Christian. He tried to charm Luther, to be fatherly to him (as Frederick had asked that he should be) and to offer an end to all the trouble by suggesting a simple empirical withdrawal—perhaps implying that the word *revoco* is not really a very important little word, possibly believing that Luther's real concern was with the practical abuses and the

[4] Of course this is a simplification. The political factor was also involved in the letter from the Emperor to Rome requesting Luther's condemnation. It remains that, given the basis on which judicial decisions were made at Rome at this time, Luther was saved on account of the intervention of purely political considerations.

Italian domination. Thus the worries of Rome, the Dominicans and Frederick might all be resolved. It was the spirit behind such a compromise which had led to the foundering of every reform proposal of the previous hundred years. Luther, however, was not just bent on 'reform', but imbued with a determination to follow what he saw to be the truth, theological Christian truth, and to witness to it if necessary with his life (the visit to Augsburg first brought the definite and immediate likelihood of such an outcome to his mind); it was a determination both highly emotional and fed by a mind deeply theological and biblically well read.

It is relatively easy to take Luther's side, and not too easy to see into the mind of Cajetan himself. But if Luther's life is to be understood (as distinct from being mythologized), it is essential to understand Cajetan and what he was after. There is a sense, at which we have already hinted, in which Cajetan was in an impossible position—first given a brief to examine Luther theologically, and then definitely told to arrest him, finally being given a countermand of all this with a view to keeping the Elector quiet. He was the servant too of his own Dominican Order, as well as of the Holy See. No doubt, however, he must have become well used to such 'impossible' positions. And we need to seek the roots of his own attitude in his theory of the Church, which was both papalist and biblical. He had thought the matter out in arguments against the Conciliarists, 'The ultimate definition of faith belongs to the Pope, though at his own place and rank, namely under Sacred Scripture whose author is the Holy Spirit.'[5]

Presumably Cajetan had at some point in his previous career made a decision that it was better to remain at the point of power in the Curia and do what he could there to further truth and goodness in the process of complying with many orders and requests from above and below (with which he would be likely to disagree) than to flee an evil administration and leave it in less able hands to the greater damage of the Church. Practical loyalty to the institution based on the Catholic view of the One Church provides the key to his position.

[5] Written by Cajetan in 1512, in *De comparata auctoritate Papae et Concilii apologia*, p. 510, cited by Tavard, *op. cit.*, p. 115.

31. *The Meeting with Cardinal Cajetan*

CAJETAN'S meeting with Luther presents a prophetic micro-cosm of the whole Catholic–Protestant controversy and rela-tionship.[1] The two great men, both notable theologians, never really 'met'. The most important reason for this failure is obvious enough. Cardinal Cajetan of the Roman Curia (aged forty-nine) was examining Dr Luther (aged thirty-five), professor of theology at the University of Wittenberg, on a citation for heresy from the Holy See. It seems undeniable that Cajetan understood clearly, as many other ecclesiastics did not, the essential points in Luther's case against indulgences, and that he agreed with many of them. He had written a piece on indulgences only ten months before, shortly after Luther had posted his theses; most of the issues he considered to be theologically open. Then, in preparation for examining Luther he wrote some further pieces, which included his agreement with Luther (and against Tetzel) that it was better to give money to the poor than to buy an indulgence; but a typically Thomist and realistic distinction then followed, that it was not a sin to omit doing the better thing for the sake of a lesser good work. These little essays also included two points against Luther, one that indulgences could remit punishment in purgatory, and the other that the doctrine of the 'treasury of merits' is not simply a pious opinion, but a doctrine of the Church —because defined by the papal bull *Unigenitus* (1343). In this latter belief, which was crucial in the interview, Cajetan was in fact largely alone as a theologian, since the Thomist view of papal infallibility as such was not commonly held. For further evidence of Cajetan's possibly friendly orientation we can look forward to the bull on indulgences, largely composed from Cajetan's report after the Augsburg meeting (see p. 160), and again to Bucer's

[1] In his play John Osborne calls on a number of authentic documents, and indulges in some conflation to achieve a strikingly accurate projection of the atmosphere of their meeting, the Cardinal patronizing both to Luther and to Luther's enemies, charming, intelligent, skilled in the diplomatic manoeuvre, finally irritable and threatening when he fails.

report that Cajetan spoke of Luther's opinions being *errores* rather than *haereses*.[2] Cajetan was among those who knew very well that the Church was in need of reform. He must have had considerable insight, on this score alone, into Luther's intentions.

On the opposite side we must weigh the fact that Luther had, by now, gone well beyond his Ninety-five Theses to positions which were at least bordering on the heretical. As Cajetan wrote in his report to Frederick after the meeting, Luther had moved from a 'disputative' approach in the Ninety-five Theses to an 'assertive' approach in subsequent writings. Then Cajetan, as an Italian, must have had some feeling of impatience, and some sense of innate superiority to the young German doctor who had created such a stir, even a touch of jealousy. Of course, he may have thought, the doctrine and practice of indulgences need reform, like a lot of other things (from the morals of the Popes downwards), but this German fuss is not the way to go about it. Then there was his official position and the political merry-go-round which led to policy being changed from one minute to another and would always lead a professional diplomat and theologian to some mildly prudent, more or less authoritarian course of action which would try, at the same time, to keep some doors open. Something of this sort must have actuated Cajetan in his choice of method and matter.

But the most important divisive feature was that Luther had already begun to question that very authority in whose defence Cajetan was foremost in his time, and for whom he was acting on this occasion. It was only the very smallest beginning of such questioning, but it prepared the way for something further as a result of the meeting at Augsburg. In Luther's reply to the citation to Rome, based on Prierias's criticism of the Nintey-five Theses, Luther had written that Pope and Council may err and that only Scripture is infallible, though he affirms that in fact the Roman Church has never definitely denied the true faith. Luther's Christocentric doctrine was being applied to ecclesiological questions for the first time, 'For me the Church is virtually present only in Christ, and it is represented in the general council'; he drew a

[2] See Jedin, Vol. I, p. 175, footnote 2.

definite conclusion about himself and the Church's authority: 'If, after a decision has been reached on the question of indulgences, I should not respect this decision, I would be a heretic'. But Luther still believed that the Church would not define anything against the teaching of Scripture. In all its past definitions the Church had always quoted Scripture to support its teaching. But there was a gap between this fact, and Luther's idea, and Luther did not yet fully recognize it. It was that the Church had always used Scripture, not alone but along with 'tradition'. Luther was thinking of the direct personal import of the great doctrines which he had understood afresh, and which seemed to him so palpably taught by Scripture. For many centuries Catholic theology had tended rather to look on Scripture as a mine for supporting texts.

The psychological implications of the meeting are important. In so far as Luther did have a 'thing' about his father, and then about God, and found himself often both revolting against and trying to appease authority, then his clash with the Roman Curia was likely to provide a concrete occasion for him to fight back, with a feeling of justification, at authority. The meeting with Cajetan would be symbolical. To meet such a man, an Italian, a Cardinal, the Cardinal Protector of the Dominican Order (Tetzel's Order), a great Thomist, a man of some charm and wit, in this case the formal representative of the Pope, the papal legate in Germany—this was a very different matter from penning diatribes against ecclesiastical abuse from his cell. It does not seem very fanciful to see that Luther found here a father figure in reverse, a figure whom he found good reason to oppose.

The meeting itself began under a cloud. Cajetan had promised the Elector to give Luther a fatherly hearing. Luther had been advised by many friends not to attend a meeting without a 'safe-conduct' from the Emperor, which would guarantee his safety. The safe-conduct document did not arrive till Luther had been in Augsburg for three days. This wait irritated the Cardinal who regarded Luther's attitude as an aspersion on his own good faith. The chances of an unprejudiced and calm examination of the theological questions were lessened by the incident.

But Luther had on his side also been put into an awkward

position. He did not know that the meeting was supposed to be simply an examination of him by Cajetan and to exclude discussion. Then when he arrived at Augsburg in the interval of waiting for the safe-conduct he was visited by the Cardinal's representative, Serralonga, an Italian with an easy tongue.

Luther was somewhat disgusted by his attempts to get him to revoke. Serralonga had come round in the evening with the talk about '*revoco*'—and a harsh word to go with it. What would Luther do, he asked, if Elector Frederick turned against him? Where could he go? '*Sub coelis*' was the famous reply, no doubt deliberately ambiguous—under the open sky, under heaven, the outcome was in God's hands. This was the reply of a prophet, and it was difficult for it to find any relevant point of impact on the politically orientated and methodical Roman theologians. At the meeting Cajetan had Italians round him, apparently with a sort of cheer leader, and free with laughter.

At the first meeting Luther prostrated himself in the accustomed fashion, and expressed a somewhat exaggerated determination to 'leave everything to our Holy Father the Pope, to support what pleased his Holiness and to root out what did not'—and to submit if 'the Christian Church desired to take exception to a single saying of his'. Cajetan then requested Luther to recant. Luther requested to be shown wherein he had erred. Cajetan selected two of Luther's theses, and declared them contrary to Catholic teaching, the fifty-eighth of the Ninety-five Theses which declared that the treasure of the Church is not identical with the merits of Christ, and a sentence in the seventh thesis of the *Resolutiones* which stated that it was not the sacrament of penance but faith that justified a man. It seemed clear that Cajetan was determined to avoid the subjects, or a method, which would have invited a compromise and intended on the contrary to take subjects on which he considered retraction could be properly and authoritatively demanded from Luther, leaving aside all theological nuance, and leaving aside other theologically open subjects. But he had misjudged both the man and the times.

Might a pastoral subject have provided the occasion for a worthwhile discussion between Cajetan and Luther, in spite of their enormous differences of approach?—Cajetan, the Thomist, the Romanist committed to the defence of existing methods and formulations on principle, concerned with the precise formulation of doctrine, the interpretation of Scripture and tradition, yet intelligent enough to know that not by any means all that was taught by the Church could be properly defended; Luther, the young doctor of theology who had become convinced that to teach theology meant to bring the Gospel of Christ, the New Testament message, to a man's inner spirit, and sure that the intellectual methodology which commonly passed as theology was in effect little more than a crossword puzzle, an intellectual game played with counters devised by philosophers, and quite inadequate to convey the Christian revelation. Perhaps. But they were both basically intolerant, as that word is now understood, though both were able to negotiate and compromise and exercise some personal tolerance. It is easier to do this from a position of authority and Cajetan was perhaps better at it than Luther. Restrained enough to be able to take part in disputations as he often had done, Luther was, all the same, entirely convinced that what he had seen, and in a substantial sense 'believed', was the truth, and that his task was to convince others. Cajetan must have understood something of the spiritual inspiration which went to make up Luther's theology and to impel his criticisms and complaints. But this understanding was narrowly channelled through a determination to surrender as little as possible from established positions, to the defence of which he was professionally and sincerely committed.

Cajetan selected the doctrine of the treasury of merits, on which he could appeal to the papal bull *Unigenitus*. As far as the second point is concerned, Cajetan simply gave Luther the direct contradiction, right on the central point of Luther's theology. The sacrament justifies, not the faith of the individual. It seems impossible to believe that Cajetan really could not see the two sides to this question: the sacrament justifies the faithful—but a man without faith is unable effectively to receive the sacramental grace, in fact far from being justified, if in bad faith he may be in a worse position than before. Was he really happy about the current teaching? It seems absurd to suppose that if he had wanted he could not have had a useful discussion with Luther about sacramental theology and grace, and about the efficacy of indulgences transferred to souls in purgatory, and about the place of indulgences in a healthy spiritual life. As it was, contradiction quickly emerged. Luther himself became truculent and intransigent in no time. And Cajetan began to remember his brief, to bring a near-heretic to heel—to deliver him to Rome, or to get him to pronounce the words 'I revoke', even though this had been modified in a 'paternalistic' direction. So Cajetan was content, apparently, to lord it over his charge with a purely conventional victory—albeit unable to resist some discussion and in fact finding himself flummoxed by Luther's many quotations from Scripture to support his case. On the main question of theological principle the meeting became geared simply to the acceptance or denial of the authority of Pope and Council.

Luther said he preferred the evidence from Scripture to the evidence from the papal bull, and claimed that Scripture does not call the sufferings of Christ the Church's Treasury. Cajetan apparently replied that the Pope and Councils are above Scripture, having the power to interpret it authoritatively. Luther denied that anyone could be above Scripture, and re-emphasized that he was ready for all that he wrote to be examined by reference to Scripture and that he would retract anything not in harmony with it. So the classic battle was joined. To Cajetan and all those who supported the old tradition it was a battle in defence of the Church founded by Christ, with the authority to teach, to expound Scripture, a battle against the contrary theory that every man could decide for himself what was the true interpretation of Scripture To Luther and his followers it was a battle against phariseeism and the claim of men to wield an authority which was really God's, a battle to defend the teaching of God-given Scripture which each man received in faith, guided by the Holy Spirit, as long as he lived in the Church and by its sacraments. (See Appendix 2, 'By What Authority', for a longer exposition of the underlying differences.)

Three meetings were held and they became progressively more

acrimonious, Cajetan repeating that he came to examine and excuse if he could, not to discuss, and that Luther's rejection of the authority of the Pope could not be accepted; Luther willing only to try to expound his own teaching in a way which was in harmony with Scripture, prepared to be shown to be wrong by Scripture, and insisting that he had no intention of rebelling—and succeeding at the third meeting in tripping Cajetan up over a verbal inaccuracy in his quotation from *Unigenitus*.

Proper communication between the one acting for authority and the young theology professor, with a possible death sentence hanging over the latter, was in fact impossible. Tetzel's counter-theses had shown Luther the worst of the inadequate response which he was to evoke from authority. The interview with Cajetan showed him the best that could be expected. It was not good enough and it marks the end of any real possibility of reconciliation. So the historian can now see. Luther himself did not yet foresee separation though he knew a death sentence was possible.

If the atmosphere at the beginning was difficult, by the end it was becoming desperate. Staupitz had come, as the local Superior of the Augustinians, to be with Luther. After the third meeting he lost his nerve, absolved Luther from his vow of obedience in case physical violence should be used by Rome and Luther might need to take rapid decisions about his movements, and then departed for Austria. Cajetan was left in a difficult position, not wishing to precipitate canonical action on account both of the safe-conduct and the wishes of the Elector, who through Spalatin was still showing himself a friend of Luther and had requested Cajetan to give Luther a fair hearing. The inconclusive nature of the affair with no communication coming for some days from the Cardinal's party at the House of the Fugger—he was staying with the bankers who handled the indulgence money and other confidential information for the Holy See—finally got on Luther's nerves too, and he made a dash for it one night, a swift decision apparently which led to an uncomfortable ride in unsuitable dress on a too lively horse. The subsequent ride back, rather like the journey home from Heidelberg, included hospitality from the eminent, and the making of useful new acquaintances, this time one of them being Albrecht Dürer.

Cajetan, it seems, had not enjoyed the meetings. Luther's flashing eyes had got on his nerves. He disliked and had failed to dissipate the tense atmosphere. Luther's departure without any further communication annoyed him.

32. *After Augsburg*

THE policy of total appeasement of Frederick by the Holy See was not yet wholly in operation. It seems that Cajetan hoped that Frederick might, at the same time, be kept sweet and be persuaded to hand over Luther. The Cardinal sent him a report of the Augsburg meeting demanding that Luther be handed over to Rome for a canonical process, on the ground now of open heresy, that of rejection of papal authority. After many messages to and fro between councillors and messengers, Frederick the Elector decided to oppose Cajetan openly and to refuse the request. For a few weeks Luther's career, and almost certainly his life, were hanging in the balance. The precise chronology is not easy to establish and the precise motives are also difficult to trace. But in essence it seems clear that Frederick, advised by his chaplain Spalatin, always felt he should remain loyal to Father Luther, doctor of theology at Wittenberg, and to the Faculty who at this time signed a memorandum to him on Luther's behalf, a memorandum about his teaching which they seem to have asked Luther himself to draw up. Finally he was persuaded personally of the validity of much that Luther preached, in particular of his claim that if he was to be condemned he must be condemned on the basis of Scripture.

The Augsburg meeting had been crucial. Luther's incipient rejection of papal authority had been strengthened, brought out a little way into the open. The previous increasingly authoritative attacks on him by a preacher and by ecclesiastical authority, first Tetzel, and then Prierias, were not disowned by Rome; no admission had been made at the meeting of what considerable justice must in any case lie with Luther's cause in its protest against widely recognized abuses. On the contrary the representative of the Holy See had pressed forward as hard as possible to prove Luther heretical. On his return to Wittenberg Luther was shown the document first sent to Cajetan from Rome in August (before any appeasement was decided on) inspired by the forgery. It had requested Luther's arrest in brutal terms. Then, certainly, Luther began to tremble. How could he put any, even the minimum, Christian trust in an authority which was prepared to cite him for heresy and attempt physical violence on the basis of an entirely unauthenticated document?

On the other hand the meeting had led to the hardening of support for Luther from his own countrymen, notably the Elector Frederick, but also from his colleagues at Wittenberg, notable among whom remained Carlstadt, and newly notable young Melanchthon. The latter, a great-nephew of Reuchlin, had recently been appointed lecturer in Greek. He was a brilliant young man, with the thin, gentle, self-possessed but not complacent face which sometimes goes with intellectual gifts. He was to become Luther's first companion in arms, co-translator and his public relations man. With Frederick's refusal to hand Luther over in December of 1518 a full policy of appeasement set in definitely at Rome. But the temper of the ecclesiastical opposition had been made clear, and Luther was given furiously to think about this authority which claimed for itself an authority given by Christ but dealt with truth and charity in a way which seemed out of character for Christians. Into his mind came the image of Antichrist, as it had come to the minds of Hus and of Wycliffe. But whilst to them it was the individual Pope in person who seemed to be Antichrist, Luther began to wonder whether the office itself was not the abode of Antichrist (and so one might be indulgent with the person—he continued very affable with Leo X in some documents). And so began to spread throughout his mind the ways in which the entire structure of the Church might perhaps need to be rebuilt, to comply more nearly with the teaching of justification by faith, with the authority of Scripture alone, with the teaching of the Word.

An ironical but important little pendant to this year was the papal bull *Cum Postquam* (November) on indulgences. It was composed from a report sent to Rome by Cajetan after the Augsburg meeting. The bull purported to settle many of the matters (and did settle them for Catholics since its contents are in harmony with what is still held by them) raised by the Ninety-five Theses. It is a typical product of Cajetan's highly intelligent and methodical theology; intolerable extremes are repudiated and indulgences defended in the same sense as in the defence given by Aquinas. The bull asserted that indulgences could not apply to guilt but that they did apply to penances imposed on earth and to punishment in purgatory. Guilt, it said, was a matter for the sacrament of penance, and this must have been remitted before indulgences could apply. The suffering of purgatory could only be relieved by way of prayer, and not by way of papal authority as such. It follows logically from this that although the value of an indulgence may be specified no guarantee could be offered of its precise (qualitative or quantitative) efficacy. In other words there was no theological basis for claiming that as soon as the 'copper in the chest rings, the soul from purgatory springs'. But this conclusion was not drawn in so many words, and the document may be called disingenuous on this score.

Luther's theses had thus led within twelve months to a formal doctrinal statement which could greatly limit some of the worst abuses—if it was strictly applied. And in practice the campaign against the Jubilee Indulgence had been successful. Tetzel himself had retired from the public scene now, almost in disgrace. Luther had achieved a practical success. But indulgences were only the rather bizarre occasion. Luther's theology was the thing—and this was now driving him into statements he had not dreamed of before he had met ecclesiastical opposition.

33. *Luther's Position consolidated*

LUTHER continued his daily round in Wittenberg, the centre of intense interest, gossip, concern. He was still the University lecturer, and Wittenberg was crammed with new pupils who were coming in rapidly increasing numbers to attend Dr Luther's lectures. He was still a very popular preacher in the parish church. The lectures and the sermons, and his status in the University faculty at Wittenberg are now of great importance. Luther was not just the giant-hero of much of the mythology which has grown up round him. But this mythology did grow up from historical fact. He was the expression, at last the articulate symbol, of the mind of a whole incipient community; the expression of religious conscience, of national feeling, and simply of a certain personal understanding of the Gospel. The expression of all this by him began to make a real community out of the common elements amongst many different classes of people. The University, the parish, the town, the Elector, and throughout Europe many diverse people, represented so far only, and somewhat inadequately, by the humanists, these stood at the back of Luther, and he was conscious of them. There was a big element of physical tension—also of spiritual horror as he moved further away from the established traditions—in Luther's personal situation, and the fact that Staupitz had released him from his vow of obedience removed another element of stability from his personal situation. However, this was counter-balanced to some extent by the massive support for him which was clearly emerging.

With almost every step that Roman or other ecclesiastical authority took, in an attempt to silence, condemn or compromise with Luther, Luther took another step in the development of his theological critique, proposing ever more drastic modifications of the framework of the ecclesiastical institutions, making this framework more supple and pliable to his theological dynamism of personal faith, personal humiliation, salvation and justification.

This process went on for the three and half years between October 1517 and the 'Luther' sessions of the Diet of Worms in April 1521. Luther's mind is continually on the move. Almost every public utterance shows some development in his position. Different parts of the eventual Lutheran picture gradually come into focus.

Soon the revolutionary focus on the 'Word of God, identified in Scripture, can no longer be fitted into the traditional ecclesiology. On the contrary it leads to a new Church theory. In this theory, the Church is a community whose confines are no longer definite to human eyes, whose essential characteristic is the faith of its members, binding them as a body to Christ and moving outwards into preaching and charitable works, a body which is no longer necessarily identifiable in a juridical sense with a single organization of human beings, and membership of which is no longer identified with communion with such an organization and its head. In May 1519 Luther coined the famous definition of the Church: 'Where the Word of God is preached and believed there is the Church', adding: 'It is called a kingdom of faith because its King is invisible, an object of faith'.[1] And no provision is made for an authority which decides whether in doubtful cases the Gospel is preached and believed. But the detail of the new Church is by no means always 'Protestant'—a place was kept in theory for the papacy, though not as an absolute sovereign by divine institution.

The last five months of 1518 had been crucial. Until August of that year Luther had received only local opposition together with a measure of more general opposition from the Dominican Order in support of Tetzel. His local bishop had opposed him at one point, but later withdrew the opposition, and a very friendly visit had been paid by his representative, the Abbot of Lehrin (March, 1518). In August came the first communication from Rome, the shocking and intellectually often puerile language of Prierias. The interview with Cajetan was Luther's first personal and direct contact with Roman authority. The iron hand in the velvet glove symbolized all that Luther detested as a German and a Christian. What was probably a matter of 'tactics', even of a rather sophisti-

---

[1] *Resolutio Lutheriana super propositione decima tertia de potestate papae*, published June 1519, shortly before the Leipzig disputation.

cated Christian courtesy from Cajetan's point of view had seemed little less than hypocrisy to Luther. Over all hung the spiritual threat of excommunication and the plain physical threat of death. From this point on Luther's path began to take a line in some ways similar to that of previous religious revolutionaries or reformers who had pondered on the existential nature of the Gospel message and had been able to evoke only contradictions from ecclesiastical authority to their insights, and their criticisms of institutions.

Luther regarded Hus as a real heretic until he had to read some of his writings in the university library at Leipzig during a disputation with Eck in the summer of 1519 and was surprised to find how much of Hus's work was agreeable to him. Luther's enemies were delighted: 'Just what we always said—a real heretic'. But the likeness was principally in relation to definitions of the Church, to belief that the community of believers and consequently the status of ecclesiastical authority were wrongly defined. But Luther's progress in this direction was not headlong; it was only gradually that he began to move away from formal recognition of papal authority. In the Spring of 1519 he was declaring the need to remain loyal to the established authority, the papacy, and emphasizing the importance for that reason of reforming the abuses connected with it.

For over a year from the time of the refusal of the Elector to surrender Luther to Cajetan the tide of official opposition ebbed. The Emperor Maximilian died in January 1519. In the summer, contrary to the wishes of the Roman Curia, Charles of Spain was elected Emperor. Until shortly before that time the Curia were all intent on pacifying Elector Frederick of Saxony and trying to get him elected and so nothing was done about his protégé Luther. After the election of Charles V it was not known what attitude the new Emperor would take to the Curia, and to Luther; he was busy settling his Spanish affairs before coming to Europe.

From the time when appeasement of Frederick the Elector was first started in 1518, the Curia was responsible for a series of more or less comic interludes centring round one Miltitz. In the circumstances they listened easily to the euphoric dreams of one with a glib tongue and something to make as a go-between, and maybe some genuine desire to make everyone friendly and happy. Miltitz was a kind of *reductio ad absurdum* of compromise and intrigue, for ever promoting meetings and agreements by persuading one party that the other had decided to agree. His sole achievement was to add one more argument to support Luther's growing conviction that Rome deserved scant respect as a genuine Christian authority. Most interesting perhaps amongst his exploits was the summoning by Miltitz of Tetzel to answer accusations of immoral life, a summons whose significance seems to have been that of the purest opportunism. By January 1519 Tetzel was the one man whom no one would any longer defend—the minor figure, the local German, thrown to the wolves. Tetzel never recovered, dying later that year; Luther sent him a letter of commiseration shortly before his death. Of the actual meetings and negotiations in which Miltitz indulged no more need be said. They are amongst the events, which from this point on are numerous, that have to be ignored in any life of Luther which is to remain within the bounds of a single medium-sized book.

The principal public event of 1519 was a disputation with Eck at Leipzig. Eck had, first, challenged Carlstadt, the older don at Wittenberg, but was really concerned with Luther. Local ecclesiastical authority tried for some months to prevent the debate taking place in the interests of preventing the atmosphere from heating up again. The subject was papal authority. The debate was inconclusive. The Universities of Paris and Erfurt were asked to adjudicate on it, but the former at first asked too high a remuneration from Duke George; Erfurt declined. The debate displayed Eck's considerable ability as a debater and his remarkable memory. It showed forth Luther's unrivalled knowledge of the Bible. It also helped Luther to articulate his own belief about the papacy and its ability to err. The writings connected with the debate are considered in Chapter 36. The principal results were twofold: (1) to bring Luther even more decisively before the public eye; (2) to introduce Luther to the writings of Hus, and to convince him that neither Pope nor Council has a final authority to interpret Scriptures. This negative, fundamental to Protestant theology in its resistance to Catholic tradition, now became firmly and finally rooted in Luther's faith. 'I am looking through the papal decretals for my disputation at Leipzig and (I whisper it in your ear) I am in doubt whether the Pope is Antichrist or his apostle, so miserably is Christ (this is the truth) corrupted and crucified by him in these decretals. I am terribly tormented by the thought that Christ's people is so fooled under this specious form of law in the name of Christianity.' So Luther wrote to Spalatin on March 13, 1519. The debate itself was a full-blown medieval theatrical-oratorical event all complete with a fool thrown in to clown about, make vulgar jokes and imitate the protagnonists.

34. *The Bull* Exsurge Domine

LATE in 1519 it became clear to the Roman Curia that Charles V was going to support them on the Luther issue. Meetings of the Curia and of committees set up by it were, therefore, convened in Rome to consider the steps necessary for formal excommunication. The details of these meetings in Rome from January 1520 to the issuing of the papal bull against Luther, *Exsurge Domine*, in May, are significant. The meeting, one and a half years before, between Luther and Cajetan showed up prophetically in a crude fashion something of the future Catholic/ Protestant controversy. The procedure in Rome which led, in the first six months of 1520, to the formal papal bull against Luther, indicates very clearly the beliefs and assumptions of the basis of the Roman Curia's action and decisions. Its members appear to have had a complete confidence in their decisions, in the sense that they believed that whatever they decided must automatically be underwritten by God. Their authority was final. Along with this went a failure to take steps to make sure that procedure and decisions were well based on established fact and proceeded from generally received or defined doctrine. The procedure reflected the manoeuvring of individuals for their own personal reputation, and an indifference to truth whether factual or theological. This attitude is consistent with the Curial action in August 1518 when

Cajetan was requested to secure Luther's immediate arrest, solely on the basis of documents which were forged, and when no examination had been made at Rome of his writings beyond that of one man, Prierias. The opening words of the bull, which was eventually signed by the Pope in May and issued in June, are finely symbolical: 'Arise, O Lord, . . . a wild boar seeks to destroy the vineyard. . . .' Leo X was at his hunting lodge, and busy with the sport of hunting the wild boar of the Italian hills—the superb scenery must have been exhilarating—when the need for the *papal bull* against the German boar was put to him in May.

The bull was contradictory, lacking in clarity, and incidentally far less effective than it might have been. It relied solely on Luther's writings prior to the Leipzig disputation. Thus the bull had in it the notorious statement that it is heretical to say that 'to burn heretics is contrary to the will of the Holy Spirit' and the anomalous statement that it is heretical to say that 'secular and spiritual princes would do well if they would put an end to mendicancy'.

Throughout the six months from January to June Cajetan attempted to bring common sense, and at least a consistent theology, to bear on the Luther problem, in the Roman Curia. He wished that a decision should be taken only after thorough examination of Luther's writings by a number of competent men; he wished that the decision should be based on proper distinctions between Luther's various writings, and between the degrees of error or heresy in them. He failed to attain these ends, although remaining a member of the committee which finally agreed on the wording of the bull, much of which he must have considered wrongheaded.

Eck came into the committee half-way through, much to Cajetan's disgust, and was largely responsible for bulldozing a decision and the miserably incompetent text through the committee. Subsequently Eck himself said that the bull was hopelessly inadequate and pointed out that in fact the committee knew very little about Luther's later 'errors'. No attempt was made to refute Luther by reference either to the Bible or to the Fathers, a remarkable and unusual omission. The bull gave Luther sixty days from

the day on which he received it to recant or be denounced as a
heretic and excommunicated.

The next step was to get the bull to Luther, and to publish it
in Germany. But the widespread popular support for Luther, at
every level, and for so many and various reasons, made this a task
of which the difficulty was much underrated at Rome. Twice in
the previous year he had had offers of physical armed support—
from the knights Hutten and Sickingen in January, from another
group of a hundred knights in June.

This was not the kind of rather doubtfully motivated support
that Luther wanted. If he wished for secular support he would
make his position clear and define what he considered were the
tasks of secular authority (so he wrote in August his *Address to the
German Nobility*. This along with other writings of 1519 and
1520 are considered in chapters 36–39). But these offers of support
indicate the growth of general support for Luther.

Naturally the Curia could not conceive that the authority of the
Church might not be on the winning side, might not be able to
compel assent. In practice Eck and Aleander who had the task of
publishing the bull found their lives sometimes in danger. The
comic interlude of Miltitz had also not quite petered out, and the
poor fellow was worried to find that just as he was making a last
minute, 'bound-to-be-successful', attempt to get agreement between Luther and Rome this tiresome bull was being published!
He asked Luther to write something for him to give to the Pope;
Luther wrote his *Treatise on Christian Liberty* and with it a letter
to the Pope which included the words: 'It is all over with the
Roman See; the wrath of God has overtaken it. It is not worthy of
the esteem of such as you and I. Satan ought to be pope, for he
certainly reigns in the new Babylon more than you do'!

35. *Luther's Reply; Bonfires; To Worms*

LUTHER would not at first credit the news of the bull. Before he had received the actual document, sealed, he began his reply to it, and entitled it *Adversus Execrabilem Antichristi Bullam*; he had no proof, he said, that it came from Rome, and thought it might be a forgery, but in any case it was clear to him that the author of it was Antichrist. He then moved into an important and solemn declaration, which, he must have been well aware, involved a possibly final and irrevocable parting of the ways, a declaration set in traditional solemn tones, reminiscent of the text used for excommunication, so much abused by Roman authority:

> You, Leo X, and you, cardinals, and everyone else who amounts to anything at the curia: I challenge you and say to your faces, if this Bull has in truth gone forth in your name and with your knowledge, I warn you, in virtue of the power which I, like all Christians, have received through Baptism, to repent and leave off such Satanic blasphemies, and that right quickly. Unless you do this, know that I, with all who worship Christ, consider the See of Rome to be occupied by Satan and to be the throne of Antichrist, and that I will no longer obey nor remain united to him, the chief and deadly enemy of Christ. If you persist in your fury, I condemn you to Satan, together with this Bull and your decretals for the destruction of your flesh, in order that your spirit may be saved with us in the Day of the Lord. . . .

This last sentence was inspired by the normal sentence of excommunication, something done on earth to the physical person with a view to his eternal salvation.

Against the Bull of Antichrist was later re-written and adapted for general circulation in German. In this vernacular form it contains the following words:

> Be it known to all that no one does me a service by despising that outrageous heretical lying Bull, nor can anyone spite me by esteeming it. By God's grace I am free, and this thing shall neither console

nor frighten me. I know well where my consolation and my courage abide, and who makes me safe before men as well as devils. I will do what I believe to be right. Everyone will have to stand up and answer for himself at his death and on the Last Day; then perhaps my faithful warning will be remembered.

This was the time of definite separation. In the previous three months Luther had written and published his *Open letter to the German Nobility* and his *Babylonian Captivity*.[1]

Eck found it impossible to publish the bull in most of north and central Germany. Aleander in western Germany tried to promote the burning of Luther's books, but he only succeeded with the greatest difficulty, and at several places the local students managed to substitute either wastepaper or anti-Lutheran works for Luther's own works. At Louvain and Liège a burning took place; but at Cologne and Mainz the students managed to rescue Luther's works. At Cologne the fire was boycotted by the Archbishop and chapter.

When Luther had definite confirmation of the burning, he determined to retaliate in kind. He would burn the Book of Canon Law. His action has often been misunderstood or misrepresented as a mere tit for tat, and act of temperament.[2] On the contrary, the burning of the Canon Law, like Luther's solemn reply to the bull, is a perfectly deliberate and symbolic act. Canon

[1] Mackinnon summed up this crucial moment finely. Writing on Luther's denunciation of the bull he said: 'In Luther the outraged moral sense of Christendom at last makes itself heard in the form of this violent ultimatum to reform itself or take the consequences of revolt and schism. The time has at length brought the man, and against this man Eck and his Bull in defence of the Papacy are but a shield of paper. In laying the blame for this dogmatic quarrel solely on his opponents—Prierias, Eck, Cajetan, etc.—he ignores the part played by his own dogmatic temperament. He had begun the attack and his disclaimers of all responsibility for the development of it is to a certain extent special pleading. But his plea for a clamant reformation in the interest of a purer Christianity, based on the teaching of Christ and the Apostles, and for the freedom of the Gospel, on which he will not give way an inch, is unassailable. The degenerate travesty of this teaching, which his opponents defend in the papal interest and which the Bull seeks to enforce by excommunication and death, had no longer the prestige and the moral force to win or overawe the people. Behind Luther were arrayed the national feeling and the moral force of a large section of Germany.' (Vol. II, p. 213.)

[2] John Osborne seems to fall into this mistake in his play *Luther*. But his transformation of this scene into a burning of the bull may well be deliberate in the service of his particular theme. He plays down the objective matter of dispute, which is so well illustrated by Luther's burning of the Canon Law, and emphasizes instead his personal struggle, his hope and despair and dependence on God, his bitter and brutal animosity against the Italian papacy. For this purpose, valid historically, the burning of the bull affords the best illustration as a moment in the dramatic bonfire at Wittenberg.

Law was the symbol of the merit-theology, and of the institution-alism which Luther considered to have practically smothered the original Christian Gospel truths, the justification of every man by Christ, the gift of faith to each. To burn the book of Canon Law was a natural way of making public and final Luther's separation of himself from the tradition and institution of the Roman Catholic Church, showing that he no longer regarded himself as owing allegiance to the papacy or being under its jurisdiction, and indicating that he regarded her Canon Law as a major cause and result of her failure to preach and live by the Christian Gospel.

A work of legalistic pastoral theology, the *Summa Angelica* of Angelo de Chiavasso, was also burnt. At the last moment Luther threw in the papal bull for good measure. The burning of the bull has become famous, but in fact almost certainly no one but Luther and his servant Agricola knew about it at the time. And many months later no one spoke of the burning of the bull. It was only the burning of Canon Law that people understood as epochal—anyone might have thrown a papal bull in the fire in a temper. The burning of Canon Law was the burning of the book which regularized the whole of everyone's religious life, the symbol of power and jurisdiction.

There followed a chaotic six months. Luther had rejected the papal bull demanding his recantation and had formally con-demned papal authority. When the three months were up the formal bull of excommunication was issued, on January 3, *Decet Romanum Pontificem*. The new Emperor's first Council was about to open at Worms, the Diet of Worms. Many people considered that the obvious course of action was to summon Luther to appear there. The ecclesiastical authorities naturally objected to this. Luther was an excommunicate; good Christians were bound to hold no communion with him, and those in civil authority were bound to take action against him in accordance with civil law. The actual course of events was as complex as Luther's affair had been from the beginning. He was invited to Worms. The invita-tion was rescinded. The Emperor tried to get the Diet to issue an edict against Luther but failed. Luther was invited again. An edict was passed sequestrating Luther's books. Finally after much coming and going, much jockeying of ecclesiastical and civil authority, Luther was requested to come to Worms. His going there was another of his journeys on which so much must depend. He had become a real storm centre now. When he arrived at Worms the herald blew his trumpet for distinguished arrivals. Luther went to the House of the Knights of St John where Elector Frederick was staying. He was visited there by a great number of the more eminent people staying at Worms for the Diet. The final showdown must now come. The Pope had spoken. Would the Emperor, the Electors and the Estates speak in the same sense? But first we must turn to the writings of the two and a half years before Worms.

36. *Writings, December 1518 – Summer 1520*

Between the last months of 1518, after the meeting with Cajetan at Augsburg, and the spring of 1521 at Worms Luther achieved an enormous literary output. He remained at Wittenberg teaching and preaching, visited and being consulted, ever more famous. His published works for this two and a half years range from theology to general political and social problems. His thought is ever on the move, and he is laying the basis, without knowing it, for the coming 450 years of Protestantism. There is so much of this written material that the mere task of setting out a precise chronological list of all the publications is something belonging to a small number of specialist historians. However, the general pattern and a big number of publications are well known.

Luther's works were among the first to achieve a great historical effect through printing. This was another of those historical coincidences so many of which met in Luther's person. All the many and very diverse motives which existed as potentials for supporting him were stimulated, fed, maintained, by the ceaseless flow of the printed word. This was in itself something novel and exciting, that there should be available frequently every month or two for quite small sums a package of pages, often with a woodcut picture on the top page, which gave people Luther's latest views, comment and teaching, a copy for each who could pay the printer-publisher's fee—Luther himself took nothing. Some were in German for anyone who could read, and were often deliberately adapted to a wider audience than the Latin productions could reach. Often Luther seems even to have restrained himself in these German works, to have avoided stirring up the people unnecessarily (one recalls how he had not always given his students or his parishioners the full story of his criticism of the Church 1514-1517). A typical example is his reply to the bull *Exsurge Domine*. The solemn sequence of condemnation and separation which he addressed in Latin to the Pope and the cardinals was not included in the German version; the Latin was a serious and more or less private communication to the Pope, not a mere gesture of impatience and publicity.

The printers, spurred on by the humanists, were soon aware that in Luther they had an author whom everyone wanted to read. Froben, Erasmus's printer-publisher in Basle, was the first to bring out an edition of the *Works*. This he did in October 1518, within twelve months of Luther's public challenge for a debate on indulgences, and two or three years only since Luther's name had begun to be spoken of in universities beyond Wittenberg. This collection had an anonymous introduction, which represents well the temper of those who supported Luther:

> Here you have the theological works of the Reverend Martin Luther, whom many consider a Daniel sent at length in mercy by Christ to correct abuses and restore the evangelic and Pauline divinity to theologians who have forgotten the ancient commentaries and occupy themselves with the merest logical and verbal trifles. And would that he might arouse all theologians from their lethargy, and get them to leave their somnolent summaries of divinity and choose the Gospel rather than Aristotle, Paul rather than Scotus, or even Jerome, Augustine, Ambrose, Cyprian, Athanasius, Hilary, Basil, Chrysostom, Theophylact, rather than Lyra, Aquinas, Scotus, and the rest of the schoolmen. May they no longer drag Christ to the earth, as Thomas Aquinas always does, but may they instruct the earth in the doctrine of Christ. May they cease

AETHERNA IPSE SVAE MENTIS SIMVLACHRA LVTHERVS
EXPRIMIT AT VVLTVS CERA LVCAE OCCIDVOS

· M · D · X X ·

5. The earliest likeness of Martin Luther
From an engraving by Cranach the Elder, 1520

6. Leo X (1475–1521), Pope from 1513
From a drawing by Sebastiano del Piombo

saying one thing in their farcical universities, another at home, another before the people and something else to their friends; and may they cease calling good men who refuse to fool with them heretics as they now do for small cause or no cause at all. . . .

Soon after the meeting with Cajetan at Augsburg Luther published an account of it, entitled *Acta Augustina*. It states his belief that the authority of the papacy is not of divine origin, and not a fundamental matter of faith. It also pays tribute, rather surprisingly, to the courtesy with which Cajetan had received him. In February of 1519 Luther published his *Apologia Vernacula* which gives a summary of his position, under six headings: (1) *Saints* may be prayed to. But they are intercessors and have no power of their own. Miracles are done by God. (2) *Purgatory* exists and souls suffer there and can be helped by prayer, and by fasting and almsgiving. (3) *Indulgences* are voluntary and the common people should be told that they are not commanded by God. They should also be told that indulgences are not as important as charitable works. (4) *The Commandments of the Church*, fasting and observance of feast days were less important than true inward piety. Eating meat on Friday was not a sin comparable to that of swearing or neglecting to help one's neighbour. (5) *Good works* can only proceed from a regenerate man. Good works flow only from God's grace; God regards not the outward action but the inner attitude of heart. (6) *The Roman Church* rightly demands loyalty. However corrupt she may be, Christians should respect her for her martyrs. The worse she is at the moment the more loyalty is needed. Luther said he had never intended to detract from the honour of the Roman Church but only to oppose those who hypocritically use it for their own purposes.

Still in the spring of 1519 Luther did not think that he might eventually consider himself to be called to separate himself from Rome. He is still sure that his own theology and the criticisms he has made remain essentially within the bounds of Catholic Christian tradition. Though Antichrist (a common symbol for 'evil' at the time) may have begun to get his claws into the papacy, essentially the public structure of the Church is Christian and ecclesiastical authority can be relied on eventually to recognize

the validity of Luther's exegesis and judgment on current practice. He intended his position to seem 'reasonable'. But his opponents were concerned only with authority. They took it for
granted that all Scripture being obscure and all knowledge
doubtful the only point of reliance was ecclesiastical authority. It
is interesting and worthwhile to notice that Luther's position in
the *Apologia Vernacula* would hardly be regarded as seriously out
of line, and certainly not necessarily heretical, today. Luther's
position is in fact still ambivalent, in its failure to say *precisely* what
force ecclesiastical authority and the commandments of the
Church have. But the statement that the fundamental authority is
God, and that the only ultimate source of good in the individual
is grace and the inward life of the spirit, is unequivocally accepted
by Catholic theology today, so long as it does not intend to
exclude sacramental grace, and Luther certainly had no such
intention.

Not long after the meeting with Cajetan, Eck had the idea of
holding a public disputation—the Leipzig meeting already referred to—to discredit Luther. The disputation itself, in his plan,
would be with Carlstadt, but the disgrace of Luther would be the
pay-off. With this in view Eck produced twelve theses covering
the points at issue. Luther issued a reply to these in February. Eck
reissued his, plus one. The last thesis on each occasion concerned
the nature of papal authority. Luther wrote a further reply
specifically against this, the thirteenth thesis, maintaining that
whilst the papacy was indeed the sovereign in the Church it was
of human, not divine origin—his work was a very thoroughly
argued exegesis of the New Testament passages, followed by a
historical and theological survey. This position was held by other
orthodox theologians at this time.

In February Froben issued a second and enlarged edition of the
Works, a third and a fourth followed in August and in March
(1520). In 1519 Cardinal Wolsey's officials found the first copies of
this book hidden in bales of wool coming into England.

Of other publications about this time Luther's *Treatise on the
Marriage Estate* is important. The first outlines of a new kind of
Christian community begin to emerge. Bringing up children,

said Luther, is much better than going on pilgrimages, building churches, endowing Masses, and doing other such things which have been called 'good works'. For people who have children their most direct way to heaven is to bring up their children well.

Towards summer Luther was busy preparing for the debate with Eck and reading up all the historical, canonical and theological material on the Roman primacy. After the debate, he set about making a revised edition of the *Resolutions* which was published in August. He had been studying the Bible more carefully and had begun to think it impossible to give anything like equal weight to every book in Scripture. If Scripture was to be the final test of truth then it was essential that the canon of Scripture was not adulterated. He expressed doubts about the authenticity of the Epistle of St James. Later in August Luther issued two more tracts in reply to productions of Eck.

In September were published Luther's commentary on St Paul's Epistle to the Galatians, and the first Section of his studies in the Psalms. The commentary on Galatians comprised the lectures, completed early in 1517, which he had since improved before giving them to the printer. This was one of the first major scriptural or theological works of Luther's to be published. He had been doing university lecturing for six or seven years, and had prepared many disputations. Then a year and a half ago he had moved into the world of publicity and publications by the accident of the popularity of his Ninety-five Theses. Since then everything he published had some direct relation to the controversy with Rome about indulgences and about papal authority. The university professor, by the publication of the Commentary on Galatians, re-asserts his academic status. Something of the content of this commentary has already been very briefly indicated in chapter twenty-one. Luther returned to this epistle of St Paul twice again, and expressed his dissatisfaction with this earlier commentary; the third version of his commentary was published in 1535 and translated into English in 1575.[1] In this first edition

---

[1] This English edition is the basis for an English text, *The Bondage of the Will*, edited by Philip Watson, issued in 1953 by James Clarke and Co. Ltd., London, at 16s. 6d.— astonishing value for 556 pages.

Luther began to broach the problem of the responsibility of civil authority, and summoned the Estates to act against usury.

The theological founts of Luther's life also flowed into the numerous sermons which he had to give, in the town church on Sundays and feast days, and every afternoon to the friars of the priory. A manuscript is extant which contains 116 sermons of Luther's delivered in the course of the nineteen months from October 30, 1519 to April 2, 1521. In the autumn of 1519 Luther composed some spiritual reading for the Elector at the latter's request. Frederick had fallen ill after the Diet at Main in June for the election of the Emperor. Luther wrote a book on 'fourteen consolations', to take the place of the usual devotion to the fourteen patron saints. Luther gave the Elector seven good and seven bad things to think about. The Elector liked the little book and asked Luther for a book of sermons for Sundays, a Sunday Postil; which Luther eventually completed for him.

In the autumn of this year, 1519, Luther also composed sermons on the three sacraments of baptism, penance and the Eucharist; the other sacraments he no longer accepted as real sacraments of the Church. In these sermons Luther began to develop the sacramental theology which he would expound more fully a year later in his *Babylonian Captivity*. He also developed some of the social applications of his theology, already begun in his work on marriage, in particular the vocational idea.

> Everyone should remain in the natural calling to which divine providence has appointed him. . . . Anyone who neglects the duties of his calling will not be helped at all by fasting, making pilgrimages, telling beads, endowing Masses, and such other 'good works' as there may be. First take care of your wife, your children, and the poor, and then make a pilgrimage to Rome, set up candles, endow Masses, erect new altar pictures, and the like! Instead of this you are constantly quarrelling with your wife and allow yourself to be deluded by the devil into doing such spectacular good works.

Every town, he said, should look after its own poor. In the pastoral line he wrote a short work on praying and understanding the 'Our Father'—this was later often republished along with 'A short form of the Ten Commandments' and 'A Short form of the Creed'.

The theological, the pastoral and the polemical can hardly be distinguished now. All the writings have as their essential inspiration the theology of personal faith and justification which Luther had developed in his Scripture lectures. Now that he was being publicly challenged, inevitably everything he wrote also received some polemical orientation by way of defence, and some justifying pastoral application. In the winter 1519–20 a new version of Luther's sermon on excommunication was published, reaffirming the position of the 1518 version that excommunication concerns the relationship of the individual to the Church, not directly to God, a position which enraged the ecclesiastics, but which is not palpably heretical.

In May 1520 was published Luther's sermon on *Good Works*, which immediately became one of his most popular works. It was a further popular exposition of the theme that man's task is to live his daily life according to his calling, to live faithfully. This is the good 'work' required of the Christian, and not pilgrimages, fasting, Masses, indulgences, etc. Luther was really coming into his own here. The *Sermon* is a fine popular exposition of the theology he had worked out in the schools. Speaking of good works and faith he draws a good analogy from the life of a married couple. When they love each other they work for each other with confidence—they do not have to keep wondering whether to do this or that for fear of losing love. So with man; he must have complete faith in God, and not worry about this little thing or that little thing, as though in some unfathomable way it might or might not be well received. It is when couples doubt each other and have no faith that one sets about the task of pleasing the other with a heavy heart. 'The first and noblest of all good works is faith.' In June Luther's *Concerning the Papacy in Rome* was published—a reply to a Franciscan Alveld who had attacked his theology. Luther developed his ecclesiology in it, on the lines already noted, that Rome's authority is not God-given, and that the Church is a visible community of believers, but that its precise extent is known only to God. Celibacy for secular priests is to be abolished. Parish priests are to be elected by the congregations.

37. *Luther considers Christian Society*

IN August Luther published his *Open Letter to the Christian Nobility of the German Nation, concerning the Reform of the Christian Estate.* The title indicates the development of a line of thought and action, to which, though appearing in his notes, he had not given much previous publicity. Luther had received the protection of the Elector, his own ruler and the patron of his university, and had shown his gratitude for it. But he had gone out of his way on occasion to emphasize his essential, spiritual, independence of political authority. He had also received offers of help from Hutten and von Sickingen, again showing gratitude and a willingness, if things came to extremes, not to reject the offer entirely. But he had not shown any wish to request the help of society at large in a campaign of fundamental opposition to ecclesiastical authority as such. Such an idea was not really possible for him in any case. He accepted the great medieval assumption that human society was made by God and that the Church included in its range civil society; altogether it was the Christian commonwealth. He did not reject this conception so much as transform it from a largely monarchical and oligarchical system into something more democratic. In this tract he spoke for the first time of the 'priesthood of all believers'. With this was linked the usual list of ecclesiastical abuses, and a statement that the priest is not made by the privileges and robes, but by his office, and this office he now defines as one which springs from the universal sacrament of baptism—the ministry, the ordained priesthood, is a way of ordering this universal priesthood, which comes from baptism and is not an independent sacrament.

Rejection of the sacrament of ordination naturally raised the status of the laity. A layman, said Luther, might call a General Council—not simply because of his civil status but because he was baptized, a responsible Christian. As baptized Christians, the Emperor and other civil rulers had a special responsibility. They must act against ecclesiastical abuses. Here was a transformation of the medieval obligation to act as the 'secular arm', when necessary to burn a heretic; the responsibility was now directed upwards instead of downwards—the hierarchy themselves must receive correction.

Luther's influence here fitted well with German traditions. It was not an entirely new conception when the First Diet of Speyer in 1526 enunciated the regional religious principle *cuius regio eius religio*. As in England, the battle of the two swords had been going steadily in favour of the civil sword; the German Princes through the institution of *Eigenkirche* had to some extent already made their churches into their own institutions. By reducing both the extent and the importance of the sacramental system as he now did, Luther transformed this tradition into a virtually 'democratic' means of criticizing and reforming the Church.

When the rulers were assembled at Charles V's first Diet, at Worms, they studied Luther's *Open Letter* with intense interest. Though, like Frederick, they were frightened of the changes in dogma, Mass and sacraments, they agreed with Luther about the enormity of the abuses which he listed, they agreed that Rome's financial exactions were often intolerable, and it seemed to them reasonable to agree that as Christians there must be some place for responsibility and action by them. The *Open Letter* is addressed implicitly to everyone with any responsibility for government, in some parts explicitly to corporate local authority, whether actually represented in the Diet or not.[1]

The lineaments of a new Church are beginning to be drawn. Mendicant orders are to be abolished or at least drastically reduced. Clerical celibacy is to be abolished—and with it the scandal of concubinage. The Hussites in Bohemia are to be tolerated not persecuted. The *Open Letter* includes an outline of educational, legal and social reform. The faculties of arts and theology are to be reformed in all universities, as in Wittenberg. Luther runs the gamut of social evils and the luxurious living which is shown in rich clothing and excessive eating and drinking—he wants the State to intervene. The public brothels which disgrace the larger towns are to be abolished.[2]

---

[1] See Mackinnon, Vol. II, p. 226.   [2] See Mackinnon, Vol. II, p. 243.

The *Open Letter* contained Luther's most searing criticism of Rome to date. The Pope is to have, still, spiritual oversight. But, he says, Rome itself is Antichrist, and anything can be bought there. The Roman Curia is the aim of all his shafts. Enough of it was palpably true for the *Open Letter* to act as a powerful agent of ferment. Written in German it has a natural continuity with Luther's previous German works. Only, now, his audience is no longer just his parishioners, nor just the laity of the district, or even of Germany at large—it is now clearly envisaged as the whole of society, the Christian world and its rulers. Luther has realized that a major work has begun, and that he is at the centre of it.[3]

38. *The Church, Sacrament and Faith*

WITHIN two months Luther published the Latin and theological counterpart to the *Open Letter*, that is the *A Prelude on the Babylonian Captivity of the Church*. In this tract Luther no longer felt any need at all to take account of the authority of Rome, or of loyalty to her or to any of the established Church traditions. All may have been subject to corruption and abuse. All must be judged in the light of scriptural theology.

Luther has now cut loose from the great anchorage of the Roman Church, an anchorage often silted or blocked, often refurbished, developed, scoured, but always till now still the anchor-

[3] Mackinnon, Vol. II, comments in the manner of another age: '*The Address* (*The Appeal*) challenges criticism when read in the calm of the historian's study. It bears ample trace of Luther's tendency to extreme, unqualified generalization. It is hardly a historically-minded statement. It is the speech of the counsel for the prosecution and sentence of the criminal at the bar, and its tone is very violent and uncompromising. It contains exaggerations of fact and mis-statement of motive. Luther, we feel, is fairly on the warpath, in the mind to swear at large. At the same time, he has undoubtedly a very strong case, so strong that one is disposed to conclude that he might well have stated it more moderately without any loss to its strength. Its vehemence, in fact, rather tends to weaken its force for the modern reader. Apart from this weakness, however, we cannot but appreciate the skill, the moral force, the impassioned eloquence with which the counsel for the prosecution handles the overwhelming evidence against the criminal at the bar, though he inclines to ramble at large at times. One feels that the hour of Nemesis has at last struck . . .' (p. 243). The classic Scottish sense of justice pours steadily forth from the calm of the historian's study.

age of western Christendom. Luther was now leaving this anchorage. He had for guide now only his own understanding of Scripture, assisted by the early Fathers, his own spiritual experience, his general knowledge of life, and the advice of his friends. Eventually his initiative would lead him to the positive acts required to initiate new traditions. For the moment Luther moved, in this tract, further towards a new theology, of Church and sacrament, a development of his theology of faith.

Like everything else Luther wrote, the *Babylonian Captivity* was only a step on the way. It was written, like nearly everything else, in great haste, and was not a carefully organized formal statement. Some of the most striking suggestions are the least radical in relation to Catholic tradition; on the other hand the theological changes are also less radical than is often supposed. It is easy to see it as a Protestant manifesto, but the text will not bear such a simple 'mythical' interpretation. Two of the superficially striking things were: (1) A demand that the laity should receive the consecrated wine as well as the consecrated bread at communion—a demand previously made by heretics, an affront to ecclesiastics, but not itself in any sense heretical (the Second Vatican Council has recently approved legislation for just such an innovation). (2) The rejection of the theory of transubstantiation—but the admission of something else which involved some kind of real presence and not a mere memorial. What Luther disliked here was the idea that a philosophical term (substance) could provide the means to a theological description, rather than the doctrine itself of a real sacramental presence.

The fundamental theology of the Eucharist, whether Catholic or Protestant, is difficult. Luther rejected the Mass as a sacrifice. But he retained the great part of the old liturgy—and a real presence of Christ in the consecrated bread and wine. Luther's primary objection to the Mass was the way in which, like the other sacraments, it was treated as a 'good work' to be done by the priest, attended by the faithful, something automatically beneficial—a sacrifice offered by a human priesthood. Luther's dissatisfaction with the theology of the sacrificial Mass as expounded in his time was shared in his time, and has been shared frequently since, by Catholics who have remained in the Roman Catholic Church to propound new theories.[1] It remains true that the straight denial of the Mass as a sacrifice in any sense was and still is intolerable to Catholic tradition. But both Lutheran and Catholic teaching were and remain at one in speaking of Christ's own sacrifice. The controversy revolves round the way, and the extent to which, Christ's sacrifice is or is not identical with, made present at, mediated by, commemorated, when the Eucharist, or the Lord's Supper is celebrated by a Christian priest or minister. Luther's words did not involve a kind of theological open-sesame, or a sudden Protestant revelation of the true primitive Church teaching, a total rejection of the whole Catholic tradition. They did, however, certainly lead to a general experience of psychological release, both for intellectuals and for the people.

Following on release from the Roman rules and regulations, and the prescribed Roman theology amongst those who accepted Luther's theories, came the desire and the need for something to take its place. Later it soon became clear that it was difficult to translate Luther's scriptural theology into new practical liturgical traditions, agreed to by all, just as it had been difficult to try to fit it into the existing Catholic and papal traditions. But the desire to do the former became present whilst it had been absent for the latter purpose.

As with the Mass, so with the sacraments. As the Mass was no longer 'a sacrifice', so were the sacraments no longer an objective 'work' which gave grace to men by their very nature (*opus operatum*—by the very action itself). And the sacraments were now reduced to the two which were explicitly to be found in scriptural texts, baptism and holy communion (confession remained something of a query). The significance now given to these sacraments referred back to the theology which Luther had been preaching since 1513. Their importance lay within the world of faith, by which man received the Word, believing and living by God's

[1] To give only one amongst numerous possible illustrations of this statement, see, for the doctrine of the Mass in the fifteenth century, the relevant pages in *The Eucharistic Sacrifice and the Reformation* (Clark) and criticism of this in 'Theological Studies' (Woodstock, vol. 22) by Rev. A. Stephenson. For recent studies on theories of the Mass, perhaps the most notable by writers who are well-known orthodox Roman Catholics and who yet differ very strongly with other such writers, see works by De la Taille and by Masure.

grace. Christ had instituted the two sacraments for the use of the Church. More important, God had given men Scripture, and Christ himself, the Word. Without faith in these, the sacraments were of no significance.

The Bible, said Luther, recognized one sacrament, The Word of God, and two (perhaps three) sacramental signs. The Christian life was an exercise of liberty and could not be tyranically imposed. The sacrament of penance had become just such a tyranny. Confession ought to be free and to be made to any brother Christian, not necessarily to a priest who had no monopoly of absolution.

> They have so taught it that the people have never understood true satisfaction, which consists in newness of life. In the second place they so insist and render it so necessary that they leave no room for faith in Christ, miserably tormenting consciences with scruples that one runs to Rome, another here, another there, to some convent or other place, another scourging himself with rods, another injuring his body with watchings and fastings, all crying out with equal zeal.

The abolition of five sacraments, and Luther's polemic against all the canonical rules and regulations associated with them, involved a decisive and public action, and clearly held important implications for the future when presumably a reformed Church was to arise to be built on the presence of the Word, on faith—and on two sacraments only. The differences between Luther and Rome were now radical and decisive. But a basic framework of Christian revelation still provided a common basis for the differences. An analogy may demonstrate this. A piece of music by Mozart is easy for many people to enjoy and to distinguish as markedly different from much other music—but there is a technical and theoretical basis to it which sets Mozart in a close relation to all other composers of music. Music has a mathematical and scientific basis. So, too, with Luther's sacramental theory. There was an underlying similarity to Catholic theory. Both were *Christian theology*. So that in spite of Luther's rejection of five sacraments, in spite of his denial of the formula *opus operatum*, it would still be possible for a theologian such as Cajetan to turn round, when no other way to

Christian unity remains, and offer terms to the Lutherans for a compromise which involved leaving sacramental practice much more loosely defined.[2] Both parties believed in Christ, the Bible and, though in different senses, the Church.

Catholic tradition assumed Luther's premise—the believer. Luther, on the other side, also assumed the Catholic premise that a sacrament is a visible, ecclesiastical action. But in each case the differing emphases were very soon magnified and inspired vast systems of prejudice often based on ignorance of each other.

The difference in emphasis may be described in this way. For Rome, the Church was the civilized world. All men in it were baptized and assumed to have faith. This assumption about faith was so ingrained that in practice it was almost forgotten; the emphasis on the public liturgy and on sacramental action itself had become so great that the necessity of faith for the objective validity of the sacrament to be *effective* in a particular person had been virtually overlooked. In the opposite direction, Luther went beyond the statement that man must *believe* for the sacramental action to be effective—he said that the sacrament's actual validity sprang simply from the belief of the recipient. This could not be logically defended along with infant baptism. It virtually denied objective value to the sacramental action.

Luther retained infant baptism—he turned, in defence of this, to his fundamental position: all comes from God, man gives nothing, even his belief is God-given, it is not for us to fathom the mystery of infant baptism. This position was in one sense close to the Catholic position: all has been given by God, including the divinely instituted sacramental order, in which God uses the material things of daily life to give his grace to Christians in the Church. The sacraments in this traditional Catholic sense are

[2] See p. 224. There are expositions of Luther's sacramental theology, supposedly at its most typical (for it changed over the decades), in *Let God be God* by Philip S. Watson and in *Martin Luther* by Heinrich Böhmer which are presented as part of Luther's reformed and anti-Catholic teaching. But the expositions are in fact often harmonious with Catholic doctrine. The authors have failed to investigate Catholic teaching, and have been content to rest their idea on particular abuses of that teaching. These expositions are an interesting witness to the fact that as far as theology, strictly so called, is concerned, Luther did not simply reject the whole Catholic tradition. He was too intelligent to turn to a mere anti-intellectual *naïveté*; his practical achievement could not have been supported by anything so weak.

gifts, entirely Christ-orientated, and harmonious with Luther's own theology. But Luther's assessment of the sacraments as they were actually used and administered was almost diametrically opposite. They appeared to be purely human works, a logical system by which man gained measurable quantities of grace or merit in view of salvation in the world to come. It is possible also to criticize Luther's own view of the sacraments as grossly human, since he made their effectiveness to depend entirely on the faith of the recipient. This is in line with a criticism of Luther's theology as reducing everything to the level of man.

Whatever the abuses, whatever the theories, it remained that, both in Catholic tradition and in the new traditions inspired in the first place by Luther, a place had to be left (1) for God, an action from him towards man, a completely free action of God, a gift to his creature, (2) for man to believe or not, to accept or reject, and to strive to do what is right or to despair. It remains true also that either of these two aspects could receive an emphasis almost to the exclusion of the other whether in a highly juridical system or in a very free personal system. And both would be liable to 'magical' or 'subjective' abuses in association with one or other aspect. A juridical system when it emphasized man's work easily lapsed into 'magic' and superstition. A free system when it emphasized God's work easily led to the confusion of purely subjective judgment.

In any religion in which a relationship of man with God is admitted, there will be moments, such as moments of worship or of 'sacramental' action, and moments of personal experience and faith, in which this relationship is said to be expressed. In the nature of the case it will always be impossible to achieve a description of this relationship which is fully satisfactory. It is not a matter amenable to positive science. Man, suddenly believing, man convinced of God's presence, of the reception of his grace, 'knows' these things. He believes. And he believes them to involve something transcendent which cannot be finally expressed. The Christian believes that Jesus Christ was and is himself the solution of this dilemma, the historical person who is also still present to all men and whose Spirit works in history. 'Present to all men'—

'works in history'. For this to have meaning there must be some recognizable standards, definitions, descriptions available to man. What are these standards, these norms? Scripture? The Church? Tradition? Luther's decisive rejection of Roman authority was concerned precisely with these things.

The Babylonian Captivity cost Luther the support of the moderates. Erasmus was horrified at the all-over demolition work. Henry VIII wrote his famous reply defending the sacraments. On the other hand it is still only a halfway house. Luther had not yet arrived at the position where he must build, and so in spite of his radical theory, his practical suggestions usually involved compromise with existing institutions.

The conclusion of Mackinnon about The Babylonian Captivity (1927) conveys remarkably well the historical status of this, one of Luther's most important works. Research done in recent years has reinforced much of his conclusion:

The Babylonian Captivity is from beginning to end a plea for spiritual religion and the liberty of the individual Christian as against medieval sacerdotalism and the medieval priestly caste. It reminds one of Paul's controversy with the Judaisers in his attempt to emancipate Christianity and the individual Christian from Judaism. Luther wages a similar controversy against the vast accretion of tradition and practice which had accumulated throughout the Middle Ages and which, he holds, has entangled and enthralled religion in a network of usages and ideas incompatible with primitive Christianity and Christian liberty. For the medieval Church he would substitute the Church of the New Testament, as emancipated by Paul, and of the first two centuries, in which the priestly conception of religion was little, if at all, developed. . . . It is an extraordinary combination of courage and prudence. He starts section by section to prove his case, and having proved it he invariably hesitates to draw the inevitable practical conclusion. He prefers to tolerate and compromise. . . . His plan of campaign seems to be to point out error and abuse in doctrine and practice and leave God to remedy them by means of the Word acting on public opinion (pp. 260–62).

We may add a rider. We know now that primitive Christianity remained deeply dependent on Judaism; we can add that Luther remained deeply dependent on the Catholic Church. Paul did not deny that the Jews were God's chosen people. Luther did not want to sweep away all the traditional and conventional practice of the Church, but to purge it.

39. *Writings, November 1520 – April 1521*

AFTER the *Open Letter* and the *Babylonian Captivity*, came *The Freedom of the Christian*. This was an evangelical tract with the ecclesiological implications. Luther shows that the justified man, the believer, is free, and owes allegiance to no one but Christ. At the same time, being the most free, he is the most free to serve. Man is identified with Christ—and we see again the traditional German mysticism (in its general, not in the pejorative Lutheran sense of merit-earning asceticism) which Luther had learnt from Tauler. Regenerated man is man who does not need to be told to do this or that. Love is in his heart, and love will tell him and urge him to works of love. There are passages here directly contradictory of the sometimes popular idea that Luther denied that man should do good works. On the contrary the justified man is the most socially conscious of all:

> Lastly we shall speak of those works which we are to exercise toward our neighbour. For man lives not for himself alone in the works which he does in this mortal life, but for all men on earth, yes he lives only for others and not for himself. For to this end he subjects his body in order that he may be able the more freely and wholeheartedly to serve others, as Paul says in Romans 14: 'For none of us liveth to himself, and none dieth to himself. For whether we live, we live unto the Lord, or whether we die, we die unto the Lord'. It is not possible therefore to take his ease in this life and abstain from works towards his neighbour. For, as has been said, he must perforce live and have converse with men, as Christ, made in the likeness of men and found in fashion as a man, lived among and had intercourse with men.

This was in November 1520. In the same month was published the public edition of Luther's piece against the papal bull to which we have already referred.

Between November 1520 and mid-April, when he appeared at Worms, Luther continued to work at numerous literary projects. These included the formal replies in Latin, *Assertio* and in German *Grund und Ursach*, to the bull *Exsurge Domine*. Luther was very relaxed by now:

> I have not pushed myself forward at all. If I could follow my own inclinations, I would always prefer to crawl back into my little corner. But my opponents have drawn me out again and again by craft and violence in order to acquire credit and honour by attacking me. Now that their game is falling through, my ambition is supposed to be the cause of everything. But, in the second place, even if they were right and I had really set myself up as a teacher, could God not have called and raised me up for this purpose? Do we not read that he usually raised up only *one* prophet from among his people, and never from the upper classes, but generally humble, despised individuals, even common herdsmen. . . . I do not say that I am a prophet. I simply say that they will have to be afraid of this as long as they scorn me and heed themselves. . . . If I am not a prophet I am at least sure of this, that the Word of God is with me, and not with them, for I have the Scriptures on my side while they have only their own teachings. . . . But do I not preach a new doctrine? No. I simply say that Christianity has ceased to exist among those who should have preserved it—the bishops and scholars. . . . I do not repudiate the Church Fathers. But like all men, they, too, have erred at times. Consequently I believe them only in so far as they can prove their teachings from the Scriptures, which have never erred (*Grund und Ursach*).[1]

Other writings continued up to and during the visit to Worms, *The Advent Postil*, *The Exposition of the Magnificat*, further parts of the *Studies in the Psalms*. In spite of public events Luther kept hard at his daily work. But the crisis was increasing. The required three months had run out since his reception of the bull. Luther was formally excommunicated on January 3, 1521. But the support for him was increasing daily in every sphere of society. The affair had reached such proportions that it must inevitably go to the other ultimate sovereign. The spiritual sovereign had spoken. The Emperor too must speak—and the German Estates have their say.

[1] Böhmer, p. 392.

7. Charles V (1500–1558), Emperor from 1519
From a painting by Jan van Orley

8. Luther disguised as 'Junker George'
From a painting by Cranach the Elder, 1521

40. *The Diet of Worms and the Beginning of the Reformation*

THE Diet of Worms cannot be described in detail here. Like so much of the years 1517–21 a great deal of the historical detail is now established, and it presents a fascinating complex of contending influences, both in the purely material and in the ideological and theological sense. It was impossible that the outcome should be a complete 'yes' or a complete 'no' to Luther. The spiritual sovereign was secure on his metaphysical foundations—*securus judicat orbem terrarum*. But for Charles and the Estates politics was the art of the possible. Charles came down against Luther in defence of the traditions of his fathers, and he did his best to jockey the local rulers into underwriting a 'ban' on Luther which would end in the latter's death for heresy in the true medieval fashion. But the support for Luther was already too massive. Civil war was now the risk. And much of Luther's position was sympathetic to the rulers in their dislike of Roman and ecclesiastical interference.

Charles's famous statement after the first session with Luther at Worms is a classic European Catholic document. At first it might seem the merest cliché. But it came from Charles's heart, and it expresses the perennial loyalty to that which has gone before, to tradition, to the Church:

> I am descended from a long line of Christian Emperors of this noble German nation, and of the Catholic Kings of Spain, the Archdukes of Austria, and the Dukes of Burgundy. They were all faithful to the death to the Church of Rome, and they defended the Catholic faith and the honour of God. I have resolved to follow in their steps. A single friar who goes counter to all Christianity for a thousand years must be wrong. Therefore I am resolved to stake my lands, my friends, my body, my blood, my life and my soul. Not only I, but you of this noble German nation, would be forever disgraced if by our negligence not only heresy but the very suspicion of heresy

were to survive. After having heard yesterday the obstinate defence of Luther, I regret that I have so long delayed in proceeding against him and his false teaching. I will have no more to do with him. He may return under his safe-conduct, but without preaching or making any tumult. I will proceed against him as a notorious heretic, and ask you to declare yourselves as you promised me.

Luther was well aware that he was pitting himself against this tradition. His spiritual struggles were at this time, and later, fires of anguish and concern lest he was doing wrong. He knew that he often spoke too sharply, and sometimes apologized for doing so— he did so in one of his speeches at Worms. His enemies' jibes remained in his ears: 'Martin, how can you assume that you are the only one to understand the sense of Scripture? Would you put your judgment above that of so many famous men and claim that you know more than they all?' So asked his accuser Eck (not the same Eck as before) at Worms.

But what alternative could he see? The Pope too was only a man. The evidence against believing that the office was able to confer true Christian authority on the man elected to it seemed to Luther overwhelming. But the anguish of responsibility remained. The man who has rejected authority has to take responsibility. Luther had his scriptural theology to support him; he turned to the Word in Scripture and inwardly to Christ. Prior to the Diet he had made his *Offer and Protest* which restated his position: he would be content to be judged, at a future Council, by Scripture. And this was what he repeated at Worms.

There were two sessions at which Luther appeared before the Emperor. The first was on April 17 at 4.0 in the afternoon. The streets were full and Luther was taken by a back way through a garden to the hall. Luther had with him Dr Jerome Schurff, a canon lawyer of Wittenberg, as his legal adviser. Eck was presiding, Johann von Eck from the court of the Archbishop of Trier, not Luther's old antagonist. After some preliminary remarks he pointed to a great pile of Luther's works and asked him both whether they were his and whether he would recant the heresies in them. Schurff intervened and asked for the titles to be read out. Twenty-five titles were read, and Luther agreed they were his books. He then asked for time to answer the second question. Possibly he was prompted to ask this by his lawyer to gain time to ponder the likely procedure and the general temper. It was agreed that Luther was to have his answer ready the next day.

The following day the meeting was scheduled for 4.0 p.m. but actually started at 6.0, Luther having been sitting in the anteroom until then. The written notes he had made for his speech on this occasion are extant, also the record of a number of eyewitnesses. Luther spoke in Latin and in German; the Spanish Emperor must have been very bored, knowing no Latin and far from fluent in German. Luther began by apologizing for his lack of knowledge of how to address important people, of the proper etiquette, etc. He then turned to the books, and suggested that a distinction should be made between those of his books which were exhortations to a moral life, etc., to which no one had ever taken objection, and on the other hand books against the Roman tyranny, and its defenders. Luther admitted that he might have been too vehement in some of these latter books, but he had been writing in Christ's cause, not his own. The Emperor and his advisers withdrew at this point. On their return Eck pointed out to Luther that he had supported Hus, denying the validity of General Councils, and that his interpretation of Scripture could not be of concern to them. The straight question was put again, would he recant. Luther came out forthrightly with what he had so often said in the last two and a half years, that he must be guided by Scripture and was willing to be convinced either by Scripture or by evident reason, but that he could not bow to the authority of Popes and Councils as superior to Scripture, and he could not act against his conscience. Whether or not he actually said *Hier stand ich, ich can nicht anders*, 'Here I stand, I can do no other', that was certainly the general tenor of his words.

The assembly was hushed whilst the words were being spoken, for in themselves they were a clear avowal of heresy with their rejection of the Church's authority to expound the certain meaning of Scripture. Then there was uproar. A wrangle followed for a few minutes, then the Emperor ended the session. Even some of Luther's enemies seem to have been impressed by his witness. His friends were all pleased. The issue was clear. The Elector Frederick expressed his usual enigmatic approval: 'Doctor Martin has spoken right well in both Latin and German in the presence of the Emperor, the Princes and the Estates. He is far too bold for me.'

Goodwill was subsequently shown on both sides by an attempt at compromise in a series of private meetings, under the presidency of the Archbishop of Trier, with a small group of theologians. But compromise was impossible. *Sola scriptura* was the beginning and end of Luther's position when it came to authority. Apparently there was the usual attempt at bribery and Luther was offered a good rich priory. It was all very friendly. Luther took lunch with the Archbishop one day. Everything was done which could be done to play down the tension. But in the end the Archbishop had to turn to Luther and ask: 'My dear Doctor, what else can we do?' So Luther quoted the advice of Gamaliel: 'If this counsel or this work be of men, it will come to nought. But if it be of God, you cannot overthrow it, unless you may be found fighting against God.' On the evening of this day, Luther wrote a final brief communication to the Emperor and the Estates, assuring them of his loyalty and claiming that he wished only to reform the Church and to have freedom to bear witness to the Word of God. The next day he left, with an imperial safeguard, a guard to protect him to his home.

The Emperor was in a quandary. A variety of factors made it impossible for him to draw up an edict immediately against Luther. The Estates would not have all voted for it. There was the risk of open rebellion. So he waited until the Diet was officially over and the Elector Frederick had returned home. Then, with a rump of electors, and to the delight of Aleander the papal envoy, the so-called 'Edict of Worms' was signed. Luther was given twenty-one days; after that he was to be considered as a convicted heretic, no one was to harbour him, his books were to be destroyed.

Luther had thought it all out many months before. In September 1520 he had written to Conrad Saum, a Wittenberg disciple:

What will happen, I know not, nor am I anxious to know. Certain I am that he who sits in heaven governing all things has foreseen from eternity the beginning, the progress, and the end of this enterprise, which I await. However, the lot may fall, it will not move me, because it will not fall except in accordance with the best will. Be not anxious therefore; your Father knows what things you have need of even before you ask him.

Ioannes Oecolampadius

Huldrijchus Zuinglius

Martinus Bucerus

Caspar Hedio

Martinus Luther

Iustus Jonas.

Philippus Melanchthon

Andreas Osiander

Stephanus agricola

Joannes Brentius

Signatures to the Marburg Convention 1529

Part Five

THE NEW WORLD

41. *Luther and the Universities*

THE universities were in a 'middle' position in relation to the conservative forces in the Church on the one side and those seeking reform on the other. They had a foot in both camps in the way common to many universities throughout European history. On the one hand the universities were 'authorities', and in medieval Catholic civilization this meant a varying degree of control of them by ecclesiastical authority, equally with much influencing of ecclesiastical authority by them. The universities were jealous of their independence, their right to seek truth and to make judgments; nevertheless in the last resort they were themselves actually part of a kind of composite authority (Pope, bishops, Emperor, lesser rulers, universities) and could never act entirely independently of Pope and bishops even though they might seek to limit their power.

The teaching authority in any university inevitably centres on tried methods and a body of knowledge passed on from previous ages. Many of those who teach will be likely to wish that things should stay as they are. So in Luther's day there was in every university a body of men, the great majority of teachers, who regarded themselves as responsible for passing on a tradition of learning and of Christian authority, however much they might sympathize to some extent with colleagues of a more adventurous frame of mind. The solid core remained faithful to one of the received scholastic schools, to the pronouncements of Popes and Councils, and regarded any radical opposition as dangerous and indeed wrong, to be put down by argument, if necessary by force, even death.

On the other hand the universities were then, as now, places where attempts were always being made to solve problems, to push the boundaries of thought further outwards. And they were institutions very jealous of their reputation and always prepared, within some measure, to oppose all other established authorities in the name of truth. In Luther's time the universities were being swept by the humanist movement, a passion for the study of Greek and Hebrew, a belief that in the pre-Christian world were to be found not only the languages which were the key to the Scriptures but principles of thought and conduct which would moderate the somewhat crude prescriptions of contemporary society. They had also taken an important part in the opposition to papal claims. But the intellectual adventure of humanism did not involve a total repudiation of scholasticism so much as a fairly radical reform of it. And the opposition to papal supremacy could be and was carried on with general assumptions about Christian authority.

The young University of Wittenberg was an ideal place for the encouragement both of the intellectual adventure and of opposition to the papacy; here above all, in a very young university, in the heart of Germany, these new elements might move out of the conservative context which held them within bounds elsewhere. After a life of only a decade and a half Wittenberg University had no long tradition. Luther gradually weaned the small theological faculty and eventually the university as a whole to his point of view. Wittenberg did not ponder the consequences of throwing scholasticism, or even the papal supremacy, aside, as the other older foundations must do.

The older foundations, whatever their wishes and tendencies in the sphere of humanistic studies and of their own independence and reputation, were committed generally to the defence of received teaching. Part of their traditional task was to refute error and to bring heresy to the notice of ecclesiastical authority. Froben's editions of Luther's work were soon being examined not only by individual *avant-garde* scholars who rejoiced to read them, and by others who partially agreed and partially disagreed, but also by many others who immediately considered it their sacred duty to refute his works and to promote their official condemnation. John Eck needed pronouncements from the universities and he was very keen that such pronouncements should be made specifically on the Leipzig debate. But the universities were never the mere tools of Luther's enemies. In fact the text of the debate did not seem to them a suitable document, and the universities did not wish to appear simply as the supporters of John Eck. They wished to make a considered judgment on Luther's views.

Louvain and Cologne universities conferred together about Froben's edition of Luther's works (the second edition), and eventually issued separate condemnations of them. This they did, Cologne in October 1519 and Louvain in November. The original initiative seems to have come from Louvain. The list of errors in the Louvain condemnation was later used, almost verbatim in parts, in the papal bull against Luther, *Exsurge Domine*, issued the following year. The Louvain list includes Luther's views on good works, merits of saints, indulgences, the Eucharist, confession, the authority of Councils, original sin. The University made little attempt to discern the root of Luther's theology, his desire to reform general sacramental practice and to return to a more deeply biblical theology. It had simply taken the standard theological formulae and measured individual statements and paragraphs from Luther's work against them in a logical fashion. It was not difficult to show that Luther was out of step. Here was the normal medieval reaction, society repulsing anyone who threatened to disrupt the conventional structure. One of the members of the University who took part in the condemnation by Louvain was the future Adrian VI, an austere man well aware of the disastrous state of the Church, but convinced that Luther's way to reform was wrong.

John Eck had been hoping that Erfurt University or Paris, the Sorbonne, might give a judgment on the Leipzig controversy. As we have seen, Erfurt declined. Paris prevaricated, at first asking too high a fee from Duke George. However, Paris did eventually institute an examination of Luther's writings, and its examination continued right up to the end of 1520; thus they were able to take stock of *The Babylonian Captivity*.

Paris was the senior university, the first university of Christendom. Its authority was held in great awe. All the greater was its authority in that it had opposed, on previous occasions, the supremacy claimed by the Pope and had inclined towards the conciliar doctrine. They could not be suspected of sycophancy. But the conservative scholastic elements at Paris were too strong for anything other than an adverse judgment on Luther. To the modern eye it might seem that the obvious and proper course was discrimination, the making of distinctions between the proposed reforms which could be harmonized with Scripture and tradition and those that could not, also between purpose and method. But the universities seemed to have felt that they must issue some kind of a black and white assessment, argued out in the logical form traditional in the schools. Such a course was death to Luther's theses, marked as they were by their origin in psychological, spiritual and pastoral experience.

The judgment of Paris was made public on the day that Luther entered Worms, but the details did not reach the city till after Luther had left. It was by no means universally pleasing to the papalist party even though Luther's doctrine was entirely condemned point by point. There were two significant omissions. First, there was no reference to the papal supremacy. On this point the French doctors were still not convinced that the Pope's supremacy was a matter of doctrine rather than of convenience or human arrangements. Secondly, there was no reference to Leipzig. Aleander the papal nuncio at Worms was disappointed on the first count, Eck on the latter. It might seem that such small matters were of little importance beside the massive doctrinal condemnation. But in the sphere of practical politics they were important, when added to all the other factors which tended against Rome, and therefore to the support of the very diverse elements gathering round Luther.

The Sorbonne had much more material to work on than Louvain and Cologne—the work of two years during which Luther had been incessantly pouring out material. Its judgment was correspondingly more elaborate. But in essence it was little different, opposing Luther in a more or less scholastic and Nominalist fashion, setting phrases of Luther's beside the received formulae. The result was manifestly inadequate as an assessment of Luther's thought. But this was not a deliberate misrepresentation. It was the result of attention to language in isolation, leading as it sometimes does with logical positivists today, to failure to communicate accurately. There is a failure to discriminate between levels of writing, between different ways of using language and a failure to assess what the writer was truly saying (not what the words 'must mean' according to the critic, but what the writer was trying to say), or to discriminate between a writer's bad grammar, and a doctrine which his writings, taken altogether, are undoubtedly teaching.

The judgment of the doctors of the University of Paris helped to confirm the Roman Curia that they had made a proper judgment of Luther. It also helped to give encouragement to some of Luther's supporters, by its implied agnosticism or antagonism to papal claims.

42. *The First Year*

LUTHER's life between the nailing up of the Ninety-five Theses and the Diet of Worms is crammed with dramatic incident. The intense interest continues in the period immediately following.

Luther left the council chamber at Worms, with the gesture of a victorious medieval knight, throwing up his hands. The victory was by no means obviously his at that stage, but he seems to have sensed that a moral victory was his. He had said all he could, and the phrase attributed to him at that moment, although not fully authenticated, yet has the authentic spirit about it. 'On this I take my stand; I can do no other.' He had satisfied his own daemon and had sensed the sympathy and support for him in the tense atmosphere, an occasion where life (and promotion) and death (or imprisonment) could be in the balance for lesser men as well as for Luther.

The journey back from Worms was also dramatic. The Emperor's herald led the party, for the journey had to be accomplished safely, with a view to Luther's eventual arrest, when the safe-conduct had been fulfilled. But the herald could not prevent public welcome being given to Luther, who was greeted with enthusiasm by many, particularly at Hersfeld where the Abbot invited him to preach in spite of a warning that this was to flout the imperial wish. The journey took them towards Luther's own country and the Thuringian Forest. A detour was made at one point into the forest to enable one night to be spent with Luther's grandmother at Möhra. Here again Luther preached in the morning in the village church. Soon after leaving this village and just before reaching Luther's old school town Eisenach, the party was attacked. Luther realized that this was part of a prearranged plan and whispered to young Amsdorf, fellow-friar from Wittenberg, that the attackers were their friends. Amsdorf affected great anger, and acted very well his part of being unable to do anything against superior forces. Luther was carried off. Amsdorf and the others rode on and expressed themselves so angrily that the imperial members of the party seem to have had no idea at the time that the attack was being made by Luther's friends. The pretence was maintained scrupulously and successfully. Luther was taken for a long but circular ride, all day, and eventually arrived at the Wartburg on the edge of Eisenach where he was imprisoned. He was told to assume the guise of a knight and land-owner, Junker George. He was not allowed out of the building for some few weeks, which usefully enabled him to grow a beard. He was meanwhile instructed in the conduct proper to a knight, and provided with the clothes and accoutrement necessary to this disguise.

Confinement and lack of regular university work, following on the kind of intense activity in which he had been engaged, upset Luther. He suffered attacks of doubts and worry. *Anfechtung*, temptation to despair, illness came on. Constipation got worse; insomnia also. However, writing materials were made available and helped to take him out of his horrors. He was soon in communication with Spalatin, and busy writing a reply to a recent attack on him by Latomus, a professor at Louvain. He headed his letters: 'From the Isle of Patmos', 'From the Wilderness'. A useful summary of his writing at this time occurs in a letter written towards the end of the year to a friend at Strasbourg: 'I have brought out a reply to Catharinus and another to Latomus, and

in German a work on confession, expositions of Psalms 67 and
36, a commentary on the *Magnificat*, and a translation of Melanchthon's reply to the University of Paris. I have had under way a
volume of sermons on the lessons from the epistles and gospels. I
am attacking the Cardinal of Mainz and expounding the ten
lepers.'[1] Soon after this he started on the translation of the New
Testament. The literary spate continued apace for the rest of his
life, and it will be impossible to do more than record some of the
titles, and look at one or two in very brief detail.

Enforced retreat strengthened Luther's faith, though giving
scope for anguish. Private life and public life were now hand in
hand and reacting strongly on each other. It was only the previous
summer that Luther had come out so strongly against the Mass in
its present form, as currently understood, with the emphasis on a
sacrifice offered by a priesthood, a means of grace and merit to
the faithful. Until then, whilst increasingly unhappy about offering Mass, and the idea of it as a ritual means of getting and giving
packages of spiritual power or merit to the living and the dead, he
had not come out in writing in a way which would lead necessarily to changes in the public liturgy in any radical sense.

In the Wartburg no doubt Luther had a chance to ponder on
all these things even more intensively. His thoughts led him
more strongly than ever into his existential personal theology,
and its spiritual and reforming implications. He would not offer
Mass by himself, for whatever form the Mass itself ought to take
—and about this he was not yet clear—he was now quite clear
that it ought not to be offered in isolation as though it was solely
some automatic grace-producing mechanism, an operation proper
to a priest without visible reference to the Church. He requested
that the priest at the Wartburg was not to say Mass daily when no
one was in attendance. Luther's position was not simply a nega-
tion of the old, or a freeing from it; his gradually crystallizing
attitude to public worship, and principally to the Mass, meant
that it was first and last public worship and was not something
that could be properly done in private. In 1522 his pamphlet
arguing against private Masses was published.

[1] Bainton, p. 152.

Luther never became anything like an 'enthusiast' (and the evidence produced by Ronald Knox in his *Enthusiasm* is as worthless as that which he brings forward against Wesley, stray quotations unrelated to any attempt to understand their whole doctrines). He did not believe in a private revelation to himself, or in the arrival of some special dispensation, over and above what is to be expected at all times throughout the life of the Church. He believed in the Gospel and all the articles of the early creeds, and in a covenant between man and God, which had a personal relevance for every man. He had reformulated this relevance in Pauline terms. In many ways the picture remains traditionally Catholic—public liturgy, sacraments, a common life in Christian parishes under an ordained priest or pastor. Luther was no mere brooding individualist. He pined in his loneliness for the Christian communities at Wittenberg, the Priory, the University, the town parish, and his intimate friends.

Luther's following at Wittenberg was solid. Carlstadt, Amsdorf, Melanchthon and most or all of the other lecturers had been convinced in the course of the previous seven years of the rightness of Luther's theology and scriptural exegesis, and following on from it of the necessity of the reforms which he advocated even though they were rejected by Rome. They followed him too when he took his thought further and questioned the authority of the Pope and of Councils as something final to which all Christians must bow. The community of Luther's supporters at Wittenberg in the University, the Priory and the town was big enough and independent enough (with the Elector Frederick always permissive though in a negative sense) and convinced enough to take actions which were the effective beginning of the dissolution of medieval Catholic social and ecclesiastical institutions. Luther had said that vows were a kind of luxury and must not be considered as meritorious. He rejected the supposition that they were like major cogs in the great machine of heavenly reward-building. A man should be free to revoke them. Luther had said secular priests should be free to marry. Very well—they would act on this at Wittenberg and they did. Secular priests at Wittenberg took wives. This was a momentous decision with tremendous psycho-

9 and 10. Luther and his wife, Katherine von Bora (1499–1552)
From paintings by Cranach the Elder, 1525

11. Melanchthon (1497–1560) baptizing
Detail from the Wittenberg Altar, by Cranach the Elder

logical reverberations. The bonds of a millennium, actions at the very heart of society, were left aside.

Luther was horrified to receive at the Wartburg a message from Carlstadt asking his opinion about monks marrying. Luther had recommended marriage for secular priests a year ago. But he had not thought of it for monks. His reaction included a statement that he himself would never be pushed into marriage. However Luther then began to search the Scriptures to work out a reply to the query and he came to the conclusion that there was no solid objection. He wrote his *On Religious Vows*—one of the great dissolvents of the sixteenth century. Luther affirmed that there was no *special* monastic vocation. On the Continent, as in England, monasticism, the biggest single constituent of medieval Christian society, needed only a small impulse for much of it to disintegrate. Carlstadt married before Luther's reply came; he was soon using German for the Mass, and communicating the chalice to the laity. The friar Zwilling, encouraged by Melanchthon, was going along with Carlstadt in the liturgical reforms, from September 1521 onwards. Carlstadt was to become the screwball of the movement later. Towards the end of the year he led an orgy of statue-breaking; later he took to peasants' clothes and work. On November 30, fifteen friars left the Priory, and this was formally ratified by the superiors in January.

Luther made his first flying visit to Wittenberg early in December. He was impelled to this primarily because Spalatin had done nothing about getting three of his recent writings into print—the piece on monastic vows, the piece on private Masses, and a blast against the Archbishop of Mainz for his continuing to issue indulgences (to which the Archbishop eventually sent a craven reply). Luther had sent them down to Spalatin who had found them very explosive and had delayed printing. Luther came in his beard, disguised, and was not recognized by many. He stayed with Amsdorf.

On his return to the Wartburg, Luther decided he would undertake the translation of the New Testament; he considered the need for it was urgent now that German was being used in the churches at Wittenberg. He said he would translate the New

Testament by Easter. He had Erasmus's text delivered to him and set to work. It was done by the time he set out to take up residence again at Wittenberg, early in March. Its verbal felicity and its accuracy are a permanent witness to the calibre of Luther's religion, to the thoroughness of his studies in the previous fifteen years, and to the power of his intellect. The translation of the Bible is at any time a matter of considerable complication, with the necessity in the New Testament of allowing for both Hebrew and Greek nuance, of recognizing very frequent references to the Old Testament and in general to the Judaic world, with the need always to bear in mind the commentaries of the Fathers and the theology which had been developed from the Gospel in respect particularly of the creeds. Luther's achievement is the work of a man who has little in common with either the popular Catholic or the popular Protestant view. A depraved revolutionary unable to control his emotions could not have done it. It was the fruit of many years of biblical study and meditation on the meaning of Christian revelation. On the other hand it was not the work of one who was overthrowing the great credal traditions; these traditions were the basis on which Luther made good sense out of a text often difficult on the face of it. He was building a reformed Church, not a new Church.

By Easter 1522 the town council was getting desperate. The priests who had left the priory were, it seems, not fitting too easily into the local society at Wittenberg, and probably found it difficult to adapt themselves to the looser discipline of society after the narrower rule of their religious order. After the statue-breaking riot the Elector had been making requests that they should go slower. Zwilling was asked not to celebrate Mass wearing his beret with a feather in it. He left the town for a parish, as Carlstadt was also to do shortly after. The town council, in defiance of the Elector, invited Luther to return. There was now a thirst for general revision and re-ordering and there was no one to lead the movement and control it. So Luther's return was not entirely unwelcome to the Elector in spite of an attempt by him to stop it.

At first at Wittenberg it was not too difficult to find and hold a middle course. Luther had already been advising from afar. To

Link, the provincial superior of the Augustinians, he had suggested that friars should be allowed to depart or to remain as they liked. It was following on this advice that the formal decision was taken to disband the priory. The Elector was very frightened at Luther's threatened return to permanent residence. On this subject Dr Martin wrote him a somewhat imperious letter, with a touch of that apocalyptic arrogance which Frederick never seems to have taken ill—but then he never did take anything ill, policy and temperament seeming to be permanently congealed like heavy putty ever slowly shifting in response to pressures. Frederick was the remarkable and indispensable context of Luther.

> I would have you know that I come to Wittenberg with a higher protection than that of Your Grace. I do not ask you to protect me. I will protect you more than you will protect me. . . . As a prince you should obey the Emperor and offer no resistance. No one should use force except the one who is ordained to use it. Otherwise there is rebellion against God. But I hope you will not act as my accuser. If you leave the door open, that is enough. If they try to make you do more than that, I shall then tell you what to do. If Your Grace had eyes, you would see the glory of God.[2]

On March 6, 1522 Luther went up again into the pulpit in the town church from which he had been absent for about a year. His task, ironically, was to steady the firebrands, to ask them to remember the 'simple souls':

> . . . dear friends, a man must not insist on his rights, but must see what is useful and helpful to his brother. . . . I would not have gone as far as you have done if I had been there. What you did was good, but you have gone too fast, for there are brothers and sisters on the other side who belong to us, and must still be won. . . . Faith never yields, but love is guided according to how our neighbours can grasp or follow it. There are some who can run, others must walk, and still others who can hardly creep. Therefore we must not look on our own, but on our brother's powers, so that he that is weak in faith . . . may not be destroyed. . . . Let us therefore throw ourselves at one another's feet, join hands and help one another. . . .

[2] Bainton, p. 164.

I will do my part, for I love you even as I love my own soul. . . .
We must first win the hearts of the people. And that is done when
I teach only the Word of God, preach only the Word of God, for
if you win the heart, you win the whole man.[3]

Less than a year after Luther's defence of his position before the
Emperor at Worms he was lecturing his followers on the need to
curb their enthusiasm.

43. 1521–1546: Loosening and Binding

THE Diet of Worms had shown support for Luther to be of
such wide extent that it would be very difficult for the Emperor or the Pope to remove or destroy him without a risk that
this would rouse violent opposition from which neither had anything to gain. The risk was not taken. For seven months no opportunity was given. The thick walls of the Wartburg protected
'Junker George', his true identity unknown to his 'gaolers' and
servants. For many months no one amongst the general public
knew whether Luther was alive or not. Albrecht Dürer noted in
his diary: 'I don't know whether he is alive or has been murdered,
but in any case he has suffered for the Christian truth. . . . O God,
if Luther is dead, who is going to explain the Gospel to us?'[1]
Dürer was an old man by then, and such a comment is a witness
to Luther's influence over a highly educated man who had only
met him once or twice.

Perhaps the trails of the messengers taking communications to
and from Spalatin and Luther's university friends at Wittenberg
could have been followed by the servants of an Emperor or a
Pope determined to dispatch Luther, and perhaps an opportunity
found of doing the deed. But no such attempt seems to have been
made or intended. Even so, Luther's first sortie into Wittenberg
early in December, seven months after Worms, was a journey,
and then a day and a night at his *alma mater*, of great excitement.
Pope and Emperor had banned him. If their law still ran he would

[3] Rupp, R.G., pp. 348–9.   [1] Bainton, p. 140.

have been apprehended, even though his beard and unusual appearance as a knight made recognition difficult.

Luther's flying visit inspired the town to send him their formal invitation to return to permanent residence. He was back in the town in March 1522, less than a year since he had left it for Worms. This time he came as himself though in layman's clothes. The town was openly defying the civil and ecclesiastical overlords, including the Elector, who with his usual prudence wished Luther not to return. This defiance was not, however, something entirely new. There was a tradition of local independence. The local Electors were never simply the lackeys of the Emperors—they were indeed precisely his electors. The local Dukes, too, still lived in a tradition of local authority, more important often than the authority of the Emperor himself. The towns themselves were of an independent mind; the invitation to Luther was sent knowingly in opposition to the Elector's wishes, although Luther himself informed the Elector before his arrival.

The historian can see a new era beginning with the actions of the Wittenberg town council. He can see a decisive stage in the disruption of the unity of Ecclesia and Empire. But the citizens of Wittenberg thought of no such thing; they were intent on justifying their famous local scholar and priest, the Augustinian Martin Luther, and putting into practice those reforms which he had recommended to them—and of continuing a tradition of opposition to Roman (Italian) authority, and indeed to imperial authority. This was the enabling context of their invitation. The immediate cause was their very urgent practical need of Luther's presence to control and direct the movements which his words had inspired.

Not Luther himself, but his fellow friars at Wittenberg, had been the first to take practical steps to act on his conclusions, soon after his confinement in the Wartburg. Priests became convinced that they might marry—it was not difficult to see that this was to be preferred to the widespread concubinage which was also expensive in terms of special fees paid to ecclesiastical authority. The populace had begun to look for a simplification of worship, and to ask for more part in it. The bonds of established institutions were being loosed. Religion was at the heart of these institutions, and a conviction of the need for specifically religious change was fundamentally disruptive of existing social forms.

From now on Luther was occupied with upholding the reform that he had initiated and opposing those who were taking it beyond what he approved. But from now on also his personal authority and advice was looked to over the whole sphere of State and society. His own personal status changed only from 'university man and friar' to 'university man and (after 1525) family man'; but his moral and public authority became almost universal in its range in local society and in the minds of many people throughout northern Europe.

The Peasants' Revolt in 1525 was stimulated at least to some extent by Luther's own personal revolt from Rome. The traditional sign of a revolting peasantry, a *Bundschuh*, a clog, had been painted on the door of the town hall at Worms one night during the Diet, and elsewhere in the town. Luther felt sufficiently implicated, and sufficiently much of an authority whose opinion was expected to be made known, to feel obliged to give his views on the Peasants' Revolt. Other similar occasions arose. But the primary significance of Luther's life remained religious. It was an acting out of the conclusions to which he had come in the previous ten years; first a purely theological conclusion about men and women, and their relationship with God according to the Christian Gospel, secondly a conclusion about the nature of the Church as something more mysterious than the single juridical unit of a human society, something which he came to believe could not be reconciled with the teaching and practice of the Catholic papal tradition.

At two Imperial Diets in Nuremberg, in 1523 and 1524, and at a further Diet at Speyer in 1526 a significant proportion of the Electors and the Estates, presenting a new power block, showed the Emperor and the papal representatives that Luther's initiative had corresponded to a widespread anti-clerical and more specifically anti-Italian mood amongst the local rulers. This in its turn was supported by a generalized discontent with political and ecclesiastical authority, which came to a specially angry head, as it had done several times in the previous century, amongst those deriving their living directly from the land, the peasants. They were able to see that their masters were taking for themselves more or less lavish rewards in the form of food, clothes, buildings, other possessions, and freedom from work. A tradition of partial self-government in the towns and villages provided an incentive to the peasants to improve their own position. Luther's revulsion, at a spiritual and psychological level, from the ancient papal and imperial tradition became an effective symbol of the mood of an important part of the German people.

Luther himself had hardly understood a great deal of this. He had no political experience at all. When set beside his intense religious convictions, this lack of political experience notably unfitted him to make judgments about public policy. The result was an apparent veering about from one policy to another, and the predication of diabolical inspiration first about one policy then about another. The princes were abjured to understand that a rising of the peasants would be a just retribution for their godless and unjust behaviour towards their subjects and that no victory in the field would set them right before God. Then, later, when Luther saw that the rising of the peasants was growing to the extent of overthrowing the whole fabric of society, he turned to the practical principle governing decisions at a political level—the civil authority must always be respected. Savage statements were then issued against the peasants on account of the indiscriminate violence to which they turned in their own cause. The princes were now abjured to uphold civil authority at all costs and to let the blood of the peasants run, and to treat them as devils incarnate.

There is no contradiction in principle inherent in Luther's two statements. Both statements were true and justified on their own principles, and the principles did not conflict with each other: (1) Princes should look to their responsibilities and duties. (2) Peasants should respect established authority. But if such statements are made in public, and are spoken with the kind of enthusiasm and gravity which Luther could command and are also given the impact and urgency which all human affairs seemed to him, under God, to have, then inevitably they will tend to incite some of the people concerned to disastrous action. General statements are commonly mistaken for short term directives if given sufficient publicity. Somebody will squeeze from them a licence for some particular action. Any politician of experience could have told Luther that to reprimand the princes in public was to effect a certain undermining of their public authority and therefore to help towards lifting the lid a little further from the stewpot of violence which was brewing amongst the peasants. His subsequent brutal anti-peasant statement displayed political inexperience and a ham-handed thoughtlessness in using what amounted to private language for public policy.

The position was ironical and complex. Luther had always stood firmly on the side of public authority in the past; his angry protests to Rome, and his sometimes very straight letters to rulers never called in question the exercise of their authority as such. In particular cases within his own monastic order, and in the affair at Erfurt in 1509 he had been on the side of established authority. Luther was now speaking as the prophet, giving what seemed to him the Christian view of a matter, leaving the consequences out of the reckoning. But prophets can seldom duplicate the office of statesman, or provide the correct practical judgment.

The princes were delighted to have Luther's support. His piece against the peasants was penned when the princes were first opposing the peasants who had had preliminary successes with their primitive weapons. It was actually published however a few weeks later when the princes were already victorious and it did nothing so much as to encourage the princes to take massive vengeance and to indulge in what amounted to a blood bath. Tens of thousands of peasants were killed.

The disastrous effect of Luther's words embittered him to some extent; his anger and impatience increased as everything he touched seemed to be bedevilled—and so also his anguish and despair. He had followed his conscience, he had followed principles worked out in the sweat of intellectual labour. He had not flinched from the limelight, little though he wanted it. He had accepted responsibility for leading and trying to control the revolution which his words had unleashed. And where had it all led? Apparently to considerable chaos in almost every field.

In another sense, however, the results would hardly seem to warrant disappointment. The revolution had visibly freed men and women from what seemed to him gross perversions of Christian truth, it had given them the chance to hear the Word of God in Scripture, and to take part in a worship which they could understand. And all this had been in some measure underwritten by local civil authority and condoned or connived in by central political authority; it had become established in quasi-permanent institutions. Wittenberg University and Wittenberg town were changed places. Even ecclesiastical authority had very soon begun to treat Luther with respect, even to express sorrow for issuing indulgences as did the Archbishop of Mainz in an astonishing (whether sincere or not) apologetic letter in December 1521 in answer to a bitter complaint of Luther's written from the Wartburg, threatening to denounce him publicly. All of this gave Luther some joy.

But in 1525 war overshadowed everything for a while. And Luther had already been engulfed by another problem, that of the *schwärmerei* or sectaries who had been taking his religious initiatives to theological and practical extremes, beyond anything he could agree to. Later with Zwingli and his followers from Switzerland, controversy centred on the Eucharist, the nature of Christ's presence and the interpretation of the words of institution as they are sometimes called. *Hoc est corpus meum*, wrote Luther in big letters in chalk on the table at Marburg, taking his stand on these words in the Vulgate, and in so doing aligning himself very closely with Catholic tradition. He had wished only to disown the particular philosophical explanation of these words offered by the medieval-Aristotelian theory of transubstantiation. Zwingli would omit the *est* (with some justification in relation to the probable original Hebraic or Aramaic construction), enabling him to understand the verb *significat*—and to treat the Mass as a memorial only.

But farther to the left there began to erupt soon after Worms a whole world of subjective religious enthusiasm, of Anabaptists and of all kinds of illuminism, a world which had come into sight from time to time throughout the history of western Christianity, and had always been disowned, usually violently put down by Roman authority. In the east of Europe and in Russia, a personal and more 'subjective' spiritual approach, at the same time deeply theological, had been well integrated with the religious culture of the Orthodox Churches. People were expected to be in some sense holy, possessed by the divine Spirit; this conception was a practical expectation rather than an exception. But in the west it was always suspect—and eventually led either to denunciation, or to canonization. The mania for finding an institutional and logical place for every religious manifestation was one of the powerful predisposing causes of the revolt which was sparked off by Luther's initiative.

The sectaries were able to arise more easily once ecclesiastical authority had been successfully repudiated. They became the most bitter of the thorns in Luther's flesh, clear results of his own repudiation of existing institutional authority, and they led him to his most violent attitudes, including agreement with the death penalty for such heretics as the Anabaptists. Luther would argue that they were undermining the whole of society and must be prevented, just as the medieval State argued (and Thomas More in *Utopia*—though it was probably not his own view). In 1527 Luther had his worst drawn-out period of *Anfechtung* after the blood-letting of the Peasants' War, and the increase in the sectaries. 1526 was the worst year at Wittenberg University for new enrolments and Luther was not to know that it would improve very greatly again; in 1526 Catholic support had been withdrawn from students going there, and the Protestants were not yet sufficiently numerous to support many entrants.

Luther's story is less and less concerned with Catholic authority as the reform takes root more and more widely. His concern was always fundamentally pastoral, based on an exegesis of Scripture; he is increasingly concerned with the general problem of bringing Christ to all people in the context of a reformed theology, of the parish and the family. Arrangements were made in co-operation with civil authority for the visitation of the parishes. As his success became more palpable, the agitation for a General Council of the Church became more intense among the uncommitted rulers, and among his own followers. Luther himself was less interested. He believed he was reforming the Church, and remained convinced that Rome, the papacy and the Roman Curia, would eventually wither away or else would remain as the permanent challenge of Antichrist. His concern, therefore, was simply to spread the reform. He himself, with the Edict of Worms and the bull of excommunication unrescinded, was never in a position to take a leading part in negotiation with Rome, and was never sanguine about the possibility of agreement.

Negotiations proceeded intermittently, Melanchthon, Luther's aide, always ready to seek unity, Contarini and Carafa notable on the Catholic side. But they became less and less a part of Luther's own story. To the historian it seems that Luther had a more clear-sighted view of things in believing no agreement to be at all likely at that time. However, he did not disown his followers whenever they set to work, with formulas to which Luther could agree, to try to find some agreement with the papalists. The disagreement goes back to Luther's original theological insights which led him to build on an exegesis of St Paul an existential theology of personal faith through Scripture, of grace which alone, through the Word (which is Scripture and Christ), brings justification, salvation, sanctification to the penitent, always sinning, always forgiven. This dynamic theology now became normative, the standard by which everyday practice, the reform of liturgy and Christian life in the Church, was judged. As such it became directly antagonistic to the Catholic tradition which in practice gave juridical and institutional factors almost a monopoly, and encouraged the people to see the sacraments and the Mass in terms not so much of God's gift, a mystery, as in terms of merit to be earned, and therefore of quasi-magic rituals. Catholic authority had never given serious and unprejudiced attention to Luther's biblical theology. Instead of a dialogue between the two, contradiction and enmity ensued. The many and various discussions about the relative authority of Scripture and of tradition which had occupied so many theologians in the previous century was

raised up to the status of a symbol of the whole Catholic/Protest-
ant disagreement. Catholics were commonly supposed to hold to
the authority of both in some kind of equality. Protestants were
supposed to hold simply to Scripture.[2] Luther's theological insights
were not concerned with this discussion in the first place. It was
the rejection of his criticisms of abuses which led to the raising of
the issue in his regard and to its eventual emergence as the supposedly classic difference between Catholicism and Lutheranism.

At the deepest level the common factors which we observed in
earlier chapters remained. Compromise formulas about the sacraments and other institutional factors which Melanchthon and
others attempted to manipulate sprang from this enabling context.
That a man of such intellectual integrity, and of such conviction
on the doctrine of papal authority as Cajetan, already so committed personally in opposition to Luther, could suggest such a
compromise (see p. 224) is a powerful witness to the underlying
unity. History is today showing that the essential Lutheran insights and expositions are ultimately able to be integrated into the
Catholic tradition; the Catholic tradition is sufficiently flexible to
be able to be modified and enlivened by Lutheran theology.

Luther's story ends with his death (1546) shortly after the opening of the Council of Trent (1545), convened to decide what
should be done about a heresy supported now by schismatic
institutions. The Council concerned itself not simply with
strengthening traditional Catholic doctrine though it did do this,
but also with a very careful and prolonged examination of
Luther's theology of justification. It was always quite possible that
Luther and his followers would be asked to go to Trent. Luther
would hardly have gone, but some of the others probably would
have done. However, they were not asked. Luther himself had
had little direct contact with Roman authorities for many years.
But the roots of his position lay deep in Catholic tradition and his
quarrel with it was working within the Catholic body to modify

---

[2] See *Holy Writ or Holy Church* by George Tavard (Burns and Oates, 1959) for a very
useful guide to the fifteenth-century sources and to the controversy as it developed prior
to Luther's work, in Luther and his disciples, in his opponents, at the Council of Trent,
and in the Elizabethans in England—a work of fascinating detail closely relevant to
present-day discussions.

that body itself, as happened at Trent, and as continued increasingly to occur during the following four centuries and more.

The inverse was also true; the sectaries were right to recognize this. In some ways Luther was as rigid as the Catholic tradition which he rejected and little room was finally left in the Lutheran tradition for that 'individualism' with which a superficial historical view sometimes equates it. The new Lutheran Church had a sacramental and liturgical life and a careful intellectual theology. The theology owed much to the biblical research and interpretation of Erasmus whose work was accomplished within the Catholic tradition. Luther's distinctive Pauline and Augustinian theology kept strong links with Catholicism.

Luther himself was denied any understanding of the extent to which what seemed to him to be at the heart of the Roman tradition was not destined to remain always so. But this would not have been important to him in any case. By the end of his life Lutheran and Protestant institutions had so crystallized his theological insights that compromise with the ancient traditions could not be thought of. Luther saw emerging a new kind of family life, a new kind of parish, a new tradition of preaching and of sacrament, a new relationship between Church and State, a more 'spiritual' Church, a more clearly recognized secular authority. All these things grew and spread in the course of twenty-five years so greatly that the old imperial-papal structures could hardly integrate them into itself whatever effort of unification was made. The efforts made by Contarini and Carafa and others were overruled by the Roman Curia before they had been fully deployed. The Emperor would never have underwritten them in any case. The Council of Trent opened with a determination on the part of ecclesiastical authority to retrench. This retrenchment, in many ways a tragic seal on division, included intellectual work of a high calibre which provided a possible basis for the *rapprochement* of four centuries later, in the middle decades of the present century.

Luther's life was a complication of many factors in the years 1517–21. After Worms it became even more so, as the public aspect became increasingly important, but the pace was no longer quite so intense. In fact the whole period from the Diet of Worms till the Council of Trent has about it the indeterminacy of an 'interim' period. And this is not exclusively an invention of the historian looking down on events with his super-century eye. A great number of individuals at the time were thinking that there could be no assurance of what was what until a full Council of the Church had been held and the matters at issue thoroughly thrashed out there. There was a sense in which ecclesiastical law seemed to be suspended. The papal, and local episcopal, authority had been flouted successfully. Priests and laity were doing things which the Pope and bishops forbad. They were doing them not only with impunity, but with the connivance, sometimes the open encouragement, of the civil authority. And eventually ecclesiastical authority began to bargain, to offer terms, and this on matters which previously had led to censure and excommunication. There was no point in repeating such measures in respect of those priests who, having perhaps left their monastery and probably married, were celebrating reformed liturgies in the churches, teaching a new theology, encouraging people to read the Bible. Sometimes a whole town would be taken up with these new ways, even whole regions, many villages, so that the 'Church' itself seemed to be a different thing. Who could tell what was right and what was wrong?

Reform had been talked of so much. Now it had come. So there was a general feeling of the 'provisional', of surprise and bewilderment at this brave new world. Luther was no doubt condemned, but condemnation no longer seemed to have practical consequences. Even some of the most rigidly orthodox, with their usual prudence, thought it would be as well not to commit themselves, to wait and see what a Council of the Church would make of it all. No one could see what Cajetan or one of the other two Cs might arrange. Astonishing changes were smiled on. After Luther had married, the Archbishop of Mainz sent his wife a present of twenty guldens as a contribution towards the household budget. People recognized that Luther was no mere runaway friar, but an intensely serious and powerful reformer. The manner and timing of his marriage in 1525 was not such as to permit an honest man to say that the motive was to escape from his vow of celibacy, for the simple purpose of giving rein to the sexual impulse; he had been free of ecclesiastical authority for four and a half years.

Perhaps the most notable thing about Luther's marriage was the ease with which it became part of his life. Wife and children did not seem to slow up his work. On the other hand they were not simply subordinated. The marriage happened in the most casual of ways. Luther had the task of settling many ex-nuns, marrying them off where he could. There was some difficulty about Katherine von Bora, her ideas and the ideas of Luther and his advisers not seeming able to coincide. So it came into Luther's head to solve the difficulty by marrying her himself. The wedding was a quiet affair, organized rather swiftly. Luther, like Wesley, probably knew that there would be those amongst his followers who would try to dissuade their leader from coming off his pedestal. But in the event Luther's marriage and family life swiftly became an integral part of his achievement, showing as in a model what the vocation of marriage could mean.

Luther remained the storm centre. Rome relaxed to some extent, once she was seen to be beaten by public opinion and in effect by *force majeure* on the essential issue. But the schwärmerei, the left-wing religious revolutionaries, added whatever Rome lacked in offence. They were soon calling Luther 'Doctor Pussyfoot' and 'Mr Easychair' for being so moderate, little better than a Catholic. Luther worked out his solutions to many problems perforce, compelled to do so by enemies accusing him from both sides.

Once Luther had married Katie von Bora in 1525 nothing outstanding happened in his own personal life. Children came. He remained at Wittenberg, Professor of Scripture in the University, lecturing, teaching, preaching—the great authority on whose every word many hung. With his growing family, and a largely open house, students in and out all the time, he became something of a legend. People copied down his every word, and the fabulous Table Talk volumes emerged. As his way of life became established he became more relaxed and jollier; and his criticisms became even less restrained than before. He grew fatter, until he was very large; he drank much and boasted of it; two characteristics being almost disconcertingly common in Catholic tradition.

44. *Luther and the Papacy, 1521 – 1546*

A PARTY which is making innovations always has the advantage in momentum over the established parties, once its first impulse has been successful. The established parties include numerous different interests. They are not prepared for making the defence now demanded of them. The innovating party is more or less single-minded, spurred on by success, and able to attack without much delay. Thus it was that Luther and his followers were able to make very rapid strides in the twenty-five years following the Diet of Worms, and the opposing forces, represented by the Pope and his advisers, the bishops, the Emperor and other Catholic rulers, found it impossible to take any single concerted action. The innovators had not been defeated by the normal means of suppression; they were at large and no routine measures for their defeat were to hand. In particular Elector Frederick was not prepared to lend his support or connivance either to the Roman excommunication or to the Edict of Worms, to which that Diet's assent was given after he had departed.

Delay became in any case inevitable in 1521 as a result of the illness and death of the Pope, Leo X. His successor, Adrian VI, was elected on January 9, 1522, whilst the tide was flowing fast at Wittenberg, and Luther had already started on his translation of the Bible at the Wartburg. Adrian has a reputation for having been a reforming Pope on account of the famous instruction which he sent by Chieregati to the First Diet of Nuremberg in November 1522 in which he publicly admitted that the sins of the Curia and the clergy were largely responsible for the present troubles in the Church and promised to grapple with the disease. Adrian, however, was no friend of Luther, and had been a member of the committee responsible for the condemnation of Luther's

12. John Tetzel
From an engraving by Bruhl

13. Zwingli
From a painting by Hans Asper

Gottes wort
bleibt ewig.

Biblia/das ift/die
gantze Heilige Sch=
rifft Deudsch.

Mart. Luth.

Wittemberg.

Begnadet mit Kür=
furstlicher zu Sachsen
freiheit.

Gedruckt durch Hans Lufft.

M. D. XXXIIII.

Die erste Epistel Sanct
Pauli/ An die Corinthern.

I.

Aulus beruffen zum Apo
ftel Jhefu Chrifti/durch den willen
Gottes/vnd Bruder Softhenes.
Der Gemeine Gottes zu Corinthen/
den geheiligten jnn Chrifto Jhefu/
den beruffenen Heiligen/ fampt allen
denen/ die anruffen den namen vnfers
HERRN Jhefu Chrifti/an allen jren
vnd vnfern örtern.
    Gnade fey mit euch vnd fride/von
Gott vnferm Vater/ vnd dem HErrn
Jhefu Chrifto.
    Jch dancke meinem Gott alle zeit
ewer halben/ fur die gnade Gottes/die euch gegeben ift jnn Chrifto
Jhefu/das jr feid durch jn an allen ftucken reich gemacht/ an aller le=
re/vnd jnn aller erkentnis/wie denn die predigt von Chrifto jnn euch
kreftig worden ift/alfo/das jr keinen mangel habt an jrgent einer ga=
ben/vnd wartet nur auff die offenbarung vnfers HErrn Jhefu Chri=
fti/welcher auch wird euch feft behalten bis ans ende/das jr vnftreff=
lich feid auff den tag vnfers HErrn Jhefu Chrifti. Denn Gott ift
trew/durch welchen jr beruffen feid/zur ᵃgemeinfchafft feines Sons
Jhefu Chrifti vnfers Herrn.
    Jch ermane euch aber/lieben Brüder/durch den namen vnfers
HErrn Jhefu Chrifti/das jr alzumal einerley rede furet/vñ laffet nicht
                                                                    fpaltung

14, 15 and 16. Title-page, page showing the opening of the First Epistle of St. Paul to the Corinthians, and illustration showing the crossing of the Red Sea, from the First Edition of Luther's translation of the Bible, 1534

writings issued by Louvain University. Adrian was one of the intellectual popes, something of an ascetic and a scholar. An eye-witness of his entry into Rome wrote: 'I could have sworn he was a Frate' (a member of the Brethren of the Common Life, an order following the individualist *devotio moderna*).[1] He intended to re-form the Curia, above all financially, by stopping the sale of offices. But finance lay far too deeply involved with everything else, and was perhaps the last thing to be amenable to drastic action. As a foreigner Adrian found it impossible to act—the Curia, in effect, would not obey him; reform means new laws carefully drafted, edicts, commands, all properly binding and valid, and the means to have them put into effect with sanctions. Adrian could not find the men to do the job. His attempt at reform was no more welcome in Germany. On the one hand he was known as an enemy of Luther; on the other the conservatives did not find his austere spirit to their liking. Chieregati's speech elicited little but jeers. The expression of sincere intentions was perhaps rather worse than useless if it could not be followed up.

Luther had appealed several times to a future Council, a free Council in German Lands, against the Roman decisions. Ironic-ally a Council of the Church in the traditional sense was the one means which the conservatives had at their disposal for a single concerted action, and they were terrified to embark on it. When a Council did finally come Luther no longer had any interest in its authority, for large areas were able by then to boast established Lutheran Christian communities, hundreds of parishes loosely joined together as a reformed Church. Luther did, however, think a Council would be valuable for the rest of the Church. The Council, when it came, established the massive counter-action of the Church, eventually to be known as the Counter-Reformation.

Adrian died, having achieved nothing. Clement VII followed him. Throughout his reign he was convinced of the dangers inherent in the calling of a Council, fearing that Catholic authority would be compromised by it. With every meeting of a lesser kind, whether inspired imperially, papally, or locally, Luther and his disciples were able to count on more and more widespread

[1] Jedin, p. 206.

support; with every month they were more and more sure of their own ground as both the literature and practical experience of the Reform rapidly grew. The Diet of Augsburg in 1530 was the outstanding public event of Clement's reign in regard to Luther and Germany. Its result was to enable the Lutherans to state their case more cogently, and to drive the Catholics into making offers of compromise solutions only to find that the Lutherans were not willing to consider them. The demand by Catholic authority for recognition of episcopal jurisdiction by the Lutherans was dropped during the Diet, and many innovations were to be tolerated, in the compromises offered. Married priests and communion in both kinds were not rejected. But the Canon of the Mass was to be restored, and sequestrated monastic property was to be given back. No fresh innovations were to be made.

These offers were obviously incompatible with the existing requirements of Luther and his followers; the ban on further progress, above all, was not acceptable. As a basis for discussion at the Diet, Melanchthon had drawn up the document which eventually became known as the *Confessio Augustana*. It was presented by him as a conciliatory document in that it emphasized, to start with, what was held in common between the traditionalists and the innovators. Luther was not sanguine from the start but was prepared for Melanchthon to do his best: 'I have read the apology of M. Philip. It pleases me very well, and I do not know of anything that I want to improve or change in it, and it would not be proper since I cannot tread so quietly and gently. May Christ our Lord help it to bear much and great fruit, as we hope and pray. Amen.'[2]

Campeggio, the papal legate, was on the whole more realistic, like Luther, about the unbridgeable nature of the gap which divided Catholic and what we may now call Protestant. It became obvious at the start of the Diet when there was a public procession of the Blessed Sacrament. Spalatin, who was there with Elector John Frederick, son and successor of Frederick the Wise who had died in 1525, wrote in defence of his refusal to attend the procession: 'The Sacrament was not instituted to be worshipped like

[2] Schwiebert, p. 723.

the brazen serpent of the Jews. We are here to confess the truth and not confirm abuse.'[3]

Three months after his note approving Melanchthon's document Luther had hardened:

> In short I am thoroughly displeased with this negotiation concerning union in doctrine, since such a thing is utterly impossible, except the Pope wishes to put away his power. It was enough to give account of our faith and to ask for peace. Why do we hope to convert them to the truth? We have come, to hear whether or not they will assent to our Confession, and they be free to remain where they are. And we ask whether they reject our side, or acknowledge it as right. If they reject it, of what use is it to try to enter into harmony with enemies? If they acknowledge it as right, why should we retain the old abuses? And since it is certain that our side will be condemned by them, as they are not repenting, and are striving to retain their side, why do they not see through the matter and recognize that all their concessions are a lie?

Thus far had things gone in nine years. Luther could speak of the uselessness of negotiating with Rome, or with any of those in communion with her. The eventual outcome of the Diet was an urgent request from the Emperor to the Pope for a Council, and Clement's official assent, but practical refusal, to implement the decision. On Luther's side Melanchthon wrote an addition to the *Confessio Augustana*, which was to become one of the classic texts of Protestantism.

Lutheranism was now openly supported for all to see by the Margrave of Brandenburg, by Philip of Hesse and by Luther's own ruler, the Elector John Frederick. His was now a public movement with its own documents, its own supporting rulers and its own theologians—and, as we shall see, its parishes, rapidly undergoing reorganization. In spite of the disaster of the Peasants' War it was also a popular movement embodying German traditions of self-government with their leaning towards some form of independence. It was now virtually recognized that religious matters were going to be settled by the local ruler who would tolerate or support either traditional Catholic practice or reformed practice as he wished. Your religion would depend on where you lived. *Cuius*

[3] Schwiebert, p. 725.

regio, eius religio. This principle was given formal sanction at the Diet of Speyer in 1526. Its existence became a political force when a league of Protestant princes and towns, the League of Schmalk-alden, was founded in February 1531.

There was a revealing epilogue to the Diet of Augsburg. The Pope, still determined to avoid a Council if he possibly could, turned to Cajetan to draw up a memorandum of possible con-cessions. This went further than before. Cajetan recommended the acceptance of married priests as in the Greek Church, and communion in both kinds. He also suggested that there need be no formal profession of faith from those who had followed Luther, only a statement that they believed in all that the Church believed. Finally there should be relaxation in regard to the legalistic approach to the sacraments. The commandments of the Church about the reception of the sacraments, and about keeping feast and fast days, should no longer bind under grave sin. The canonist Accolti was so shocked that he warned the Pope that he might endanger his own position, running the risk of deposition by a Council as a disturber of ecclesiastical discipline.[4] Needless to say Cajetan's memorandum was relegated to the Roman archives, a monument to inertia.

Pope Clement died in 1534 and was followed by Paul III, a Farnese, who was determined from the start of his reign to have a Council of the Church. He was an intelligent and energetic man and it is a measure of the difficulty of bringing such a thing to pass that it took him eleven years to convoke and open a Council. The Curia and international politics both erected endless barriers. Much of his efforts in this direction have little direct relevance to Luther's life. In 1536 Luther invited Paul III's papal nuncio to dinner. The Pope had sent him to Wittenberg to see whether the way could be prepared for a Council. The nuncio was shocked and angered by Luther's patronizing comment: 'Our group does not need a Council, for we already have the firm Gospel teaching and order

4 Jedin, p. 274. On the following page Jedin implies his own disapproval: 'It was impossible to go further in an endeavour to facilitate their return to the Church: the uttermost limit of what was possible had been reached, it may even have been crossed'. Cajetan, however, had no sense of having 'crossed' a limit. And Luther of course did not think in terms of having left the Church.

of service; but Christendom needs it, so that the part which is still held captive may discover error and truth'.[5]

But the general desire for a Council in Germany itself was the cause of meetings there which involved Luther. One of the more important was the meeting at Schmalkalden in 1537 where the Elector summoned a number of rulers and theologians to discuss a definition of the Protestant position, so that they should be prepared to give a coherent and united witness if and when a Council was summoned. Luther prepared the Schmalkalden Articles for it; the important point in them was a complete denial of the Pope as head of the Church by divine right, and an assertion that he was only Bishop of Rome. Luther fell ill, and Melanchthon took the lead and the Articles were somewhat modified. But the statement remained radical, and there was with it a refusal to have anything to do with a Council as Paul III was preparing it, for he was preparing it in Mantua, not in Germany, and the extent to which a German would be able to call it a 'free' Council was in much doubt. The meeting at Schmalkalden marked a stage in the public cohesion of the general anti-Roman, anti-Italian feeling amongst both rulers and people, on the one hand, and Lutheran, theological, anti-papal convictions on the other. Luther's theology and his practical reforms now had the complete protection of political rulers. The Lutheran *landeskirchen* are no longer just the expression of a revolutionary theology but component parts of Protestant political bodies. The final failure of any possible reconciliation was due not to the theologians but to the politicians during this meeting.

The continued progress of Protestantism along with the absence of a Council led to independent conciliatory moves being made within Germany. The Catholic Duke George of Saxony attempted such moves more than once. In 1539 he tried to arrange a conference at Leipzig at which the Protestants should be free to express themselves as they wished, in the hope that reconciliation might be achieved. A reunion draft was drawn up, of a highly liberal character. The awkward subjects were omitted—the papacy, and the sacrificial nature of the Mass. Duke George himself attended Catholic and Protestant services indifferently. But it all came to nothing.[6]

A strong reforming movement arose at Rome, heir to a century and more of reform proposals, a selection of which we referred to in Chapter 20. This movement was led by the layman Contarini, later Cardinal, and by Carafa, later to be elected pope as Paul IV. Paul III encouraged them, and during the years 1537–39 a great struggle was waged to reform the Roman Curia, a struggle which saw amongst other things the publication of the plan entitled *Consilium de emendanda Ecclesia* signed (amongst others of the reforming committee set up by the Pope) by Carafa, Contarini and the Englishman Cardinal Pole. It came to nothing but it was an important part of a prolonged overture to the opening of the Council of Trent. Clearly the reforming party within the Church would not succeed without a Council of the Church to support it. But the reforming party had shown themselves, with the Pope's support, to be strong. They had much to occupy them. Whilst struggling for radical reforms within the Church's organization they were also engaged in trying to see how to come to terms with the Lutherans. Contarini was himself profoundly convinced of the rightness of Luther's essential theology of justification. He wrote to a friend in 1523: 'No man is justified by his own works; we must have recourse to God's grace which we receive through faith in Christ'. He made a special attempt at Ratisbon in 1541. A layman and cardinal, he was the first papal legate to receive a great ovation on his arrival in a German town for many a year. But things had gone too far. Luther did not come. Melanchthon had been told not to move from the text of the *Confessio Augustana*. The Curia put paid to the attempt at reconciliation before work had even started, by appointing a new nuncio, Morone, opposed to all parley with the Protestants.

Although neither the reform of the Curia, nor a reconciliation had been achieved, a way had been prepared by Paul III for a successful summoning of a Council. Luther remained indifferent on this matter, and then increasingly bitter about the papacy itself,

[6] Jedin shakes his head: 'Thus even the most faithful of the faithful had not completely shaken off the fatal delusion that there was no real schism'.

its representatives and policy. He had first appealed to a Council in his own case in 1518. Since then many people had taken up the cry for a reforming Council. Clement VII had assented verbally. Paul III had expressed his strong intention of summoning a Council. But the strength of the entrenched Roman Curia and the very grave difficulties in the political sphere, including that of war, prevented the summoning of a Council until 1545 when the Council of Trent finally opened in that place of geographical compromise, high up on the Brenner pass, where both Italian and German were spoken. But long before that Luther had concluded that there was no sincere intention of holding a Council, and that with Rome, as ever, it was nothing but talk, intrigues, the man-oeuvres of Antichrist. In 1539 in a booklet *On Councils and Churches*, and then again in 1545 in *Against the Papacy*, he poured forth a more or less vitriolic polemic. There were many well-presented arguments, recapitulating his established teaching. He insisted that the early Councils of the Church, in particular the first four, had limited themselves to what could be deduced from Scripture. The second booklet, inspired by the Pope's solemn admonition to the Emperor who had yielded, as a matter of policy, to various Protestant demands at the Diet of Speyer in 1544, and had further promised them a Council, was replete with Luther's most righteous anti-papal anger.

The Council of Trent finally opened in 1545, with the Protestants uninvited, and Luther with no will to go. Many of his followers with closer interest in the political situation had expected from the promises of the Emperor that a final attempt at reconciliation would now be made, but were inclined to reject the Council as not the free Council in German lands which had been talked of for so long; the general impression was that they would refuse to go whether invited or cited. Luther undoubtedly felt he had better ways of occupying his time. His experiences with Catholic authority, and his success in establishing new Christian communities, permanently integrated with the social and political structure, gave him good reason for thinking this. The first sessions of the Council opened in December 1545. In the following February Luther died.

45. The Reformed Mass

ESSENTIAL to Luther's own spiritual experience and the theology which owed so much to his own experience is the idea that though we should pray to God, we should never do so with the idea that we can offer anything of any value to him. We are too poor to give him anything. Christ has made the one all-sufficient sacrifice. As a newly ordained priest, the pattern of his theology was set when, as he was about to read the words at the opening of the petitions in the Canon of the Mass—*Te igitur clementissime Pater*, 'Therefore, O most loving Father'—a horror had come over him of addressing God, even though he was to do so through Christ. Catholic theology teaches, not that a fresh sacrifice is offered at Mass, but only that the same single sacrifice of Christ is offered. However the principal emphasis in Luther's day (and often since) was on the objective idea of the Mass as 'a sacrifice', and the value which it had in terms of spiritual goods—so that Luther considered that the popular idea of the Mass was simply that of a 'work' done by man, a 'sacrifice' offered by him.

Once Luther himself was conducting a programme of reform, his first thoughts included the deletion of all references to sacrifice and to petitions linked with the idea of the Mass as something of value offered to God the Father (whether or not offered in Christ's name). The Canon of the Mass was cut down, by him, to little more than the recitation of the words of institution: 'Who, on the night that he was betrayed, etc.'

In 1523 Luther published his *Formula missae et communionis*. It was a careful and considered work. He knew that it was useless to try to change everything all at once. He insisted only on what he regarded as the essential changes, and left the development of a generally simpler form of liturgy to take place in due time. 'We assert that neither now nor in the past has it been our intention to abolish entirely the whole formal *cultus* of God, but to cleanse

that which is in use, which had been vitiated by most abominable
additions.'

The *Formula* was followed two years later by the *Deutsche
Messe*, the Mass in German to enable the people to take as full
part as possible. Both the consecrated bread and the consecrated
wine were to be communicated to the people. The Canon was cut
down as in the *Formula*. The epistle and gospel were to be audible,
the sermon was to be an important part of the service. Beyond
that, much of the service looked just like a Roman Mass with
vestments, incense, and the elevation of the host and the chalice
(other Protestants abolished these long before they disappeared
from Wittenberg in 1545).

Gradually, later, what were regarded as 'Roman' frills were dis-
carded; and more congregational singing came in. Luther was
fond of music and sufficiently knowledgeable of its technique to
be able to take a hand in directing the musical side of the reformed
liturgy, and it is probable that he composed some of the hymns
himself, including the famous 'A mighty fortress is our God'. A
great musical tradition was enabled to grow up, a tradition which,
in its own way, often became nearly as specialized as the traditions
it had replaced—but not entirely. In the corrupt 'Roman' traditions, still extant (at the time of writing) in St Peter's, all the singing parts, congregational and choir parts, may be usurped by a
specialist choir. But in the Lutheran tradition, even when Bach
wrote his great oratorios and chorales, a place was reserved for a
massed choir, with melodies that could be learnt and sung by a
determined congregation. And generally, throughout the
Protestant tradition, vocal and musical participation of the congregation, whether in the formal parts of the liturgy, or in
newly composed hymns, became an appropriately significant
mark of 'reformed' worship.

But there was no extempore praying or other marks of the more
radical kind of Protestant worship. Luther retained the idea of a
very carefully disciplined liturgy. In some ways he wished to
tighten up the discipline. For a time at any rate in some places
communicants had to announce themselves to the priest before-
hand, a rubric also written into the Anglican reform, with the idea

that the priest had a duty to ensure that a communicant was not scandalously unprepared or himself a public scandal. Then the discipline of the confessional was made more public and democratic and extended to control not only morals but knowledge of doctrine. There is a woodcut picture showing princes and nobles on the confessional chair. Once a year they might be examined in their knowledge of the Catechism, the Creed and the Lord's Prayer.

Luther instituted a 'reformed' liturgy, not at all a new liturgy. At the centre of it was the sacramental communion. Apart from the suppression of all references to sacrifice, the important changes were all positive and related to hearing the Word of God, in Scripture and through preaching.

46. *The Bible*

THE translation of the Bible was one of Luther's perennial tasks from the first month of 1522 onwards. He continued to revise the translation up to the last year of his death. His own copy, his own *handexemplar*, became the source for the final edition after his death—with the usual intricate and detailed problems, lasting for centuries, as to authenticity. The first complete edition of Luther's translation was published in 1534. The Old Testament, with its Hebrew problems, had taken twelve years. The New Testament, as we have seen, Luther completed very swiftly in the first three months of 1522. On arriving at Wittenberg for his permanent return to the city in the spring he was able to go through the translation, which he had already made, with young Melanchthon, the professor of Greek. It was published in September 1522.

Luther had intended to have Amsdorf as his principal helper with the Old Testament, but in the service of the Reform the latter had gone off to be parish priest at Magdeburg. In his place was Aurogallus whom Luther found helpful. Melanchthon also helped. Luther published the translation bit by bit as he got it done. The work of translation was taken with professional seriousness and an attempt made to present the full meaning to the German readers, in real German, not a mere verbal transposition. Of the translation of the Book of Job he wrote: 'if it were translated everywhere word for word (as the Jews and foolish translators would have done) and not mostly according to the sense, no one would understand it'. He speaks of the grandeur of the language in this book, and, in the middle of this task which he thought to be taking too long, jokingly says that Job seems to be more impatient with their translation than with the consolation of his friends.

The work was done with great method; a famous description of the meetings which had to be held brings a sense of the business very vividly before one. The description relates to the revision work which went on after the publication of the full Bible in 1534:

> . Dr M. Luther gathered his own Sanhedrin of the best persons available, which assembled weekly, several hours before supper in the doctor's cloister, namely D. Johann Bugenhagen, D. Justus Jonas, D. Creuziger, M. Philippum, Mattheum Aurogallum; Magister Georg Roerer, the *Korrektor* was also present. . . . M. Philipp brought the Greek text with him. D. Creuziger a Chaldean Bible in addition to the Hebrew. The professors had their rabbinical commentaries. D. Pommer also had the Latin text. . . . The President submitted a text and permitted each to speak in turn and listened to what each had to say about the characteristics of the language or about the expositions of the doctors in earlier times.[1]

The success of Luther's translation owed much to Luther's theological study, study rooted originally in late medieval methodology, corrupt maybe but still the product of a millennium and a half of reflection, meditation and hard intellectual thought about Christian doctrine. Luther had superimposed on this his own personal return to the Bible, and transformed the doctrine which he inherited into a dynamic biblical theology. He was thus in a unique position, in translating the Bible, to express the fundamental doctrinal themes in a coherent but dynamic fashion—a task at which more recent translators have failed in

[1] Schwiebert, p. 649.

spite of great progress in biblical research, because they lacked a sufficient theological grasp. A fundamental principle relates to the unity of Scripture and the several senses in which it can be used to interpret itself: Luther had already expressed this in 1519: 'The Spirit is nowhere more present and alive than in His own sacred writings. . . . We must let Scripture have the chief place and be its own truest, simplest and clearest interpreter. . . . I want Scripture alone to rule, and not to be interpreted according to my spirit or that of any other man, but to be understood in its own light [*per seipsam*] and according to its own Spirit.'[2] Modern biblical research has uncovered much in the way of divergences and differences, but Luther's translation has lasted.

All this is not to deny that Luther's hobby-horses received undue emphasis at times, the great example being the addition of the word 'alone' after 'faith' in the reference to justification by faith in the Epistle of St Paul to the Romans. The Greek text simply has 'faith'. In this case Luther was determined that his version should avoid the possibility of interpretation in terms of the old merit theology. 'Justification by faith' just like that, he felt could still be argued to include 'works', and he considered, rightly enough, that St Paul's sense is to state unequivocally that faith, in its fullest sense, justifies. To bring out the meaning properly he felt, at that time anyhow, the German must have the word 'alone'.

If theology provided an important contribution to the success of Luther's translation, Luther's blunt-at-the-same-time-sensitive, personal, human, down-to-earth character had as much to contribute. Having settled the fundamental meaning and sense of a passage, in the deepest redemptive and theological sense, he then had to convey this to Germans. 'One must not ask the letters in Latin how to express the idea in German . . . but the mother in the home, the children in the street, and the common man in the market place and inquire of them how it should be expressed, and then translate it accordingly. They understand it and notice that someone is speaking to them in German.'[3] There had been previous translations, and German editions of the epistle and gospel

---

[2] Quoted by P. S. Watson in his introduction to the translation of Luther's commentary on Galatians (James Clarke, London, 1956).

[3] Schwiebert, p. 661.

passages were easily obtained, especially with a commentary in the popular Postils. But nothing like the methodical comprehensive translation work of Luther's had been attempted before.

The effect of Luther's printed works, disseminated far and wide, Latin and German, professional and popular, was a major factor in the support which he elicited between 1517 and 1521. Almost certainly this it was that prevented the judgment of Catholic authority from being triumphant—the argument of the other side had been heard and understood. From 1522 onwards it was first Luther's text of the New Testament, and then his text of the Old Testament which perhaps more than anything else enabled the reform to spread fast and solidly, providing a norm and a tangible basis to the teaching. 'The need for a Bible in German is so great that no one can imagine it. No one realizes the insight which it has offered to our world today. What we once tried to accomplish through continual lecturing and great industry and still could not attain, this text now offers clearly by itself; for none of us realized in what darkness we were living because of the former translations.'[4]

The New Testament probably sold 200,000 copies between publication in 1522 and the complete Bible publication in 1534. Many printers in many cities were involved using Low German and High German. Numerous illustrations printed from wood-cuts accompanied the texts.

47. *Wittenberg: The University, the Parishes (and Civil Authority), Luther's House*

WITTENBERG became the model and centre of the reform at several levels. In the University, Luther and Melanchthon between them adapted the courses, with the Elector's approval, according to plans which Luther had been working out for many years previously—he had been writing to Spalatin about what a

4 Schwiebert, p. 663.

Christian university really should be like as early as 1515. The parish became a model parish for the Reform. Luther's personal household in the Black Cloister became a centre at a more personal level.

The enrolment at Wittenberg University sunk in 1525 and 1526 to about 50 and 80 respectively, lower than it had ever been, since its foundation in 1502—the previous lowest being about 125 in 1505.[1] This drop was partly due to the Peasants' War, but also partly due to the withdrawal of Catholic support. However, the enrolment in 1527 shot up to 300 and from then on there was a satisfactory enrolment, reaching peaks of just under and just over 700 in 1543 and 1544, the previous peak being 550 in 1519 at the height of Luther's new reputation. The University prospered, and its pupils carried the message of the Reform far and wide; as many pupils came from southern as from northern Germany. The organization of the University was gradually adapted so that it became precisely based on Lutheran theology. Melanchthon drafted new statutes in 1523, which demoted the philosophical disputations so that they were held less frequently. More changes were made between 1533 and 1536. It was then that the University became definitely confessional: 'As in the churches and boys' schools throughout our territories, so in the University, which should be the chief guide and censor of doctrine, we wish to have the pure doctrine of the Gospel taught in accordance with the confession which was presented to the Emperor Charles in August 1530, which doctrine we assert with certainty to be the true and eternal teaching of the Catholic Church of God, to be piously and faithfully proclaimed, preserved, and propagated.'

From Wittenberg Luther and his followers worked for other educational reforms elsewhere. In some towns Luther introduced the provision of funds from the town for gifted students who were too poor to pay (Nuremberg was an example). In other towns an extra-mural foundation for adult courses, under the name *Lectorien*, was instituted.

---

[1] A diagram of annual entries at the University from its foundation until some time after Luther's death is given in Schwiebert's book which is also the authority for a great deal of the factual information appearing in this chapter, and indeed for that relating to much of the post-Worms time, not available elsewhere.

The policy of reforming and invigorating the schools, and of founding new ones was typical of Luther's method and ideals. The wilder of his supporters, like Carlstadt, reacted violently against their past and tended towards a demagogic anti-intellectualism. Some of the most well-educated of his supporters, like Amsdorf, tended to judge that the best thing they could do would be to get out amongst the people into the parishes and do the work of a parish priest. But someone had to remain at the helm, to plan the Reform and organize the training of teachers and pastors. Plans needed to be drawn up and put into execution—a purely haphazard shower of activities was not enough. In 1524, probably, Luther addressed his *Weckruf* to the mayors and aldermen of the German cities pointing out the indispensable role of schools in society and particularly in teaching reformed Christian doctrine. In 1530 he published his *Sermon on the Duty of Sending Children to School*. He gave figures in it to show the crying need for more pastors to work in parishes and more masters in the schools.

At Wittenberg a new school was founded under the direction of Luther and Melanchthon in 1533, the Wittenberg Latin School, divided into three levels, elementary, secondary and high. In the same year a new school for girls was founded as a result of Luther's campaigning.

After completing some elementary steadying work in Wittenberg on his arrival in 1522, Luther made a tour in the district, and then began to formulate some organized means of improving the life of the parishes, and of controlling them and reforming them doctrinally. In his writings prior to Worms he had reached the conclusion that the civil authority in a Christian country had a specific duty particularly when standards had slipped and the ecclesiastical authority seemed unable to instigate a reform by itself. The precise basis for this pluralism in effective Christian authority was never perfectly elucidated; however, it fitted well enough with the rest of Luther's theories, all of which implied the individual responsibility of each person to play his full part as a Christian in a vocational society. Obviously, then, those who had authority in such a society could not remain indifferent in specifically religious matters.

Essentially Luther's position is a development of the classic medieval theory of the two swords—a Christian Commonwealth in which there are two authorities both demanding obedience in the name of a divine sanction. Basically there are 'two kingdoms', God's kingdom of grace and mercy, and the world's of wrath and severity, and they should not be confused.[2] But Luther takes the duties of the civil power further than they had commonly been taken before, far enough for it to be possible to envisage the single 'Christian' Nation-State, in which the Church was in practice totally subordinate to the State. But so long as Luther remained alive and where his authority was effective this did not happen. The spiritual authority of those who had founded the Reform remained effective. Indeed Luther's whole purpose was of course radically opposed to Erastianism. His political philosophy (sufficiently well-articulated to warrant such a description) is tied to his theology at all points. The two biblical sources for his twofold teaching have been singled out as 'let everyone be subject to the higher powers, for the powers that be are ordained by God' (Rom. 15.1), and 'We must obey God rather than men' (Acts 5.39).[3] He wished to raise the standard of secular life and political practice: 'I hope to instruct the secular authorities in such a way that they shall remain Christians and that Christ shall remain Lord, yet so that Christ's commandments need not for their sake be changed into "Counsels".'[4] Although Luther has many passages recognizing the existing and perhaps inevitable low level of political conduct, his attitude tends towards hopefulness. The emphasis laid on the religious duties of civil authority opened the way to the Erastian Nation-State. The new situation was underwritten by the Diet of Speyer with its implication of relative religious indifferentism by which a ruler could be responsible for deciding which should be the dominant religious tradition in his land.

Visitations of the parishes began in 1528, as a result of the Diet of Speyer, and with detailed instructions drawn up by Luther, with the assent of the new Elector John Frederick, son of Frederick the Wise. Inquiry was made into finance, liturgy and the personal

[2] Rupp, *R.G.*, p. 292.   [3] See Rupp, *R.G.*, p. 301.   [4] See Rupp, *R.G.*, p. 295.

life of the incumbent—and the visitors returned again later to see if their recommendations had been put into effect. Some of the pastors turned out to be genuine followers of Luther, others seemed to be merely toeing the line, others again definitely held to the old traditions, others were incompetent and did not have even an elementary grasp of the Gospel, or were regularly drunk, or convicted of sexual misdemeanours. Those in these last two categories were usually removed. They were numerous in some parts and in general seem to have been between a third and a half of all the incumbents.

Finance was a big trouble to start with. The abolition of cash offerings made to the priest when he celebrated Mass had made many priests poorer than they were before, the problem being most severe in the country districts. In the towns the priests were often able to marry into the local nobility, and in any case the prosperity of the town was sufficient to ensure their salaries. The supply of priests was also a severe problem at first. And Luther's conviction that ordination was not really a sacrament made further complications; he had to produce a new form by which a man would be ordained, a form which declared the universal priesthood of the baptized and made of ordination no more than a formal selection and direction of a man to the task of pastor. Luther raised up a class of emergency preachers, laymen, drawn mostly from among the professions, consecrated to the ministry in their spare time. Luther wrote many Postils, for use as sermon material by the less well educated priests. And for them and their flocks in particular he composed the *Small Catechism*. Luther has a forthright passage introducing this which describes the dreadfully low standard he found in sòme parishes, and the way in which the Reform movement had enabled the bad to be even worse, giving them more freedom in some immediate respects:

> The deplorable, wretched conditions which I experienced recently as a visitor constrained and forced me to put this Catechism of Christian teachings in this small common, simple form. Dear Lord, how much misery I saw everywhere! The ordinary man knows almost nothing about Christian teaching, especially in the villages. A good many of the ministers are almost wholly unprepared or else

unfit to teach. Yet they are all to be regarded as Christian; they are supposed to be baptized; and they receive the Lord's Supper. Still they do not even know the Lord's Prayer, the Creed, and the Ten Commandments. They live simply like cattle and act like pigs, as though they had no conscience. And now that the Gospel has come, they have also learned how to abuse all their Christian liberties in masterful fashion.[5]

It was in 1529, after the shock of the first visitations, that Luther sat down to write the catechism, to be based on the essential core of material that all should have off by heart: the Ten Commandments, the Creed, and the Lord's Prayer. All should understand the two sacraments of baptism and the Eucharist. Simple explanations were given of these. The *Small Catechism* was well adapted, in its simplicity, for use by the parent. Luther also thought of it as useful for the examination which he considered should be made of communicants (on an annual basis) when they came to confession before communion—sins were still to be confessed though not in order to obtain sacramental forgiveness. The *Small Catechism* Luther came to hold in very high regard amongst his writings—once saying that all his writings might be destroyed, but he would like to keep the *Small Catechism* and the answer to Erasmus on the *Bondage of the Will*.

The Postils had an effect parallel to that of the *Small Catechism*, doing for the run of the clergy what the Catechism did for the laity. The Postils also sometimes became happy hunting grounds for theologians wishing to understand Luther's theology more fully. Sometimes in such popular productions he would express a doctrine more forthrightly and significantly than elsewhere. When Luther first began writing them in greater number it was partly, or largely, in order to protect priest and people from going after any and every new idea, and giving themselves into the hands of anyone who claimed spiritual insight. Luther eventually covered the whole of the Church's year—the epistles and gospels for each Sunday, with his own commentaries and notes for preachers.

The Postils lead us easily to consideration of Luther's own home

[5] Schwiebert, p. 631.

as the centre of the Reformation, for he began in 1532 to preach
on Sunday evenings at his house to whomever might be gathered
there. And these sermons were subsequently gathered together
and published as *Hauspostille*. One is apt to think of Luther as
rather a hard man, with the grit and courage a man must have who
will face death for an idea, with perhaps the bitterness, the re-
pressed sadness, which must always go with such a life when
friends come and go; and we are almost bound to think of Luther
as a dominating man with little time for human detail. But the picture of the Luther household in the Black Cloister does not really
bear this out. Luther's sensitivity, a great personal openness and
kindness are shown forth. He practically held permanent open-
house, and any refugee might find a place there. Carlstadt, fleeing
from parishioners and others who would have none of his illuminism and his neo-simplicity, knocked on Luther's door on his
wedding night to ask for lodging. Carlstadt had done very grave
disservice to Luther, opposing him, damaging his works. His life
had tended towards the ruin of any kind of orderly reform. But
he could dare to knock on Luther's door; and he was taken in.

An authentic picture comes in a letter to Prince George of
Anhalt from someone advising him not to try to spend a night
with Luther:

> The home of Luther is occupied by a motley crowd of boys,
> students, girls, widows, old women, and youngsters. For this reason
> there is much disturbance in the place, and many regret it for the
> sake of the good man, the honourable father. If but the spirit of
> Doctor Luther lived in all of these, his house would offer you an
> agreeable, friendly quarter for a few days so that your Grace would
> be able to enjoy the hospitality of that man. But as the situation now
> stands and as circumstances exist in the household of Luther, I would
> not advise that your Grace stop there.[6]

It was a typical writer's house—Katie could not find her way
about for the papers and books. But she was an efficient house-
keeper, and the picture of something like a lively idyll does not
seem to be too far from the truth. After the dry and rather
monotonous life of the monastic enclosure both husband and

[6] Schwiebert, p. 597.

wife must always have relished in quite a simple sense the mere
freedom they had. There was the suffering, usual at the time, of
seeing no more than half one's children grow to maturity. Their
daughter Magdalena died in early adolescence, a veritable picture
of sanctity, doing as her mother and father had taught her and
saying she wished only for God's will.

Luther seems to have stormed more on paper than in person,
even though he undoubtedly had a quick temper. But it seems
clear that although Luther ordered Katie about, she held her own.
Undoubtedly Luther could speak in very forthright terms; he
detested any kind of temporizing, and was a bad tactician. His
followers often deplored the blunt way he dealt with his
enemies.

As far as language is concerned, we have already shown that
the Roman Curia itself could measure up well to Luther himself
on this score. This matter is the one on which people have sometimes taken the greatest scandal from Luther, but its significance
is perhaps different from what has often been imagined. It seems
certain that Luther's addiction to excremental and coarse words
owes something to his personal psychological history. But there
are other considerations too. Apart from the matter of common
usage, the extra special verve of Luther's language could be quite
deliberate—an attempt to bring before his opponent the brute
facts as an ordinary man would express them; it was all part of the
departure from the scholastic abstractions back to a vocabulary
for the Gospel in which the nouns, verbs and adjectives were
those in everyday use. The sense of evil, of the battle on earth
between the things of God and the things of the devil, was strong
amongst the great majority of Christians, and remained strong in
Luther. He could not call evil things anything but what he believed them to be. So also with all his theology—its existential
nature led to the use of expressions which could be easily ripped
out of their context to make an enemy's thesis. 'Pecca fortiter'
('sin properly'), he wrote to Melanchthon from the Wartburg,
but meant it in much the same bantering way as Staupitz when he
had told Luther to stop being so scrupulous and to stick to real
sins in his confessions, such as murdering his father. 'Be a sinner

and sin thoroughly. But at the same time confide and rejoice still more boldly in Christ who is the conqueror of sin and death and the world.' And scandal has been taken by those who do not read Luther but hear that Christ has been called a fornicator—Christ, said Luther, took all our sins on himself, and he expressed this in his usual way. No one who has read Luther with honest care and application could call him a blasphemer. We have seen already how Luther easily presented a poor image of himself in public affairs, during the Peasants' War. Another occasion for criticism was when Luther, ignorant of some of the facts, agreed to a bigamous marriage by Philip of Hesse in 1540.

The anti-Lutheran myth of the foul-mouthed German beast, barely in control of himself, will not hold together. In some of the early disputations between 1517 and 1519 eyewitnesses spoke of Luther's patience in debate, as well as of his outspoken phrases and the impressive nature of his rather ascetic features and his piercing eye, the latter a feature which Cajetan found so disturbing. If the picture will not hold together even for the public life, it becomes absurd for the home-life. Luther becomes rather more like a kind of Chesterton, jolly, cantankerous, obstinate, deep-drinking, expounding, contradicting, brilliant, human, adored, lovable, prayerful. This angry fellow was unable to refuse refuge to a hunted hare (one day of exercise when he was at the Wartburg) that took refuge in the sleeves of his cloak from the baying hounds which, however, bit its throat through the cloth of his coat.

There was music and games, and a garden. While he was away Luther would write to Katie, and to the children. Hans, aged four, had a long, somewhat laboured letter in the full medieval morality tradition, all about a marvellous garden Luther had found where there were purple and yellow plums and pears and cherries, and the children wore gold jackets, and rode ponies with silver saddles, etc., etc. The conditions of eventual entry were to pray, to study hard, and be very good. Three paragraphs of it, but all very jolly and fatherly.

Luther had the remarkable opportunity to practise the virtues of the married vocation about which he began to preach quite frequently in 1518, if not before. He seems to have practised them

and to have set an example, in his own person, of something like
the new kind of Christian household he had dreamed of. We
should not overemphasize the difference between it and the
typical good Christian household in the previous 200 years. In
some ways it was a distinct step forward in responsibility, but the
family still owed much of its stability and many of its customs to
the tradition gradually established throughout the whole Christian era, and Luther would have been the first to say so.

48. *The Religious Left and Luther's Idea*
of the Church

ALTHOUGH much of the borderlands of psychology and religion still remain unexplored today, and the discoveries already
made remain largely unorganized, yet we are today actutely aware
of the existence of these borderlands and of the need to explore
them more systematically. In describing the varieties of reformers
to the left, and very far to the left, of Luther, it is necessary to set
them in their medieval context. These borderlands had not even
been recognized as an area for objective investigation, except by
the occasional genius. For the most part there was simply a general
idea that there were 'mystics' to whom 'special revelations' were
made. And there were other people unhappy to be possessed by
evil spirits. The sphere of direct supernatural or praeternatural
intervention was considered to be large[1] and the Church was considered to have an important task in regulating the resultant
activities. Regulation was the point. And we have already contrasted this attitude to that of the Eastern Church[2] in which it was
rather taken for granted that everything and everyone was in
some measure a subject for this kind of direct divine activity, and
that the 'holy' was ever hovering over all life, spirits being
'familiars' rather than aliens.

Once juridical authority in the Western Church ceased to be

---

[1] Cf. pp. 7–13   [2] Cf. p. 214.

effective, once its authority as a 'regulator' was removed, a dangerous 'freedom' was given to all those in whom religious experience was strongly felt. The Church had been seen less as a mother who encouraged and nurtured this kind of thing within herself than as a schoolmaster. The occasional individual with strong religious interests and experience had as a result always tended to feel 'special'. When he was released from the schoolroom of the Roman regulations the result was a proliferation of illuminism and 'wildcat' spiritual initiatives, which Luther recognized very well as the result of 'freedom' in the sense of release from convention, and it often saddened him.

Wittenberg was at first thought of as a centre to which such people might turn for help. So it was that in December 1521 the 'Prophets' arrived from Zwickau, the town where Thomas Münzer was preaching a doctrine of the enlightenment of special individuals by God. He believed that he himself and others held converse with God, that the Church should be reformed in conformity with their ideas, that those who opposed them might be eliminated by violence. Melanchthon was flummoxed by the prophets, particularly their leader. He made no headway by argument, and told the Elector he did not know what to do. Meanwhile Carlstadt had been leading his iconoclastic riots and changing the liturgy without permission, and talking wildly. So it was that Luther came, four months later, and began to preach his go-slow sermons. The 'prophets' and their like he condemned on a common-sense basis. Their activities were not compatible with charity. Münzer eventually became one of the leaders of the peasants in the Peasants' War and was beheaded when they were defeated.

Carlstadt retired from Wittenberg in 1522 to the parish of Orlamunde where he dressed and lived like a peasant. Luther on his tour visited the parish and tried to replace him. Eventually Carlstadt roused everyone against himself. But there were others who managed to get considerable followings and Luther felt bound to issue warnings against them. In 1524 he published *Against the Heavenly Prophets*. Luther maintained in it, amongst other things, the real presence of Christ in the Eucharist, against the opinion of Carlstadt, which involved its contradiction. This pamphlet was aimed at Carlstadt but it drew a reply from the Swiss reformers Zwingli and Oecolampadius, who had been inspired by their humanistic studies, and encouraged by Erasmus's translation of the New Testament, to a reform movement of their own. Their line was Platonic and inclined to a 'puritan' interpretation of the text: 'The letter kills but the spirit gives life'. There followed a pamphlet controversy between Luther and Zwingli. Luther produced arguments based both on his exegesis of Scripture and on his theology; Zwingli was addressed in the tones Luther kept for his enemies. In 1527, when he wrote the last of three pamphlets on the subject, he was ill physically, and deeply depressed by the widespread lack of control amongst his followers, by the Peasants' War which had been partly fomented by the wild spirits like Münzer, by the bloodshed and his own inability to control what to some extent he had engendered, and by the deplorable state of the many parishes which he had been visiting. On top of this was the controversy, as it were within the camp, between himself and Zwingli which he had not asked for; it brought out all the bile there was in him.

In 1529 the Protestant princes felt that a united ideological front was required—the princes of Saxony, Hesse, Nuremberg, Strassburg and Ulm, also the Margrave of Brandenburg. As a result of their requests the Wittenberg theologians drew up the Schwabach Articles, as a basis for discussion. The two parties then met at Marburg. As usual Luther was a little easier in a face-to-face meeting though even then there were some harsh words; at the end of the meeting he said to Zwingli: 'Pardon me, please, for now and then speaking rather harsh words against you, for I am after all flesh and blood'. The Marburg Articles were drawn up at the end, fourteen points which formed the basis of the Wittenberg Concord of 1536. A fifteenth point on the Eucharist asserting that the Lord's Supper is a sacrament of the true body and blood of Jesus Christ was not signed by the Swiss. The latter were all the same hurt that the Lutherans would not admit them to a final joint communion service. The grounds of refusal were the same as those on which Christian groups make similar stands today—that it is dishonest to cover doctrinal disagreement by a liturgical act whose essential meaning is in question.

Zwingli had already been faced by more or less perfectionist sects in his own party, a kind of Protestant monasticism which included rejection of infant baptism (the Anabaptists); they gathered together in religious communities, adopting the Sermon on the Mount as their ideal. With Zwingli's assent, their practice and belief was made illegal in Zurich in 1525 and the death penalty invoked against them. No way in fact was found in these first decades of Protestantism to tolerate or in any way digest the extremists any better than Catholic authorities had done. Luther himself was finally driven to approving the persecution of Anabaptists by the civil power, in spite of his earlier tolerance. The bitter polemic with Münzer and the latter's influence on the bloodshed of the Peasants' War convinced Luther, for good, of the danger of allowing free range to individuals who repudiated all established ecclesiastical authority.

Closely associated with Zwingli were Oecolampadius and Martin Bucer. Oecolampadius had been a force for unity, but he died after the Marburg meeting. Martin Bucer, a determined and changeable man, owed his original enthusiasm to Luther's success at Heidelberg in 1518 at the meeting of his order. Subsequently Bucer had gone further and faster than Luther, accepting the protection of the Knights. He had also villified Luther. However, eventually he was convinced that Luther's position was correct; he and Zwingli were finally prepared to agree that the body and blood of Christ are truly present at the service of the Last Supper. They did not hold this in exactly the same way as Luther, but they rejected their previous idea that the presence depended on the faith of the communicants. The result was the agreement known as the Wittenberg Concord. It was only achieved after some difficult testing meetings and discussions since Luther did not find it easy to believe that Bucer was sincere, and suggested they might be better to remain honest enemies. However, eventually agreement was reached and a common liturgy was celebrated. This was not organic unity, but it was doctrinal agreement and inter-communion.

Organic unity would in any case hardly have been looked for. Luther's ecclesiology did not go beyond the establishment of local ecclesiastical authority within a given area of civil authority. He had repudiated the centralized authority and was not looking to replace it by some other universal system. On the contrary he may be said to assume the absence of any such thing. The really important things, the souls of the justified, are known only to God. Luther did not, except possibly for a short time, think in terms of a Church reduced to the 'elect', a tiny body of 'saints' within the known Church. He kept to a theory which said that the true boundaries of the Church could not be known for certain, and that the Church could not be a cut and dried juridical body. A passage of Gordon Rupp's explains Luther's ecclesiology finely. It starts with a quotation from Luther:

If you ask the Pope, why are you the People of God? he replies, 'Because I sit in the seat of the Apostles Peter and Paul. I am their successor. Thence have I my cause in Scripture. Thou art Peter and upon this rock will I build my Church.' But a dog or a pig can sit in the seat of Peter. But to have vocation, that is believe the Word, over and above that succession, this constitutes the Church and the sons of God . . . but we do not doubt we are the Church, for we have the Gospel, Baptism, Keys, Holy Scripture, which teach that man is lost and damned in Original Sin and that it is required that he be born again through Christ.

Rupp continues:

The point about the pig and the dog is characteristically blunt but not frivolous. It is simply that historical continuity, alone and by itself, is not the differentiation between the true and false Church, but the divine vocation and promise. . . . Abundant testimony could be given that Luther constantly believed in the need for a continual succession of believers on the earth, and, above all, for the continuity of the ministry of the Word.

Rupp cites passages to support the contention. He goes on to quote further passages which provide a useful pointer to Luther's beliefs about the Church:

The fellowship of believers is twofold, one inward and spiritual, the other outward and bodily. The spiritual consists in a unity of faith, hope and love to God. The bodily consists in sharing in the same sacraments, i.e. the signs of faith, hope and love, which, however, extends further to things, matters of use and language, buildings and other bodily circumstances.

The Church is a number or gathering of the baptized and believing people who belong to a pastor in a town, or in a whole countryside, or in the whole world.

This is our trust and glory, that with good ground we confidently boast and say: We are holy and holy brothers towards one another at Wittenberg, Rome, Jerusalem and where the Holy Baptism and Gospel are.

Finally a definition orientated towards the differences and agreements with Rome, for these always remained the important controlling factors:

We have the same Baptism, the same Sacrament of the Altar, the same Keys, the same Scripture and Word. And then, we arise from the same apostles and Church, as from one mother Rebecca. Where then do we differ? We take hold of the Word in the Sacrament, we follow our vocation, and we treat things according to faith. They according to a visible appearance. We say that the Word is to be regarded 'in usum Sacramenti' and to be received in faith. They make it an 'opus operatum'. Thus that is the true Church which adheres to the Word, and faith which does not lean on works but which hears and follows the calling of God.[3]

49. Erasmus and 'Free Will'

AFTER Luther's return to Wittenberg, his writing in a sense took second place to his actions. He became the leader of a movement. And his own books took second place to the work of biblical translation. But some of the writings after Worms are of major importance. The Catechisms and Postils we have already referred to. There are many others including the final version of

[3] Rupp, R.G., pp. 338–40.

the Commentary on Galatians.[1] The 'Bondage of the Will' (*De Servo Arbitrio*), Luther's reply to Erasmus, is also of fundamental importance. It confirmed the deeply theological nature of the Reformation as a movement of Christian and evangelical reform founded by Luther. It is still a good guide to one of the dominating themes of Luther's theology. The title is off-putting—both sombre and immediately rousing prejudice as to Luther's ability to psychologize; but once beyond the covers one finds a doctrine which is intelligible, and is concerned in fact not with psychology but theology. The most recent English edition[2] greatly facilitates understanding of it, both by the presentation of the text itself, and by an excellent introduction.

Erasmus and Luther never met, although they were the two most notable figures of the ecclesiastical scene in the first half of the sixteenth century. However, their various disciples and go-betweens did meet and correspond; and they themselves corresponded to the extent of a few letters over about nine years.

The most notable work of Erasmus, as we have seen, was to provide a new text of the New Testament, much more accurate than that of the Vulgate, St Jerome's Latin translation from the Greek. Erasmus's text was used by Luther to great benefit. It was made from the original Greek and had notes and commentaries, or rather, more frequently, pastoral applications. It was a godsend not only to scholars, but to preachers as well. However, Erasmus was concerned, in the tradition of scholarship, primarily with the

---

[1] See p. 259.
[2] *On the Bondage of the Will* by Martin Luther, a new translation of *De Servo Arbitrio*, by J. I. Packer and O. R. Johnston (James Clark and Co., London), 1957. The only fault in an excellent introduction seems to be a slight exaggeration of Gordon Rupp's opinion of this work of Luther's. The introduction quotes Professor Rupp quoting Bishop Normann's high opinion of the work. This needs to be counter-balanced with Professor Rupp's own view, which interestingly differs from that of many other people: 'As a controversy, it is not one of the great literary duels. Both writers have an eye over their shoulder at the listening world. Erasmus is bent on clearing his own reputation. Luther suffers from major and minor inhibitions: angry and disappointed and alarmed, still, by the defection of Erasmus, engaged in a subject touching some of his deepest convictions, yet restrained at the entreaties of such friends as Philip Melanchthon, who had to keep friends with both parties: and perhaps with a too lively inferiority sense about his own Latin style when contrasted with the magisterial elegance of Erasmus.' He adds: 'Many readers of it as a controversy would, I imagine, give Erasmus a victory on points'—a surprising opinion to the present writer. But a similar view is implied by some words of Professor Joseph Lortz, who says that few experts would dare to claim that the theses of this 'violent book' express the 'veritable pensée' of Luther (Chapter 25, *Découverte de l'Oecuménsime*, Cahiers de la Pierre-qui-vire, Desclée de Brouwer, Paris, 1961).

establishment of an accurate text. He was not a theologian and said so. Like many scholars he also had a dry wit and was often tempted to poke fun at his fellow academics in the faculties of philosophy and theology. He liked a simple comfortable life and to stand apart both from the verbal battles of the theoreticians and from the pious practices of the mass of the faithful.

Erasmus has become a hero for one party and a villain to two other parties ever since he began to write. He is the hero of those who think a middle-way solution of the Reformation problems could have been possible, and who still sympathize with Erasmus's attitude towards theology and his dislike of the Protestant and Catholic extremes. He is a villain both to many orthodox Catholics and to many orthodox Protestants who villify him for what they consider to be his shallow, woolly and sceptical approach. Erasmus himself uses the word scepticism in his own preface to his work, *The Diatribe on Free Will*, to which Luther's *On the Bondage of the Will* is a reply. He said that he would 'readily take up the Sceptic's position wherever the inviolable authority of Holy Scripture and the Church's decisions permit'. The temptation of this passage has been too much for many; the 'sceptic' has been kept and the 'inviolable authority of Holy Scripture and the Church's decisions' ignored. So Jedin, a Catholic, considers him as basically a Sceptic.[3] J. I. Packer and O. R. Johnston, Protestants, consider him a barren moralist.[4]

Erasmus fascinates historians and everyone who touches this period feels bound to make some judgment. Often this involves a man in judging Erasmus in purely ideal and universal terms, rather than depicting him within the limits of his own lights. He saw himself as a servant, a scholar who would provide good texts, but who, if pushed about by warring parties with other interests, would be unable to provide the theological weapons they wanted, and would probably react with something like a snarl. He did not like wasting valuable time. He admits freely that he was not made of the stuff of martyrs. Perhaps the need felt by most historians to make a judgment is best explained by the vast

[3] See references to him in *The Council of Trent*, Vol. I.
[4] See introduction to *The Bondage of the Will*.

influence which Erasmus seems to have had. Professor Knowles considers the influence to have been very great[5] and at the same time admits to the complexity of Erasmus's mind. 'In this respect resembling an Abelard or a Newman, [he] is one of those men of genius whose complex minds present so many facets that any summary judgment stands self-condemned, and any precise labels can at once be criticized.' Later he writes: 'Thus, while never denying what had been defined, or flouting what had been ordained, by the supreme authority of the Church, he remained as it were agnostic to the thesis that a religious truth could be contained within a theological formula, or a virtuous life regulated by a disciplinary code'. The professor goes on to speak of Erasmus's 'distrust of metaphysics and of theological speculation and formulation' and finally of 'a low-tension Christianity, a despiritualized religion'. This is not far from the case made against Erasmus by Luther, as by other theologians of the right and the left. Such judgments do not directly concern us here, but the extent to which Erasmus's personality and work still remain a matter of controversy are a useful indication of the importance also generally given in the Europe of his time to the work he wrote against Luther, after six years during which he had sometimes spoken up, though with circumspection, on Luther's behalf.

Erasmus had written his own pieces against the degenerate aspects of the Church from soon after the turn of the century, notably his *Encomium Moriae* ('In Praise of Folly', in Latin a play on the name of his friend Thomas More), where his weapon was that of the scholar's light sophisticated wit. This book became something for his fellow humanists to chuckle over, but it was not likely to worry theologians unduly. When he first heard of Luther Erasmus recognized immediately the signs of a courageous reformer well justified in what he was saying in his witness against indulgences, basing himself on Scripture. As a man of commanding position in the world of letters and of religion, a statement of his position in the *affaire* Luther was, inevitably, eventually required. Erasmus managed to put off a final commit-

[5] *The Religious Orders* (Cambridge), Vol. III, chapter XI.

ment remarkably long, in spite of being consulted by both sides
a number of times. Before Worms he did not hesitate to express
himself in general in Luther's favour, but carefully avoiding particulars, and always counselling Luther to go more quietly. Luther
on his side had great admiration for Erasmus as the man who had
restored a worthy text of Scripture, but with his customary sense
of discrimination he realized as early as 1516 that Erasmus was a
somewhat detached humanist scholar concerned solely for the
text itself, and was not much interested in its theology.

Fourteen years or so older than Luther, Erasmus was consulted
about Luther by Elector Frederick at Cologne soon after the
coronation of Charles, in the autumn of 1520. Erasmus said that
Luther had attacked the monks in their bellies and the Pope in his
crown and so of course he was unpopular—a typically aphoristic
attempt to defend Luther without endangering his own work.
Erasmus was even induced at that time to write down a rather
compromising summary of his opinion in which he said that the
Church should look more kindly on Luther. At Worms Erasmus's
letters showed that he feared Luther would be burnt. When the
outcome was otherwise and everyone was beginning to take sides,
pressure began to be brought on Erasmus to declare himself. In
the past he had been suspect of radical tendencies but friendships
in England and Rome, and his own notable work, had saved him
from trouble. It was becoming imperative on him to make his
position clear if his own work was to go on unhindered.

Meanwhile it was true that Erasmus had become increasingly
out of sympathy with Luther. Erasmus believed that the Church
should be reformed, but he did not believe in the radical changes
which Luther had recommended in the *Babylonian Captivity*.
Above all Erasmus found Luther's loud-mouthed approach very
unsympathetic, the denunciation of evils as works of the devil,
and calling the papacy Antichrist. But ultimately it was Luther's
thoroughly doctrinal and theological approach which he found
tiresome, and so it was that the thing which irritated him more
than anything was precisely a theological statement, and in fact
one of the statements which lies at the heart of Luther's work, and
of the whole Reformation. This was Luther's frequent reference

to man's inability to take any act towards his own salvation by his own free will, Luther's references to man's will as enslaved by the devil or by God. The freedom of the human will to take some meritorious steps towards salvation was one of the current, Occamist, assumptions and Erasmus accepted it as seeming to be a reasonable part of every man's normal cultural baggage.

Erasmus seems to have thought that Luther's talk about man being unable to will his own salvation was just one of his extreme statements, an indefensible paradox drawn from some over-literal interpretation of Scripture. He thought he had found a subject which would enable him quite honestly to express his disapproval of Luther's extremes and thus to dissociate himself publicly. Erasmus set about defending on the one hand the com-monsense (philosophical) view that man has freedom of choice in his actions, and on the other the current rather muddled theological position which was a kind of compromise, assenting on the one hand to the sovereign nature of God's grace, but on the other hand unable to dispense with the idea that man could merit, and therefore could take real steps simply in his own powers to-wards his own salvation. In the course of this latter defence Erasmus sometimes fell back on the agnostic approach, saying that Scripture is obscure and the whole matter therefore in doubt. He spoke of 'probable' views on matters which were precisely what he was debating. The general upshot was that he accused Luther of propounding something quite unreasonable about a rather obscure theological point on which the only obvious thing to be said was that man *has* freedom of choice.

Luther replied that he had never asked anyone to deny a choice to man in the ordinary affairs of life. He is concerned, in speaking of man's lack of freedom of will, simply with the affair of his salvation. And here he makes it clear that, by definition, freedom of will, quite unqualified, can only be possessed by God. Here he articulates the insight of Augustine: 'Freedom is the knowledge of necessity'—man is only free in a limited sense within the areas in which he is already obliged to remain; and can only exercise this freedom properly when he has recognized this fact. Briefly Luther makes out an overwhelming case for the

17. Erasmus
From a painting by Holbein the Younger

18. A composite group
From a painting by Lucas Cranach the Younger
Luther is in the left foreground. Far right is Melanchthon, next to him Creuziger,
then Jonas (cf. Luther's translation committee, p.231), then Erasmus, then
Bugenhagen. Hatted behind Luther is Spalatin.

19. Luther holding the Bible. The writing on the pages shown is that of Melanchthon.

From a portrait by Lucas Cranach the Younger, painted during the last ten years of Luther's life

fact that in the affair of salvation man has always to rely on God's
grace, which is always the initiator; only after that can man act,
and then he is no longer 'free' in any sense that enables one to
speak of man having freedom to will his own salvation. More than
once Luther uses Erasmus's own words about grace to drive this
point home.

Louis Bouyer has written[6] that the whole controversy was bedevilled by the lack, in both Luther and Erasmus, of a traditional
Catholic theology of grace. He claims that the degenerate theology
and philosophy against which Luther was reacting precisely prevented either of them from being able to expound the full traditional theology of grace in which man's work here is a work of
response; he has the obligation and the capacity to respond but
grace remains sovereign, and response to grace is only made with
the help of grace itself. This suggests, perhaps with justification,
that the differences between Luther and Erasmus are not quite so
enormous as Luther makes out. Both are in some sense seeking for
a tolerable theory which saves God's sovereignty, yet does not
deny a sane psychology of man. It is true that there seems sometimes to be only a verbal difference—Erasmus using 'free will' of
man's ability to choose to respond (with God's help), Luther of
man's ability, which he denied (and which Erasmus would have
denied too), to initiate. In his tract Luther settles the matter at the
start by defining free will as something only God possesses. From
then on all he can really say is that Erasmus is using the wrong
term for whatever kind of freedom it is he is trying to describe.

The controversy, however, is of greater importance than might
appear simply from a comparison of the two arguments in themselves in the course of which both authors found themselves in
great logical difficulty. The significant point is that for Erasmus
this matter of the freedom of the will is rather a tiresome academic
matter, on which he thinks Luther has been opposing common

[6] *The Spirit and Forms of Protestantism*, chapter 7. Bouyer is perhaps too hard on Luther
and too assured that Catholic doctrine answers all the questions. Certainly Rupp has
shown that it is simply false to state as Bouyer does that 'Luther diverges, not only from
the tradition of the Church, but from the Gospel and St Paul himself, in creating the
chimera of a salvation which should save us, without drawing us in the least from the
state of sin'. The last phrase does not adequately convey the general drift of Luther's
teaching (explicitly dependent on scriptural definition), on sin. See Rupp, *R.G.*, pp. 241–6.

sense, whilst for Luther it is a crucial theological matter and illustrates perfectly his own conviction that in religion, in everything pertaining to the spiritual, in everything in fact which is really of any import in life, God remains dominant. God rules the world which he made, so that the creature sustained by God the Father, but alienated from him by sin, can only come back to him through the Son, with the inspiration of their Spirit. Man in fact could only claim freedom of will if he was himself divine. And this enables Luther to drive home again the great practical and pastoral point which lay at the origin of all his reforming initiative; man cannot merit, he does not have the potentiality to do anything of spiritual, religious worth, simply from his natural powers, without first turning to God. It was the whole fault, he claimed, of the religious practices and the theology he was opposing that man was taught to do such and such a thing to gain merit.

Luther congratulates and thanks Erasmus for giving him the central theme of his theology for debate: 'You have not worried me with those extraneous issues about the Papacy, purgatory, indulgences . . . you and you alone have seen the hinge on which all turns, and aimed for the vital part (*ipsum iugulum petisti*)'. This is an important statement. Even in 1525 at the height of Luther's early practical work in establishing the Reform, against all the forces of the Catholic world, he does not think of the papacy as being the major issue theologically. He is still first and foremost the biblical theologian whose lectures in the period 1513–1518 formed the basic bedrock of his life and its work. And they involve a transformation of that tenet of Nominalist theology (which made theology something sharply distinguished from philosophy, dividing the world into two), that the sovereignty of God could not be defined; but instead of a matter of 'revelation' merely, as in Nominalism, something which man need not, indeed must not, take account of in his everyday understanding of life, God's sovereignty becomes in Luther's thought the thing which can practically obliterate every created reality if this thought is erected, as it would later be, into a logical formula-theology. However, with Luther himself the dynamic, personal and sacramental outlook remains strong enough to prevent such an outcome.

This was a classic debate, and displayed one of the major factors in the Catholic/Protestant debate, just as the meeting with Cajetan had displayed another. In that meeting it was authoritarianism and the juridical element against conscience. In the controversy with Erasmus it was a certain complacency, 'common sense' and a theological slackness against a deeply biblical and theological awareness of the overwhelming reality of the divine. This is to express matters to Luther's benefit. Expressed with an opposite bias the controversy with Cajetan becomes the unity of the Church and the authority of the papacy against the subjective judgment of the individual rebel; the controversy with Erasmus becomes the practical statement of what man's situation really is, a pilgrimage during which he is tested and must make responsible choices against a statement of the domination of the spiritual so extreme that man seems to be predestined either to heaven or to hell. It is true that although the judgment of God and the punishment of hell ceased to be a personal difficulty and the cause of anguish for Luther, they did remain doctrinal difficulties to which he could find no purely logical solution and in face of which he falls back on 'faith' and in practice on an intellectual agnosticism superficially similar to that of Erasmus. These things have remained difficult to many theologians since that time.

Some quotations will indicate the essence of Luther's position as he stated it and provide also some idea of the force with which he expressed it and his consciousness of his own rough and ready speech compared with Erasmus's more gentle and sophisticated manner. More than a glimmer of ironical humour appears in his expression of this.

> I yield you the palm—an unprecedented thing for me!—not merely for far outstripping me in literary power and intellectual ability (we all grant you that as your due, the more so since I am an uncivilized fellow who has lived his life in the backwoods—*barbarus in barbarie semper versatus*).
>
> Fortune (or Chance or Fate if you prefer) has led you to say nothing at all on this whole vast topic that has not been said before,

and to say so much less about, and assign so much more to 'free-will'
than the Sophists [i.e. the Scholastics] did before you that it seemed
a complete waste of time to reply to your arguments. I have already
myself refuted them over and over again, and Philip Melanchthon,
in his unsurpassed volume on the doctrines of theology,[7] has tram-
pled them all in the dust. That book of his to my mind deserves not
merely to live as long as books are read, but to take its place in the
Church's canon; whereas your book by comparison struck me as so
worthless and poor that my heart went out to you as having defiled
your lovely brilliant flow of language with such vile stuff. I thought
it outrageous to convey material of so low a quality in the trappings
of such rare eloquence [from Luther's introduction].[8]

First, we will begin as we should, from your actual definition.
You define 'free-will' thus: 'Moreover, I conceive of "free-will" in
this context as a power of the human will by which a man may
apply himself to those things that lead to eternal salvation, or turn
away from the same'.

Cautiously, indeed, you here propound a bare definition, but give
no account of any of its parts, as others normally do. . . . The thing
defined, if closely examined, is undoubtedly of greater extent than
the definition. This is the kind of definition that the Sophists called
vicious (vitiosam)—that is, one in which the definition fails to cover
the thing defined. For I showed above that 'free-will' belongs to
none but God only. You are no doubt right in assigning to man a
will of some sort, but to credit him with a will that is free in the
things of God is too much. For all who hear mention of 'free-will'
take it to mean in its proper sense, a will that can and does do, God-
ward, all that it pleases, restrained by no law and no command; for
you would not call a slave, who acts at the beck of his lord, *free*. But
in that case how much less are we right to call men or angels *free*;
for they live under the complete mastery of God (not to mention
sin and death), and cannot continue by their own strength for a
moment. Here then, right at the outset, the definition of the term
and the definition of the thing are at odds, for the term connotes
one thing and what is really in mind is another. It would be more

[7] The *Loci Communes*, a work of Melanchthon's composed in 1521 in an attempt to
reduce Luther's theology to terms which other traditional theologians could understand
and which could afford some kind of norm or term of reference—a thing which of course
Luther never did, always developing, adding, rewriting, expounding the fresh insights
which were ever suggesting themselves to his fertile mind.
  [8] *Bondage*, p. 62.

correct to call it 'vertible-will' or 'mutable-will'. In this way Augustine, and the Sophists after him, diminish the glory and force of the term 'free', qualifying it with this limitation, which they call the 'vertibility' of 'free-will'. And it becomes us to speak in the same way, lest we befool men's hearts with swollen and vainglorious words; as Augustine also thinks. We should speak according to a definite rule, in sober and proper terms; for what is wanted in teaching is simplicity and legal correctness, not the high-flown figures of a rhetorical persuasive [from the beginning of the section headed Review of Erasmus' 'Arguments for "Free-will"'].⁹

Erasmus informs us, then, that free-will is a power of the human will which can of itself will and not will the word and the work of God. . . . Yes, it can will all things when it can will the contents of the word and work of God! What can be anywhere below, above, within or without the word and work of God, except God himself? But what is here left to grace and the Holy Ghost? This is plainly to ascribe divinity to 'free-will'! For to will the law and the Gospel, not to will sin, and to will death, is possible to divine power alone, as Paul says in more places than one.

Which means that nobody since the Pelagians has written of 'free-will' more correctly than Erasmus! For I said above that 'free-will' is a divine term, and signifies a divine power. But no one to date, except the Pelagians, has ever assigned to it such power.¹⁰

You grant that without special grace man cannot will good . . . and this is just to grant that it can *not* apply itself to what bears on eternal salvation—which was the burden of your definition! Further more: a little earlier, you say that the human will after sin is so depraved that it has lost its freedom and is forced to serve sin, and cannot recall itself to a better state! . . . Now here, I think, no way of escape is open to Proteus; he is caught and held fast by his own plain words, namely that the will has lost its liberty and is tied and bound in slavery to sin! Yet when Luther said the same, 'nothing so absurd was ever heard of!', 'nothing could be more useless than that this paradox should be broadcast!'

Perhaps nobody will believe me when I say that Erasmus says these things. Let doubters read the Diatribe at this point; they will be surprised! Not that I am particularly surprised. A man who does

⁹ *Ibid.*, p. 137.   ¹⁰ *Ibid.*, pp. 140–1.

not treat the question seriously and has no interest in the issue, whose mind is not on it and who finds it a boring and a chilling and a distasteful business, cannot help uttering absurdities and follies and contradictions all along the line; he argues his case like a man drunk or asleep, blurting out between snores 'Yes!', 'No!' as different voices sound upon his ears![11]

Luther is faced with many passages in Scripture, adduced by Erasmus, where a 'reward' is spoken of. His contention is that this 'reward' is a simple consequence of right behaviour, and not a prize for meritorious action. This perhaps is the weakest part of his argument. It is not too difficult for him to establish that Scripture sets all man's actions in a divine context where good actions are only good if they are truly motivated, that is done for love and for God's glory, and not for selfish reasons. But it is difficult to evacuate entirely from Scripture the idea that within this context a 'goal' and a 'reward' is spoken of as a kind of encouragement to man in a way which allows some place for motivation which is not entirely altruistic. Such an admission would not really damage Luther's fundamental thesis about the freedom of the will, because in seeking a reward the will is already working under grace. We do here enter the psychological rather than the theological sphere and the weakness of Luther's wish to apply a completely black and white picture of theological principle to every aspect or every action relating to salvation must seem crudely expressed in the light of modern psychology. A theological solution is possible in a more articulated understanding of the human personality and of its life in relation to a theology centred in the person of Christ—a solution which remained in sight with Luther himself, in his dynamic and christocentric theology.

The last words of Luther's text—before he turns in a conclusion to final personal remarks to Erasmus—state the great principle of the universality of Christ's mission in a way which was Catholic and traditional: 'Finally if we believe that Christ redeemed men by his blood, we are forced to confess that all of man was lost; otherwise, we make Christ either wholly superfluous, or else the

[11] *Ibid*, p. 146.

redeemer of the least valuable part of man only; which is blasphemy and sacrilege'. 'Redemption' and 'blood' here were not the pass words of an emotional revivalism or illuminism; they contained a theory of the universe and of God, of flesh and spirit, which Luther had laid hold on through years of hard study and personal experience, a theory at whose centre was a historical person, a hypostasis as the scholastics called it, which Luther believed the medieval Church to have betrayed by compromises, practical and doctrinal.

50. *Luther's Later Theology: The Commentary on Galatians*

ALTHOUGH St Paul's Epistle to the Romans was the primary scriptural source of Luther's doctrine of justification, his favourite epistle was that to the Galatians. Jokingly he once said it was his 'Katie von Bora to whom I have plighted my troth'. A letter from St Paul to some recent converts warning them not to be persuaded by Jewish Christians who said they were bound to observe every item of the Jewish law, including circumcision, it was a perfect vehicle for Luther's theology of the free gift of grace through faith as opposed to a doctrine of works. St Paul contrasts 'The [Judaic] Law' with 'The Spirit', and Luther expounds his teaching that the Spirit frees man from the Law.

Luther lectured three times on this epistle at Wittenberg in 1516 (published in 1519),[1] in 1523, and in 1531. The first course owed much both to St Jerome and to the recently published New Testament text and commentary of Erasmus. In 1523 Luther departed considerably from them both. When he took up the epistle for a third time in the University lecture hall in 1531, he produced a new text again. Luther's mind was then full of the opposition he must show to both his enemies, on the one hand, to the followers of 'Enthusiasmus', as he sometimes called those who looked first to inner inspiration as superior to all objective norms,

[1] See p. 104.

the 'Schwärmerei', who included followers of Münzer, and, earlier, of Carlstadt, also the Anabaptists, and the 'prophets of Zwickau', and on the other hand, to the papists. Three separate members of the audience, all of considerable intellectual ability, took notes during the lectures, and the Latin text, on which the currently available English text is based,[2] was produced by them, and then approved by Luther who wrote a preface.

This book is typical of the later Luther. His enemies had become almost an obsession. An attitude of opposition had become part of his very life-blood, a psychological necessity. He had begun life by an intense inner struggle. Having solved this struggle he found that his solution led him logically to oppose much of the common practice in the Church. Becoming subsequently a public figure, at the same time retaining his theological position, he inevitably had enemies to right and to left. They all became the subject for sweeping condemnation, sometimes in arguments which cannot bear too close examination. Sometimes they are all lumped together as in Luther's preface to this Epistle:

> The Papists and Anabaptists are today agreed on this one point against the Church of God (even if their words disguise it), namely, that the work of God depends on the worthiness of the person. According to the Anabaptists, baptism is nothing unless the person is a believer. From this principle (as it is called) it must follow that all the works of God are nothing if man is not good. If baptism, which is a work of God, ceases to be a work of God when man is evil, it follows that the married state, the office of a magistrate, and the station of a servant, which are works of God, are no longer works of God because men are evil.

This is a good example of how Luther built up in his own mind the idea that a 'works' theology, the mark of the devil, was the doctrine of all his enemies. He attributed it left, right and centre to anyone on whom it could be pinned with any semblance of justification. His argument in the above passage is that instead of relying entirely on God, the Anabaptists and the papists rely on

[2] George Rörer was the principal editor, his helpers were Veit Dietrich and Caspar Cruciger. Details of the currently available English text are referred to in the note on page 232. This text is based on the second edition of the text prepared by Rörer.

man—the former in that they deny all value to the sacrament of baptism unless the person being baptized has faith, the latter in the usual way for the meritorious works (indulgences, pilgrimages, offer Mass as a good work, etc.) which Catholics were encouraged to do. But the only possible implication of Luther's argument here about baptism as a 'work of God' is that the sacrament is precisely, as in the traditional Catholic teaching which he had so strongly opposed, an *opus operatum*, a work of God which cannot be evacuated of content by the absence of faith, even though it be rendered ineffective for the moment. Luther was defending a doctrine which he usually attacked, and was denying to an opponent his own very teaching of the necessity of faith for a sacrament to be of any significance. This brings into sharp focus the difficulties of Luther's teaching about the sacraments, in particular over infant baptism.

The passage, however, is of interest in that it gives a good idea of the way in which Luther saw all life as sacramental—he propounds a vocational-sacramental view of life in which a man's status, though undoubtedly the result of indifferent accidental factors, is one which God recognizes as proceeding from his work of creation and which he again takes up and re-establishes as a new Christian thing, a sacramental part of the new order established by his Son. Thus, in Luther's words, the married state, the office of a magistrate and the station of a servant all become 'works of God', all part of the sacramental life of the baptized Christian. So it is that a modern Lutheran theologian has claimed with considerable reason that the Christian life recommended and lived in Luther's terms gives a more central and more profoundly Christian place to the sacraments than did the traditional Christian life of the late medieval centuries.[8]

Luther expounds in the course of the introductory part of the commentary his conception of the good works which the moral law, given to the Jews by God, rightly demands, until a man is freed from its burden and acts morally from love, not from fear of the law. But he says that Catholics misinterpret him when they claim that he forbids good works. He is saying only that man

[8] R. Prenter in *Spiritus Creator*, p. 164.

cannot achieve any spiritual good in a 'good work' by itself. He returns to the theme often in the course of the commentary which provides many obvious occasions for it:

> Paul then did not reject circumcision as a damnable thing. . . . But he rejected circumcision as a thing not necessary to righteousness. . . . So we at this day do not reject fasting and other good exercises as damnable things; but we teach that by these exercises we do not obtain remission of sins. When the people hear this, by and by they judge us to speak against good works. And this opinion the Papists do confirm and increase by their preachings and writings. But they lie, and do us great wrong.[4]

Later Luther says that whilst remembering that they be free from the curse of the law, the godly should remember that, 'as touching the body, they are servants, and must serve one another through charity, according to this commandment of Paul. Let every man therefore endeavour to do his duty diligently in his calling, and to help his neighbour to the uttermost of his power.'[5]

Luther elaborates on the necessity for actual good works, acts of charity, contrasting this opinion with the idea that a good intention is what really counts, and again turning to the inadequacy of putting one's trust in ritual acts when one omits essential acts of charity:

> The faithful have this temptation, that if they omit never so light a matter which they ought to do, by and by their conscience is wounded; but they are not so troubled if they neglect charity (as they daily do) or bear not a sincere and brotherly love and affection towards their neighbour. For they do not so much regard the commandment of charity, as their own superstitions, from the which they be not altogether free during this life.

Luther is harsh on the scholastics. He says:

> The opinion of the schoolmen concerning this word 'love' is utterly cold and vain; for they say that to love is nothing but to wish someone well, or that love is a quality inhering in the mind, whereby a man eliciteth that motion of the heart, or that act, which is called benevolence. That is altogether naked, barren and mathe-

[4] *Galatians*, p. 94, commenting on Chap. 2, v. 3.   [5] *Ibid.*, p. 483.

matical charity, which is not (so to speak) incarnate, neither proceed-
eth to work.[6]

No doubt some of this criticism was justified, but Luther is blind
to anything good in his enemies, and fails to see that at the root
of this scholastic idea is the simple Christian idea, one with which
he is well acquainted, that kind acts can be done in such a cold
spirit and with such an inadequate motive that they virtually
cease to be acts of charity—it is the inner spirit that counts. To
use Luther's language, works are useless unless done by the man
justified by faith.

Luther returns to the subject of works and justification in a
massive way towards the end, commenting on St Paul's words:
'Behold, I Paul say unto you that if you be circumcised Christ
shall profit you nothing'.[7] I quote at length here because the
passage displays Luther's bedrock conviction of the universality
and comprehensive nature of God's power in the world and in
man, his specifically Christian idea of the grace of Christ and the
work of the Trinity, together with his burning concern about
those who deny this teaching, indignation expressed in emotional
terms. This indignation involved an overt recapitulation of his
own personal past, his own anguish, an anguish which had its
roots in his own special individual experience, including his relationship with his father. It was also a powerful symbol for others
of the psychological attraction of release from the legalism of the
Roman Catholic structure. Luther is expounding a set theme,
which whilst wide open to criticism in various particulars, has now
become for him, his followers, and for German Protestants,
parishes and dioceses a typical form of the Word of God, possessing, in this quasi-sacramental way, an ability to convince and
inspire others.

Paul here wonderfully stirred up with zeal and fervency of spirit,
thundereth against the law and circumcision: and these burning
words proceeding of great indignation, the Holy Ghost wresteth
from him, when he saith: 'Behold, I Paul' etc., I (I say) who know
that I have not received the Gospel by man, but by the revelation
of Jesus Christ, and have commission and authority from above, to

[6] *Ibid.*, p. 485.   [7] *Ibid.*, pp. 447 ff.

publish and to preach the same unto you, do tell you this new but undoubted truth,[8] that if ye be circumcised, Christ shall profit you nothing at all. This is a very hard sentence, whereby Paul declareth, that to be circumcised is as much as to make Christ utterly unprofitable:[9] not in himself, but in respect of the Galatians, who, being deceived by the subtlety of the false apostles, believed that besides faith in Christ, it was needful for the faithful to be circumcised, without the which they could not obtain salvation.

This place is as it were a touch-stone, whereby we may most certainly and freely judge of all doctrines, works, religions[10] and ceremonies of all men. Whosoever teach that there is anything necessary to salvation (whether they be Papists, Turks, Jews, or Sectaries) besides faith in Christ, or shall devise any work or religion, or observe any rule, tradition, or ceremony whatsoever, with this opinion that by such things they shall obtain forgiveness of sins, righteousness, and everlasting life; they hear in this place the sentence of the Holy Ghost pronounced against them by the Apostle, that Christ profiteth them nothing at all. Seeing Paul durst give this sentence against the law and circumcision which were ordained of God himself, what durst he not do against the chaff and dross of men's traditions?

Wherefore, this place is a terrible thunderbolt against all the kingdom of the Pope. For all of them, priests, monks, hermits, etc. (I speak of the best of them), have reposed their trust and confidence in their own works, righteousness, vows and merits, and not in Christ, whom they most wickedly and blasphemously imagine to be an angry judge, an accuser and condemner; and therefore here they hear their judgment, that Christ profiteth them nothing. For if they can put away sins, and deserve forgiveness of sins and everlasting life, through their own righteousness and straitness of life, then to what purpose was Christ born? What profit have they by his passion and blood-shedding, by his resurrection, victory over sin, death and the devil, seeing they are able to overcome these monsters by their own strength? And what tongue can express how horrible a thing it is to make Christ unprofitable? Therefore the Apostle uttereth these words with great displeasure and indignation: 'If ye be circumcised, Christ shall profit you nothing;' that is to say, no profit shall redound unto you of all his benefits, but he hath bestowed them all upon you in vain. . . .

---

[8] *sententiam novam quidem, sed certam et veram.*　　　[9] *ociosum.*　　　[10] *cultus.*

This is therefore a most certain and clear sentence, that Christ is unprofitable, that is to say, he is born, crucified and risen again in vain to him that is circumcised, that is, which putteth his trust in circumcision. For (as I have said before) Paul speaketh not here of the work of circumcision in itself (which hurteth not him that hath no affiance or opinion of righteousness in it), but of the use of the work, that is to say, of the confidence and righteousness that is annexed to the work. For we must understand Paul according to the matter whereof he intreateth, or according to the argument which he hath in hand, which is, that men be not justified by the law, by works, by circumcision, or such-like. He saith not that works of themselves are nothing; but the confidence and righteousness of works are nothing; for that maketh Christ unprofitable. Therefore whoso receiveth circumcision, with this opinion that it is necessary to justification, to him Christ availeth nothing.

Let us bear this well in mind in our private temptations, when the devil accuseth and terrifieth our conscience to drive it to desperation. For he is the father of lying, and the enemy of Christian liberty; therefore he tormenteth us every moment with false fears, that when our conscience hath lost this Christian liberty, it should always be in dread, feeling itself accused and terrified.[11] When (I say) that great dragon, that old serpent the devil (who deceiveth the whole world, and accuseth our brethren in the presence of God day and night, Rev. xii) cometh and layeth unto thy charge, that thou hast not only done no good, but hast also transgressed the law of God, say unto him: Thou troublest me with the remembrance of my sins past; thou puttest me also in mind that I have done no good; but this is nothing to me: for if either I trusted in mine own good deeds, or distrusted because I have done none, Christ should both ways profit me nothing at all. Therefore, whether thou lay my sins before me, or my good works, I pass not: but removing both far out of my sight, I only rest in that liberty wherein Christ hath made me free. I know him to be profitable unto me, therefore I will not make him unprofitable: which I should do, if either I should presume to purchase myself favour[12] and everlasting life by my good deeds, or should despair of my salvation because of my sins. . . .

Therefore whensoever the devil transforming himself into the likeness of Christ, disputeth with us after this manner: This thou oughtest, being admonished by my word, to have done, and hast

---

[11] *ut semper sit in metu, ac sentiat reatum et pavores.*   [12] *gratiam.*

not done it; and this thou oughtest not to have done, and hast done it; know thou therefore that I will take vengeance on thee, etc.: let this nothing at all move us, but by and by let us think with ourselves: Christ speaketh not to poor afflicted and despairing consciences after this manner; he addeth not affliction to the afflicted; he breaketh not the bruised reed, neither quencheth he the smoking flax (Matt. xii. 20). Indeed to the hard-hearted he speaketh sharply: but such as are terrified and afflicted, he most lovingly and comfortably allureth unto him, saying: 'Come unto me all ye that travail and be heavy laden and I will refresh you' (Matt. xi. 28); 'I came not to call the righteous, but sinners' etc. (ix.13); 'Be of good comfort my son, thy sins are forgiven thee' (ix. 2); 'Be of good cheer, I have overcome the world' (John xvi. 33); 'The son of man came to seek and to save that which was lost' (Luke xix. 10). We must take good heed therefore lest that we, being deceived with the wonderful sleights and infinite subtleties of Satan, do receive an accuser and condemner in the stead of a comforter and saviour: and so under the vizor[13] of a false Christ, that is to say, of the devil, we lose the true Christ, and make him unprofitable unto us. Thus much have we said as touching private and particular temptations, and how we should use ourselves therein.

Interestingly Luther in commenting on the next verse goes on to an overtly personal reference:

And this which I say by occasion of Paul's words, I have learned by experience in the monastery, both in myself and others. I have seen many which have painfully travailed, and upon mere conscience have done as much as was possible for them to do, in fasting, in prayer, in wearing of hair, in punishing and tormenting their bodies with sundry exercises (whereby at length they must needs have utterly consumed them, yea although they had been made of iron), and all to this end that they might obtain quietness and peace of conscience: notwithstanding, the more they travailed, the more they were stricken down with fear, and especially when the hour of death approached, they were so fearful that I have seen many murderers [and other malefactors] condemned to death, dying more courageously than they did, which notwithstanding had lived very holily.

[13] *larva.*

Therefore it is most true, that they which do the law, do it not. For the more men go about to satisfy the law, the more they transgress it. Even so we say and judge of men's traditions. The more a man striveth to pacify his conscience thereby, the more he troubleth and tormenteth it. When I was a monk, I endeavoured as much as was possible to live after the strait rule of mine Order: I was wont to shrive myself with great devotion, and to reckon up all my sins (yet being always very contrite before), and I returned to confession very often, and thoroughly performed the penance that was enjoined unto me: yet for all this my conscience could never be fully certified, but was always in doubt, and said: This or that thou hast not done rightly; thou wast not contrite [and sorrowful] enough; this sin thou didst omit in thy confession, etc. Therefore the more I went about to help my weak, wavering and afflicted conscience by men's traditions, the more weak and doubtful and the more afflicted I was. And thus, the more I observed men's traditions, the more I transgressed them, and in seeking after righteousness by mine Order, I could never attain unto it: for it is impossible (as Paul saith) that the conscience should be pacified by the works of the law, and much more by men's traditions, without the promise and glad tidings concerning Christ.

Wherefore they that seek to be justified and quickened by the law, are much further off from righteousness and life, than the publicans, sinners and harlots. For these cannot trust to their own works, seeing they be such that they cannot hope to obtain grace and forgiveness of sins thereby. For if righteousness and works done according to the law do not justify, how can sins justify which are committed contrary to the law? Therefore in this point they are in far better case than the justiciaries: for they have no affiance in their own works, which greatly hindereth true faith in Christ, if it do not utterly take it away. Contrariwise, the justiciaries, which abstain outwardly from sins, and live holily[14] and without blame in the sight of the world, cannot be without the opinion of their own righteousness, with which [the true] faith in Christ cannot stand: and for this cause they be more miserable than the publicans and harlots, who offer not their good works to God in his displeasure, that for the same he may recompense them with everlasting life (as the justiciaries do), for they have none to offer; but desire that their sins may be pardoned for Christ's sake.

[14] *religiose.*

There are some remarkable passages in this work about the unity of the Church, the importance of concord in order to keep unity and the impossibility of preventing atomization and disintegration once the unity is broken. Luther, as we have seen, regarded himself as a reformer of the Church, working within the one Church. These passages then are really intended for the followers of Münzer and the others, but they are a useful witness to Luther's concern for the visible Church in its unity of life and doctrine: 'If the foundation, that is to say, if faith in Christ be overthrown by wicked teachers, no peace or concord can remain in the Church, either in doctrine or life. .... And when once the concord of the Church is broken, there is no measure nor end of that evil; for the authors of schisms, dissenting among themselves, do teach, one that this work, one that another work is necessary to righteousness.'

Luther's doctrine of the sin which remains in man throughout his life is stated towards the end of the commentary. This doctrine has often been misunderstood to mean that justification is something purely exterior in Luther's teaching, 'extrinsic' justification. But this has been shown conclusively to be incorrect on the basis of Luther's own work.[15] Luther's most cogent Catholic interpreter of modern times is in agreement.[16] Luther is not denying the efficacy of the sacraments, or proposing any sort of Manicheism. He is doing no more than state that there is a flaw in man, that there is always a tendency, remaining until death, towards actions which a man himself believes to be wrong. In principle he is teaching the Catholic doctrine of original sin. However, he does finally arrive at astonishing statements in another direction, the result of using scholastic logic to draw out further meaning from existential theological affirmations. He declares that the sin of the faithful is not imputed to him, whilst the sin of the unbeliever is mortal. His words convey a proposition which goes beyond the paradoxes of the Gospel. An unbeliever is to be punished personally for something for which he is not personally guilty. It was the kind of failure into which the earlier Augustine fell, reducing his

[15] Rupp, R.G., particularly pp. 241–6.
[16] Lortz in his chapter in *Découverte de l'Oecumenisme*.

20. Luther preaching
An illustration from an early edition of his prayers

21. Luther dead
From a drawing by Furttenagel

theological concepts to a too jejune pattern and following a strictly logical argument to arrive at a conclusion obviously unharmonious with the Gospel. The same process we have observed to occur in *The Bondage of the Will*. But we should not linger on this point. Luther was not concerned with the problem of the unbeliever but of the believer, the ordinary German Christian whose faith seemed to have been whittled away almost to nothing by Roman legalism, preoccupied with sin and judgment. Luther's message was that of an enlightened director of souls today: 'Do not concentrate on your sins but on God in whom you trust and hope. Trust in him as your loving Father.'

Luther's meaning is only adequately interpreted when any particular proposition is related back to all the rest of his teaching. This is no doubt true in some degree of every thinker. But in Luther the point is of special importance. He cannot be said to be a careful or methodical writer. He retained the habits of polemical debate which he learnt in the early days at the university, a discipline imposed on thought from outside for the purpose of presenting points to be debated one by one. This method can mislead. It certainly does so in Luther. Individual texts may well be put against each other to show what a contradictory fellow he is or what a careless writer or a bad logician. But if an attempt is to be made to find out what he really thought and what in general was conveyed to his followers, if an attempt at generalization is being made, individual texts must be set back into the context of all his thought. To some extent generalization itself may be out of place in that Luther was often concerned with special or particular objects in his writing and was not, in any particular writing, concerned with overall consistency in relation to other writings. Then again his thought develops and changes. The great influence Luther had was not related stringently to the total of all he said or wrote. By no means everything was read by everyone. Many who were indirectly influenced by him never read anything of his. But it remains that a general consistency is not difficult to discern.

Interpretation by the Cranach School of the distribution of the Lord's Supper
to the Protestant Saxon princes. Note John Frederick confessing to Luther
at upper left. Painted about 1560

51. *Summing Up*

LUTHER had lived about half his adult life as a religious in a community of Augustinian friars, and about half as a layman and public figure, family man and religious reformer, seventeen years as the former, and twenty-two as the latter. With his death there disappeared from the scene an unrepeatable and unique experience, a person whose life exactly bridged the end of one era and the beginning of another. The shorter of the two halves was the first. But the first seventeen years of a man's adult life exercise a fundamental influence on the remainder. Luther's life was Catholic and Protestant.

It is superficial to divide history rigidly into periods, and a good case can be made out for saying that greater and more important changes occurred in the eighteenth or the twentieth century than in the sixteenth. In some ways the Catholic Church itself, even the majority of Christian communions, are only today coming to grips with assumptions of medieval Christianity, not all of which are to be judged as flowing from the Gospel—and a time will be coming perhaps when primitive Christianity itself can be grasped more thoroughly, and its assumptions faced out. But it is true that Luther's death in 1546 and the Council of Trent which began in 1545 marked in a definitive way the establishment of Protestantism as a Christian sociological phenomenon, finally separate from the Roman Catholic Church. While Luther was alive his own sense of reforming an existing Church rather than founding a new one remained a dominant factor at Wittenberg where all matters of doubt continued to be referred. An oracle remained, the great man, who had achieved the seemingly impossible, rupture from Rome followed by survival, growth, respect from the world, and the flowering of Christian ideals.

The primary positive achievement is not difficult to discern— a new Christian vision, directly based on the Bible, with a renewed conviction of the sovereignty of God, of man's life as built on faith in him; a new face for religion, expressed in the people's language, taking them up into its practice in a more democratic fashion. The negative is more difficult to assess. Some of what Luther himself rejected has since returned. Much of what his followers rejected has returned. Today instead of a rapidly increasing rift between two traditions, there is a slowly returning respect for and interest in each other, backed by an urgent realization that Christian unity is more important than anything else. Catholics dare to look the facts of Luther's vision and achievement in the face. Aquinas and the 'rancid philosopher' Aristotle can be looked at by Lutherans with some measure of calm; and it can be seen that Christian unity must be something more than purely caritative or transcendental. On some of these issues Luther's most strongly-worded statements are those which survive least successfully.

In the work of Aquinas and other scholastics, Christian theology became an achievement of a high intellectual order, scrupulously confined within the areas where the intellect can give significant expression, admitting its limitations, proceeding with logical consistency from one point to another. This achievement was insufficient by itself to convince Christians of the need to do the 'one thing necessary'; indeed the achievement became the subject merely for further intellectual speculation. Many of the valid and good things in it were obscured, and finally lost for a time. Luther was convinced that the whole thing was just a mess of abstractions, not only useless but a corruption of the Gospel. Convinced, like many others, of the futility of the scholastic method, Luther turned to a theology of affirmation, a biblical method. But he could not forswear his own intellect, nor his logical training. He still believed firmly in the power of the reason as a tool (as distinct from a source of truth, or a guide to life). In practice he then ended up with propositions which are mutually contradictory; where Aquinas turned to analogy, Luther turned to 'faith' in a way which implied agnosticism in the strictly intellectual sense. Having no rationale for infant baptism Luther turned to faith. But once the intellect abdicates, one is left with faith only fitfully supported by reason, and so with fideism—which is where the Nominalists had got to, a faith whose revealed propositions were accepted purely on the authority of the Church. And so the way is open for a renewal of the authoritarian bigotry and prejudice traditionally associated with religion, and to the easy way out offered by biblical fundamentalism, the precise words of Scripture being consulted like a crystal ball, not that this was Luther's intention.

To the Thomists of his time, to Cajetan and other Catholic theologians, Luther's disavowal of the authority of the Church, and the substitution of Scripture, without any precisely defined and known authority to interpret it, seemed fatal. They held to a belief in the guidance of established ecclesiastical authority by the Holy Spirit in the sense of a protection from any final corruption, a proposition set in a context in which faith, assisted by the intellect, was able to penetrate further into the meaning of Scripture. They knew the extent to which corruption had in fact proceeded, and therefore had sympathy with the revolt both against the overbearing use of papal authority and against the general corruption of popular practice. But they were convinced that the reform of the latter was not to be obtained by the rejection of the former.

Luther's later writings recapitulate his essential insight, setting it now in an argument which makes a rigid distinction between the followers of his teaching and the Papists to the right and the Protestants to the left of him. Disagreements which had been for a few years divisions within the schools were now built into divisions between separate bodies of Christians. This was far from Luther's intention. From the University Hall at Wittenberg he and his followers had watched their reforms spread with an extraordinary rapidity, just as the first wave of interest in Luther himself had spread almost unaccountably in the winter of 1517–18. Soon they were sure of their reform; success against the overwhelming ecclesiastical establishment spread like a tidal wave before their eyes. They had no thought that they were preparing centuries of division to come. For instance, Luther was not thinking primarily, or probably at all, in his final commentary on Galatians, of producing a normative writing, a commentary over which we might pore in centuries to come—he was not particularly interested in publication, leaving this to his pupils. The shafts against his enemies were the shafts of a university lecturer on his home ground—shafts which in any case his listeners had come to expect, perhaps demand. But the shafts struck exceedingly deep and built part of a wall between Christian bodies which lasted four hundred years and more. Within the palisade built by those shafts was nurtured that strong tradition of personal religion which is Protestantism. Perhaps a bridge exists in the Orthodox tradition with its great respect for the individual and its institutional nature. But this is to dream. Neither Pope nor Luther knew that tradition—nor could they foresee other bridges.

I have tried to select facts, and judgments on them, to convey a true picture of Martin Luther, the man of history, religious reformer and theologian. In my introductory chapter I referred to the relevance of such a study to the contemporary problems facing those who work for Christian unity. I disclaimed any wish to make this an 'ecumenical' study, since such a claim might imply an attempt to select only the factors in Luther's life which tend towards unity. No such attempt has been made and it would be absurd. Luther's life is a story of exchanges with those with whom he disagreed, a story of dialogue and of battle. But a study of these exchanges and all the facts of his life should assist ecumenical study. We must be done with Luther the giant-villain or giant-hero. He was an Augustinian friar, of good intellect, piously bred, deeply anguished in his spiritual life, solving his personal dilemmas in a re-thought biblical theology. This theology led him to fulminate against the superficial legalistic religious practice of the time. He became the leader of the European religious breakaway from the western Roman Church which became Protestantism.

Many factors met in the life of this man which lifted him higher and higher so that he became a kind of multiple symbol in which nearly everyone could find a rallying point. He became the symbol of the *gravamina* which the Estates so often brought before the Emperor for righting, of the northern European attack on ecclesiastical and Italian abuses, of the Church's own internal

movement for reform already a hundred years old, of the humanist emphasis on original texts. But the bedrock factor is theological.
The reader was warned that he must submit to theological categories in facing a theological complex. He may well say he has
had indeed to submit—if he did not give up. But there is no
other way. Luther was grappling with the ultimate problems
which face all men, about the nature of the world and of men; he
faced them in the context and form in which Christian theology
attempts their solution.

Luther became something of a myth even in his lifetime. This
is never good for any man, and it must have tended towards the
exaggeration of his defects. If his wife usually seems to have stood
up to him, some no doubt were frightened to tell him off when
he waxed too vehement. They were frightened for his health; and
they revered him for his astonishing achievement. They were in a
certain awe of a man who had done what he had done. And there
remained an element of anguish, and an element of fear in Luther's
own personality, which communicated itself outwards; there was
something frightening about success in his particular venture, success which in papist eyes was sin and damnation.[1] Such fear always
found an echo in Luther's own psychological make-up. His
tirades increased in violence if anything as he grew older. But they
were not the major thing. We have seen something of his massive
achievement. He remained a man of charity to the end of his life.

His death came to him partly as a result of a long and tiring
winter journey in answer to a plea in the autumn of 1545 to come
and solve and end a family quarrel between the princes of Mansfeld, at Eisleben where he was born, eighty miles away. By the
middle of February the work was done. On February 18 Luther
died after only a few hours illness. On the 19th was held the
funeral service in the church of St Andrew not far from the house
in which he had been born. The body was taken back to Wittenberg where it was buried in the castle church on February 22,
having entered the church through the door on which the Ninety-
five Theses had been nailed. Melanchthon was one of the
preachers, the other being Bugenhagen.

[1] In Appendix 2 will be found some further considerations.

After the death of one of his children Luther commented that he had had an experience which no Christian priest had had for a thousand years—this was an exaggeration in various ways, but it expressed vividly something of the true significance of his life, a turning again to what might be called the human values at the heart of the Gospel. That Luther could speak as he did of human fatherhood is a comment on the extent to which the idea of spiritual fatherhood had been absent from the Church.[2] Luther's message was not solely the rather austere theology of justification, but a return to the New Testament themes of the Fatherhood of God, the sending of the Son, and the Son's message of forgiveness and love for all men. Beneath the polemics and the theology lay this concern for man, the personal appeal. He spoke of Christ the man who had suffered for them, and had taken on the bitter life of the world. Luther himself lived out his life as one who shared all things with others, an ordinary honest man.

[2] I am indebted for this insight to the Rev. A. M. Allchin who was amongst those who kindly read the typescript and gave me advice and criticism.

Appendix 1

INDULGENCES

This is an attempt to provide a brief account of the theory and practice of indulgences in relation to Luther's criticism, in language as far as possible non-technical without losing any theological nuance. It is impossible to make a really simple explanation. Twentieth-century Roman Catholic preachers find it hard to explain indulgences to congregations. For a more complete exposé, together with extracts from many of the most important historical documents see *Sacraments and Forgiveness*, Paul F. Palmer, S.J. (Volume II, Sources of Christian Theology, pages 321–369). Among these texts is a masterly theoretical *rationale* provided for indulgences by Aquinas. Nothing short of Luther's 'dynamic' theology would suffice to contradict the answers provided by Aquinas to the obvious objections. But his *rationale* ends with an economically worded warning whose implications are exceedingly far-reaching and implicitly add a very strong rider to any conclusion that might be drawn from his doctrinal exposé such as that indulgences should be widely granted and the people strongly encouraged to use them: '. . . yet other works of satisfaction are more meritorious with respect to our essential reward, which is infinitely better than the remission of temporal punishment' (the words are also quoted in the text on p. 110). There are two points in that brief sentence, and the failure of the medieval Church to observe them or to reform its practice in conformity with them is highly typical of the general failure to reform itself, with which Luther was so radically concerned. There are those in the Catholic Church today who think that the final and total abolition of indulgences would, on balance, be spiritually advantageous.

Indulgences existed and still exist in the following Catholic framework. A Christian does not live a perfect life; he sins. He sins, offending against the Gospel, against a moral principle or breaking a commandment of the Church. Subsequently he is sorry for this lapse, turns to God inwardly and is forgiven. His sin was not only an act against his own nature destined for glory with God, it was an act against God's Church. It was an injury to every member of the Church, for all depend upon one another, the health of one works for the health of another, the sickness of one for the sickness of another. So, as when a Christian first joins God's Church, he does so through the formal Church rite of the sacrament of baptism, and as when his life further progresses it is marked and strengthened by other sacraments of the Church, so when he has damaged his relationship with God and his Church, and, by doing so, threatened or injured that of others, a sacrament of the Church makes provision for formal statements of sorrow by the sinner, of God's forgiveness by his Church, and for a means of spiritual help, grace, to help the sinner to carry out his intention to amend. The questions then arise whether the sinner needs to make reparation or satisfaction, and whether he must receive some punishment for sin. The Church seems to have given an affirmative answer in principle to all three questions from very early times. This does not affect the forgiveness always and immediately forthcoming from God to a repentant sinner who turns inwardly to God; reparation, satisfaction and punishment were linked with the Church's formal sacramental ratification of repentance and forgiveness. In the early Church the sinner was only formally reconciled after doing penance, sometimes public penance in which the parish might join with him on his behalf, for a certain number of days. The sinner was excluded from the Eucharistic liturgy (a form of excommunication) until the penance was complete. Clearly the early Church only bothered itself with what Staupitz called 'real sins'; shortness of temper cannot have been a cause for confession unless it led to murder or grave slander or some other such definite abrogation of the law. But people soon felt a need, apparently, to express their sorrow for the lesser things. In time they confessed more frequently; smaller penance was done, and this was subsequent not prior to the sacramental reconciliation. The sin hardly deserved excommunication.

When penances became small the possibility occurred to men that at the time of his death a Christian might not have done all the penance which his sins deserved in the sight of God. He might still be due to receive some of what the theologians later came to call the 'temporal punishment due to sin'. It was assumed that this remaining debt must be paid after death. The sinner had been completely forgiven, but he might still in justice have some reparation or satisfaction to make, or punishment to bear. To state it in another way, perhaps more in tune with the Gospel, the forgiven sinner might still need a further time of preparation or purging before he was fit for the marriage feast of heaven.

The Church then said that a Christian who had received the sacrament of penance, could by various good works, the saying of particular prayers or doing such pious works as assisting in the building of churches (by a cash payment) achieve release from some part of, sometimes all of, whatever 'temporal punishment' he might still be due to undergo after death. An indulgence was a statement to this effect—the Church promised release to the repentant sinner, duly shrived, on the condition specified, of undertaking such good works. And if the release was not plenary (a 'plenary indulgence') it was measured, and the amount specified. How measure punishment in purgatory? Only by some equivalent. The standard used was that of the old traditional penance which was measured simply by days of visible penance and exclusion from the liturgy. So indulgences were issued as releases from so many 'days of exclusion', and they were intended to release the sinner from the equivalent in purgatory, whatever it might be, of so many days penance in the early Church.

All this was in harmony with the general doctrine of the authority which the Church understood that Christ had given her: 'Whatever you loose on earth, it shall be loosed in heaven. Whatever you retain on earth, it shall be retained in heaven.' Salvation itself is not at issue. It is only a question of relationship to the Church on earth, and in so far as it was linked to it, of punishment in purgatory.

Meanwhile the medieval theologians had propounded an explanatory, mechanical theory of 'merits' which further rationalized the use of sacraments, and of indulgences. The saints and Christ had been good, and gained 'merit', far above what was necessary to avoid damnation and achieve heaven. The principle of solidarity, of the health of one working for the health of another, was transformed into an accounting system by which the merit of each member was theoretically measured in heaven, and all of it beyond what that member required put in a bank for the help of others. 'The treasury of merits', a typically medieval gambit, was not really necessary for a theological justification of the granting of indulgences, but it helped to explain the solidarity principle for the canonically-minded theologians of the time, who also found it easier to encourage people to gain indulgences with this ingenious and readily intelligible theory. In practice this theory was translated so widely that it tended to overshadow the simple theology of the redemption of all men by Christ once for all. The scale of indulgences became a principal source of income for ecclesiastical authorities.

Indulgences left plenty of room for abuse, both in a basic doctrinal sense, and in their being granted for cash payments. When more emphasis was given by preachers to the gaining of indulgences—for instance, by the good work of making a cash contribution to the building of a church—than to the sacraments, the liturgy and ordinary acts of charity, then it was made to appear as though the values of the Gospel were being abandoned. Ordinary Christians were appealed to as though their first concern should be to obtain release from sufferings in purgatory by a cash payment. If the sermons were frequent enough, and enough publicity and external pomp accompanied the offer of an indulgence it could very well be that the matter of salvation itself could become confused in the popular mind with what could be obtained by an indulgence. Then it was commonly supposed, and the Church seems specifically to have encouraged such a supposition, even though theology could not and did not finally support it, that a cash payment could in appropriate circumstances buy an immediate release from purgatory for the souls suffering there. The Church had always encouraged Christians to pray for those who had died; when indulgences began to be issued with the idea that they might be transferred to the souls in purgatory this was seen, not without reason, as a praiseworthy raising of the motive for gaining an indulgence, from something selfish to an act of charity towards others. It was commonly supposed and preached that a transferred indulgence certainly guaranteed a soul's immediate release. But this cannot be maintained, in traditional Catholic theology, and the Church has not maintained it on the few occasions when the matter has been directly and authoritatively treated. This became one of Luther's more bitter points of protest[1] on a matter which was controversial and in fact remained in some doubt, dogmatically, for several centuries. Abuses in connection with indulgences were recognized and combated from an early time. The Fourth Lateran

[1] Palmer makes it clear that though there must have been some doubt, dogmatically, about this in Luther's time, and in the nineteenth century, the conclusion must be drawn that the Church has definitely declined to believe that a plenary indulgence transferred by prayer to a soul in purgatory can guarantee its release, though the Church hopes, as it were, that Christ will respect her wishes in the matter (note, p. 357). It seems to be true that in this respect an abuse against which Luther fought still exists, since many Catholics seem still to believe that when they gain a plenary indulgence it can be applied at will so as to obtain the automatic release of a soul from purgatory. And the dogmatic implications are important, for they concern the matter of the claim of the Church to exercise a certain direct executive rule in purgatory.

Council of 1215 was an early case of a formal attempt by the Church to prevent abuse.[2] The doctrine itself was regarded by the more scrupulous as one to which not too much emphasis should be given. The conclusion of Aquinas makes this clear.[3]

It is not difficult to see that the whole theological atmosphere in which indulgences thrive is inimical to the dynamic theology of justification which Luther had been working out. This juggling with 'days' of penances, equivalent to time in purgatory, this concern with how many 'days' could be got for how much monetary contribution, or how many prayers, the very idea that something one did oneself could produce a change, could cause God to act—all this would seem unworthy of one who owed a complete surrender to God, who could never be of himself worthy of the sovereign creator, but who had in fact been saved and justified by the Word of God, made one with the saints by the free act of Jesus. From a more abstract point of view, as we have seen, Aquinas puts out a very stringent criticism, sober and terse, though it is in the final sentence on this subject.

But the incompatibility was not absolute. Luther did not at first contradict indulgences in principle. He knew the value of simple explanations for the people. He never turned away from the broadly sacramental—in the sense of a visible formal rite—attitude to religion, nor from the Church doctrine of solidarity in Christ which provided the theological background essential for indulgences. Luther's theses include a proposal (thesis 38) for a 'correct' interpretation of them: 'The Pope's remission and distribution are in no way to be despised since, as I have said, they are a declaration of divine forgiveness'. But on the other hand they are to be given only a minor place, less than that of acts of kindness: 'Christians must be taught that it is not the Pope's intention that the purchase of indulgences is in any way comparable with the works of mercy'.

Luther's primary concern was that the palaver accompanying the offer of indulgences, their mechanical side, and the emphasis laid on them had radically covered over that first essential—sorrow for sin, turning to God, use of the sacrament of confession. The tremendous publicity given in 1517 to the preaching of the most recent indulgence by Tetzel and his preachers confirmed him in the feeling that the people were being encouraged to forget the essential inner realities and to substitute a commercial transaction for it. In the first place, then, it is a matter of emphasis. Instead of the Word of God the preachers are preaching a commercial and almost magical recipe.

But Luther was also concerned specifically with that part of the doctrine which involved a claim by the Church to release souls, whether on earth or in purgatory, from the punishment which they might need to undergo before they would have fully expiated their sins, or would be fit for heaven. The theses were of course at first a controversial technical matter, intended for debate, and intended no doubt to focus public attention on the undoubted abuses, theological and practical, involved in the preaching of the indulgences. It does not seem to be certain that Luther believed them all, explicitly, at the time when he drew them up. Quite probably his mind was open, he was prepared for some of the theses to be contradicted, proven wrong in public debate. In the course of such a debate, the theological bases of the granting of indulgences

[2] See Palmer, op. cit., p. 336.   [3] See note 1, p. 279.

might be more clearly expounded, perhaps modified, and the abuses perhaps exposed and those responsible for them reprimanded. This would seem to be Luther's position from his *Appeal to Leo X* in 1518[4] in which he states clearly, even at this later date, his entire willingness to abide by the authority of Rome: 'I shall acknowledge your voice as the voice of Christ who is enthroned in you, and who speaks through you'.[5]

The theses express precisely the kind of objection which flows naturally from the basic theological position which Luther had established. He was deeply concerned at the extent to which the Church seemed sometimes to claim an authority not confined to the authority given to it by God, but equivalent to the divine authority itself, an authority which would allow it to rule in purgatory as well as on earth. Furthermore, the very concept of 'ruling' struck him as alien to the Gospel which spoke of a 'ministry' rather than rule. Although there must be an authority in the Church, it should exercise authority in this sense of serving the Church.

Luther therefore put forward the thesis that by indulgences the Pope could only be intending to release souls from the precise penances which the Church herself had canonically applied, and that they are simply statements of divine forgiveness of those who are truly contrite. Basically, this proposition was revolutionary in that it proposed, in harmony with Luther's presentation of the theology of justification, that a contrite man is not only forgiven but has also full remission of punishment. Although not logically inevitable this theory of the full remission of punishment is a harmonious adjunct to the theology of the act of justification of a man by the Word of God. A man believes in God, and God takes him to himself. There are no half measures in God, he makes up for all that in which man fails—only believe, only accept this all-satisfying, all-achieving grace, and a man has the essence of what makes him acceptable to God, the essence even of sanctity, in spite of his remaining tendency towards sin.

Whatever Luther's own attitude may have been at the time of the composition of the theses, subsequent events had the effect of convincing him that they were all in fact correct, and they do doubtless represent his own attitude a few years later, and for the reasons we have adduced.

---

[4] See Palmer, *op. cit.*, p. 359.

[5] This appeal implies that the theses were a sort of sighting shot in an attempt to attack specific abuses: 'I thought it right to show at least a modicum of opposition to the preachers: I therefore called their doctrines in question, and proposed a public debate.' The exaggerated terms in which Luther, flinging 'himself prostrate at the feet of your holiness', describes the authority of the Pope, applying semi-mystical terms ('Christ enthroned in you') was typical of the time, and of some later times. The wide, but in many ways imprecise, authority of the Pope implied by these terms was more far-reaching by a long way than that stated by the definition of infallibility of 1870, ringed around as that definition is with provisos and conditions.

Appendix 2

BY WHAT AUTHORITY?

A GUIDE TO THE THEOLOGY OF AUTHORITY AND THE TERMS 'SUBJECTIVE' AND 'OBJECTIVE' IN RELATION TO LUTHER'S INITIATIVE

Luther's life up to the time of the Diet of Worms was a gradual and personal development, his writings and his action proceeding, not according to some plan of his own from which everything could be easily deduced, nor as an inevitable unfolding of a predestined pattern, inherent in his own teaching or temperament. His theology has been shown to be based on certain simple and fundamental aspects of the teaching of the New Testament. This theology led him to make stringent criticisms of current Christian practice. This criticism—in effect criticism of established Catholic practices and institutions and of persons currently in authority—was undertaken from within the Church and was projected with the clear purpose of reform, similar in intention to that of many other criticisms made at the time. Luther explicitly affirmed his complete adherence to the one institution and its teaching, and to papal authority, in making these criticisms, well into 1518, and in modified senses into the early part of 1519. This criticism led to a response in the form of a personal and canonical attack on Luther by supreme Catholic authority. Luther's reaction to this was further to develop and articulate his theology, beyond the point of criticism from within, until it brought him, on some matters, into direct contradiction with Catholic tradition, in particular concerning the authority of Popes and Councils, and the status of Scripture. He proceeded to an explicit rejection of traditional ecclesiastical authority, papal and conciliar, also of parts of Catholic teaching on the Mass and the sacraments, and was duly excommunicated by the Pope.

There is, then, a fundamental contradiction between Luther's two positions: (1) early in 1518 when he retained faith in the papacy as the ultimate authority within the Church, and in the Mass and sacraments; (2) in 1521 when he had rejected this authority and some of the Catholic teaching on the Mass and the sacraments. By what authority did Luther advance from one position to the other, from a position in which he wished to promote a more dynamic theology within the existing structure of the Church, and reform abuses associated with the generally accepted theology, to a position in which he denied some of the traditional doctrines and the authority of the Roman Church? By what other authority did he challenge established Christian authority? If the rule of the Pope, and the traditional institutions associated with him, were irreformable, and if Christians should no longer acknowledge them, what would he put in their place? To what authority should ordinary men and women look in their daily lives—where did Luther look himself?

Since Luther's own day answers to these question have been supplied vigorously by Christians, Catholics and Protestants agreeing at least that the authority to which Luther appealed is different from that which Christians in communion with the Roman and Catholic Church had until then commonly recognized. Catholics said it was a new and bad authority, and amounted in the end to the authority of 'private judgment'. Protestants said it was a return to the old authority from which the Church had fallen away, the authority in fact of God as distinct from the authority of man, the papacy and its court, masquerading as divine authority.[1] These replies, of a partly polemical nature, have often failed to do justice to the real problems.

Luther's own brief answer to these questions would indeed be 'The Word of God', Christ, found in Scripture, and living in man by faith.[2] This is the only ultimate Christian authority. However, in its fundamental assertion, that the ultimate authority for all Christians is Christ, this statement is also affirmed by Catholic tradition, and has always been inherent in papal teaching. And Luther had worked out his fundamental theology of faith in and obedience to Christ without finding it contradictory of the tradition he had received, whilst still a full and a willing member of the Catholic and papal Church. Luther's theology of faith could in fact support adherence to more than one theory of the Church. Ecclesiologically it is ambivalent. The important question is: How is the authority of God *manifest*? Luther eventually took the road which rejected the theory of its manifestation in the Pope and the Councils of the Church, the theory that they possessed (or better, were possessed by)[3] a fundamental and final authority to mediate God's Word on earth. He said that Rome claimed such a mediating authority falsely and that in practice her exercise of authority amounted to an abrogation of God's divine authority, practically equating canonical and juridical authority directly to divine authority.

This was the truly important point, that, *in practice* authority was exercised autocratically and dictatorially as though God had no traffic with each person, in the sacraments, in prayer and charity, giving grace. Luther said that the authority of the Word is directly manifest not in a single institution, but in Scripture, and in a sense in the individual Christian who receives the Scripture in faith.[4] However, Luther continued also to believe in the Christian Church as something instituted by Christ, a visible body. He evolved a theory of 'marks' (preaching the Word, baptism, the Lord's Supper) which distinguished the Church in any place and time (Catholic tradition spoke also of 'marks'—one, apostolic, holy). He did not believe that these objective marks were sufficient to enable any man to apply them as a rule of thumb to find the exact confines of the Church at any time. The Church is a spiritual community.[5] Where the

[1] For an exposition of this see the last chapter in *Let God be God* by Philip S. Watson (Epworth Press, 1958 edition).

[2] 'Christ and the Word are virtually interchangeable terms for Luther', says Watson at the beginning of the chapter referred to in the previous footnote, and demonstrates his point.

[3] See P. Fransen, 'The Authority of Councils' in *Problems of Authority*, ed. John M. Todd (Darton, Longman & Todd, and Helicon Press, 1962).

[4] Cf. the famous words from Luther's exposition of the *Magnificat*: 'No one can rightly understand God or God's Word, unless he receives it directly from the Holy Spirit. But no one can receive it from the Holy Spirit without experiencing, proving and feeling it.' Quoted by Philip S. Watson, in his editor's preface to Luther's *Commentary on the Galatians* (James Clarke and Co., 1956).

[5] This does not mean spiritual in the Platonic sense. Luther understood the Hebrew use of 'spirit' and 'flesh' and did not use them in a 'dualistic' sense. 'Spiritual' was not simply a synonym for 'invisible'.

Word is preached, and where men have faith in Christ there is the Church, and these things cannot be simply equated with a juridical institution by the purely human criteria of human society.[6] The Church is made up of the men who are redeemed by the Word of God. It is an objective fact of the spiritual order, visible but not always fully known to man. But the Church cannot wield God's authority. The authority to which Christians must look is the primary authority of God himself, the Word, Christ, manifested in Scripture and living in them by faith. All human ecclesiastical authority must be subordinate to the 'Word'.

But who is to say when the Word is truly preached, who is to say when the sacraments are administered? To this comes his answer which refers us both to the individual Christian and the Church, but not finally or authoritatively to either. In this case, then, must we not say that the authority in which Luther trusts is, ultimately, subject to 'private judgment' and to all the vagaries of all 'subjective judgment'? If he abandons the binding authority of the institution is he not delivered into the anarchy of private choice?

In giving some answers to this question, and showing how the problem (referred to above) is more complex than is commonly assumed, we must distinguish between this problematical level and history. History gives a various answer. It shows certainly that to abandon the authority did mean deliverance into the anarchy of private choice—the anarchy of the numerous sects who plagued Luther for the rest of his life. Equally history had already shown that in practice Catholic ecclesiastical authority did often act as though it believed that God had delivered himself into its hands and it could dispose of spiritual goods how it wished. (Again of course history did also show the contrary of both these facts—Luther's initiative did bear fine spiritual fruit, the Catholic body had done the same.) History also declares that Luther did act precisely on the ground that he was turning away from a human authority which pretended to a guarantee and a history which it did not possess, and that he considered that he was turning back simply to the authority of God, an authority which must be mediated, but not by means of a single all-powerful juridical Church. It is at this point that the pure 'problem' is relevant to the historical reality since Luther's action must be set fully in the context of his life and writings which as a whole illustrate and in effect pose and answer the problem; and equally so must the Catholic institution be set in the full context of its historical theology. With this necessity in mind, we can properly elaborate the various assumptions and implications either at the back of Luther's mind or implied by his life, and the doctrinal assumptions which always lay behind the activities of Catholic ecclesiastical authority. So we return to the question posed at the end of the last paragraph, and give the following threefold answer which we then elaborate.

[6] And it follows naturally that it does not require to be theoretically identifiable down to its last member with the precision of a slide rule. Cf. Gustaf Aulen's exposition in *World Lutheranism Today*: 'Therefore the Church is not only a human or social institution, but nothing less than the Church of Christ, the Body of Christ. Thus this Church is a living reality in the present world. She is not "of the world", but she lives and works and fights in this world for the Kingdom of God. It is not possible to decide who are the true members of the Church and who are not. It is not possible, from this point of view, to fix the frontiers of the Church. As regards this question the only thing that can be said is that the Church reaches as far as the dynamis of the Word and the Sacraments performs its work. Through this work the Church appears as a living reality.'

1. The contrast between subjective and objective is not wholly justified. There is a basically subjective element in every act of faith.

2. 'Objective' (Roman Catholic) ecclesiastical authority does not in itself claim to dispose simply of God's authority, its authority being analogous and mediatory, and its criteria being subject to the sinfulness of the men who exercise ecclesiastical authority. These criteria include the authority of Scripture, and indeed the authority of the teacher of theology, like Luther, and of the 'prophet'.

3. Luther eventually worked out an ecclesiology, and a theory of State and society, in the course of answering people's practical problems. His theory and answers included institutions which he invested with objective Christian authority.

1. At the heart of every sincere Christian faith lies a free act of assent, of adherence and submission to the one God, first revealed to the Jews. Their monotheism, their assertion of a single Creator, Jahveh, having lordship over all men is to be distinguished from every other religious faith known to history, having about it, so they believed, a unique element of revelation. Their God is not the tyrant to whom men must pay the kind of satisfaction demanded on a deity's behalf by a witch doctor, ritual acts, essentially arbitrary. Nor is he an oriental wise man. He is the Creator of all and the Father of his people. The Christian Church maintained and maintains the same faith. The teaching of Jesus was given within the Jewish revelation, and is built on it. There is one God, Creator of everything and all men, the Lover of all men, the Saviour of all men, from whom all come and to whom all will return. Christ added to this the revelation of God's trinitarian nature, and all that pertained to himself, the incarnate Son, the Word of God on earth.

It is impossible to avoid the fundamentally subjective element in an act of faith in these doctrines. They are not logically demonstrable. And an act of faith once made cannot, humanly speaking, bind a man for the rest of his life. A man can reassess the matter; or he can cease to assent to what he assented before. As a matter of experience, commonly, a Christian will continue to penetrate more deeply into the content of such a 'faith', an activity which may sometimes involve asking himself questions precisely about the truth of that in which he believes—'Was Jesus really God?'—and a Catholic will ask himself: 'Did he really found a united and visible Church specially protected and guided?' His repeated affirmative answer to such questions must always have about it a subjective, mysterious, personal, unfathomable element, which no human authority can be properly said to 'control'. The authority may provide objective criteria, but these are not of themselves necessarily convincing. They are received in and by faith.

It is clear, then, that to speak simply of Luther moving from a faith which involved an objective authority to one involving a subjective authority begs a primary question in so far as it may ignore the fact that the faith of every Christian is always in some sense subjective. The ultimate authority to which Luther appeals is the same ultimate authority to which Catholic tradition appeals, divine authority, God, Catholic assent to which necessarily has a subjective element in it.

There is a sense, however, in which a defence of Luther's approach as not subjective only begs the question: it simply asserts that the authority he recognizes is the authority of God grasped by faith, a determination to 'let God be God'.[7] However, this existential answer, which leaves the charge of subjectivism unanswered from the human standpoint, is important in its deliberate eschewal of criteria, rightly dismissing the naïve idea that Luther really thought Scripture could provide a more or less oracular authoritative guidance. It only yields an answer to one who believes.

We note here, in passing, something of the incorrigible tendency in human nature to devalue, to simplify and eventually to transmute all religious faith into a simple abandonment to magic. Luther's trust in Scripture was a trust exercised in the full context of an incarnational theology, of justification by faith, of the daily life of Church, sacrament and society. But it often degenerated in later centuries into the dependence on Scripture alone, regardless of all else. In the same way Catholic teaching on the authority given to Peter as first and leader amongst the twelve, and the authority established in the Church in one bishop as first amongst his brother bishops, an authority which is a service, has been continually devalued into authoritarianism, legalism, and pharisaism of the most blatant sort. Both devaluations, Lutheran and Catholic respectively, involve a lazy attitude which prefers a 'magic' religion, faith in which need not be rationally grasped and which requires the minimum of personal effort. Such a 'magical' approach had its equivalent also in the fideism of the currently accepted philosophy, Nominalism, which emphasized the autonomous nature of the spiritual factor to the detriment of a rational faith, integral with human experience.

2. It is misleading to speak of the objective authority, and the objective criteria, of Catholic tradition as though these spoke either with a single and unambiguous voice, or as though if they did what was said could be considered, on their own principles, to have an absolute authority. On the one hand authority in Catholic tradition is not solely a matter of Popes, bishops and Canon Law; on the contrary there is in it the authority also of Scripture, and indeed of the teacher of theology such as Luther himself was, and of the prophet. On the other hand the authority inherent in the criteria is analogous to, mediatory of, divine authority; it is not simply a species of divine authority. Men exercising institutional and juridical authority in the Church are possessed by God's authority, which is exercised by them as fallible men in the service of the Church, fallible though guarded from grave error.[8]

The analogical and mediatory nature of Catholic institutional authority is rooted, like revelation itself, in the Judaic religion. And we can find there also a variety of forms of authority, including the authority of the teacher such as Luther, and of the prophet such as Luther might well seem to be. Luther came to reflect on the authority, which he, unavoidably in his situation, began to exercise, and whilst he never claimed to be a prophet, the authority which he did exercise and recognized in himself could be classified as the kind of authority claimed by prophets in the Old Testament. If the Jews asked by what authority such a man claimed to speak, his reply was similar to Luther's—'by the authority

[7] Watson's exposition, see footnote 1 of this Appendix.
[8] See *Problems of Authority*, especially chapters by Bishop Pailler, Père Congar and Père Fransen.

of Jahveh'. The prophet's message is recorded in the sacred books thus: 'The Word of the Lord came to Ezechiel . . .' (Ez. I. 3). The prophet recognized and obeyed the established religious authorities and the Law, but claimed to have an authority in addition to or alongside them for a particular purpose. The Jews found it difficult to recognize a true prophet, and more than one perished as a martyr. However, it is clear that God's authority was recognized as potentially revealed in a prophet; and the prophet would have denied that his message was subjective, on the contrary it was a gift, a command, a message from God to his people in a particular circumstance.

St Paul's teaching about *charismata*, special gifts of the Spirit, given to particular Christians, has something similar about it. And there is a theology of prophecy in the Catholic tradition.[9] The life, for instance, of St Catherine of Siena may be understood in this category. Although she had a great reverence for the Church, referring to it as an extension of the Incarnation, and would speak of the Pope as 'Christ on earth', she clearly understood these phrases in an analogical sense, and as referring to the office and not the person since she sent the Pope highly critical letters, upbraiding him severely.

In rejecting the authority of the papacy and of General Councils, Luther was turning not simply from an objective institutional authority to a subjective personal authority. He was turning from a belief that the authority of the Word was mediated through the papacy and Councils, Catholic tradition and Scripture, to a belief that omitted the papacy and the Councils and raised Scripture to the first place in this mediation, Scripture as understood by the faithful. As far as immediate executive authority was concerned Luther was openly searching at first. To the problems which began to confront him as a public figure he gave empirical decisions, and gradually worked out new theories in order to justify particular authorities. In turning away from the papacy and the Councils, as he knew them, he was turning away from an exercise of authority which did often act as though it considered itself to be divine, and left little place for the analogical description of it to which we have referred, or for the human failings of those who hold office.

3. Luther did not simply set up subjective interior, mysterious and personal criteria. Having been convinced that the papacy and the Councils were not valid Christian authorities he had to hammer out a development of his theology of the 'Word' which provided new day-to-day authorities. He was faced, *ad hoc*, by numerous practical problems. His answers were practical, workable solutions, implying approval of various institutions as integral parts of Christian society, and setting a plan (though he hardly realized this) for the growth of the Lutheran churches.

Luther's advance, then, from a Catholic position in 1517 to one which contradicted Catholic tradition on some points four years later, did not involve some sort of intellectual somersault, without rational foundation. What is in question is a theory of the Church, not common sense or honest reasoning. The points on which Luther first began to come into conflict with authority were points commonly considered to be open. Even his denial of the papacy and of

---

[9] Père Congar has provided a sketch of this in both *Vraie et Fausse Reforme* (Editions du Cerf), and in *Lay People in the Church* (Geoffrey Chapman in London, Newman Press in U.S.A.).

Councils began at a common problematical level—many theologians, including the lay theologian Sir Thomas More, considered the papacy not necessarily to be of divine institution, and all were doubtful about the exact relationship between conciliar and papal authority. The subsequent sacramental and liturgical developments grew up from Luther's newly established positions about the authority of Scripture. Basically these could have been the subject of discussion within the Church, but instead, together with the criticisms of sacramental practice, they became the occasion for ecclesiastical authority to confront Luther with one of their possible implications, that is that he was propounding heresy.

By what authority? By the authority of the Word of God in Scripture, thundered Luther, much as the Old Testament prophets thundered. The considerations in this Appendix are intended to help a reader to put aside irrelevant controversy in understanding Luther's position.

Index

This is an index of names of people and places only. No index has been made to subjects or events for which the 51 headings in the table of contents provide a general guide. From this present index the names Martin Luther and Wittenberg have been omitted since references occur throughout the book and the information provided would do little more than duplicate that provided by the table of contents.

Accolti, 224
Adrian VI, Pope, 199, 220–1
Agricola, 120, 170
Albert, Elector, Abp of Mainz, 114,117–20, 124–6, 129, 140, 205, 213, 218
Aleander, 167, 169, 192, 200
Alexander VI, Pope, 100
Amsdorf, Nicholas von, 105, 202, 204, 230, 235
Aquinas, Thomas, 42, 52–8, 106–11, 160
Aristotle, 20, 44, 45–7, 52, 89, 105
Augsburg, 144, 146, 152, 154, 158, 160
Augustine, St, 46–51, 79, 88, 105, 252
Augustinians, 31–3, 43, 63–5, 133, 207
Aurogallus, 230–1

Basle, 124, 172
Bernhardi, Bartholomew, 104
Biel, 42, 47, 54, 75, 79, 113
Bora, Katherine von, 219, 239–41
Bramante, 60
Brandenburg, Bishop of, 120, 124, 142
Brandenburg, Margrave of, 223
Braun, John, 41, 44
Brethren of the Common Life, 16, 17, 58, 221
Bucer, Martin, 135, 245
Bugenhagen, 231, 275

Cajetan, 103, 129, 143–60, 162–73, 224, 255
Campeggio, 222
Capranica, 100
Carafa, later Pope Paul IV, 215, 217, 226
Carlstadt, 105, 125, 159, 164, 204–6, 235, 239, 243, 260
Charles of Spain, subsequently Emperor, 137, 144, 148, 163, 165, 170, 179, 189–93, 223
Chiavasso, Angelo de, 170
Chieregati, 221
Clement VII, Pope, 221, 223–4, 227
Cologne, 169, 199
Contarini, 215, 217, 226

Dietrich of Niem, 99
Domenichi, Domenico, 100
Dürer, Albrecht, 158, 208

Eck of Ingolstadt, 143–4, 163–9, 174–5
Eck, Johann von, 190–1, 198–9
Eisenach, 18, 41, 202
Eisleben, 3
Erasmus, 6, 16, 47, 82, 89, 98, 124, 172, 186, 217, 248–59
Erfurt, 19–25, 31–59, 64–5, 86, 112–13, 136, 154, 199

Frankfurt, 127, 129
Frederick, John, Elector, son of Frederick the Wise, 222–3, 236, 251
Frederick the Wise, Elector of Saxony, 96, 112, 118–20, 126, 133, 138, 140, 148–61, 163, 167, 192, 204, 206–7, 220–2
Freud, 5
Froben, 172
Fuggers, 117

George, Duke, of Saxony, 114, 164, 199, 225
Grefenstein, John von, 34, 36, 50
Grünenberg, John, 120, 143
Guldennapf, Wiegand, of Fritzlar, 18
Gunther, Francis, 113

Heidelberg, 133–7
Henry VIII, 143, 186
Hus, 159, 163, 191
Hutten, 167, 178

Jäger, John, of Dornheim, 20
John of the Cross, St, 108
Julius II, Pope, 60, 101, 114

Lang, John, 64–5, 86, 105, 136
Lehrin, Abbot of, 162
Leipzig, 19, 43, 124, 143–4, 163–6, 198–200, 225
Leo X, Pope, 114, 139, 159, 166, 168, 220
Liège, 169
Link, 207
Lombard, Peter, 42, 44, 46–51
Louvain, 103, 169, 199
Luther, Hans, Martin's father, 3, 4, 5, 10, 32, 37–42
Luther, Hans, son of Martin, 241

Luther, Magdalena, 240
Luther, Margaret, Martin's mother, 3, 4, 5, 10

Magdeburg, 14, 16–18, 60, 118, 124, 126, 230
Mainz, 169
Mansfeld, 3, 20, 24
Mantua, 225
Marburg, 213, 244
Marsiglio of Padua, 17
Matthew of Cracow, 99
Maximilian, Emperor, 138, 148, 163
Melanchthon, 6, 159, 203–5, 215, 222–3, 225–7, 230, 235, 240, 243
Michelangelo, 60
Miltitz, 163–4, 167
Möhra, 202
More, Sir Thomas, 98, 124, 143, 214
Morone, 226
Münzer, Thomas, 243–4, 245, 260, 268

Nathin, John, 42, 45, 60
Nicholas V, Pope, 100
Nicholas of Cusa, 100
Nuremberg, 60, 63, 113, 134, 210, 243, 244

Occam, 42, 44, 46–7, 50, 54–6, 113
Oecolampadius, 244–5

Paris, 164, 199–201, 203
Paul III, Pope, 224, 226–7
Paul IV, Pope, see Carafa
Philip of Hesse, 223, 241, 244

Pius II, Pope, 100
Prierias, 147, 152, 162, 166

Ratisbon, 226
Rome, 59–64

Savonarola, 62, 72, 100
Schalbe, Henry, and family, 18
Schmalkalden, 225
Schurff, Jerome, 190
Serralonga, 154
Sickingen, 167, 178
Spalatin, 96–7, 106, 112, 133, 138, 140, 143, 165, 202, 222
Staupitz, John, 43–4, 47, 59, 64–7, 73, 75–7, 93, 134, 142, 157, 240
Stotternheim, 24

Tauler, 92–3, 106–8, 135
Tetzel, John, 114–9, 124–5, 127–9, 142, 151, 160, 164
Trebonius, John, 18, 19
Trier, Abp of, 190, 192
Trutvetter, Jodocus, 19, 44, 54, 105, 125, 136

Wartburg, 18, 202–7, 240
Wimpina, 127, 142
Worms, 141, 144, 162, 170–1, 188–201
Wycliffe, 159

Zwickau, 243, 260
Zwilling, 205–6
Zwingli, 213, 244–5